ROUTLEDGE LIBRARY EDITIONS: COLONIALISM AND IMPERIALISM

Volume 29

GOVERNMENT IN WEST AFRICA

GOVERNMENT
IN WEST AFRICA

W. E. F. WARD

Routledge
Taylor & Francis Group
LONDON AND NEW YORK

First published in 1965 by George Allen & Unwin Ltd.

This edition first published in 2023
by Routledge
4 Park Square, Milton Park, Abingdon, Oxon OX14 4RN

and by Routledge
605 Third Avenue, New York, NY 10158

Routledge is an imprint of the Taylor & Francis Group, an informa business

Revised edition 1966
Reprinted 1967
Third revised edition 1968
Second impression 1969
© 1965, 1966, 1968 George Allen & Unwin Ltd.

All rights reserved. No part of this book may be reprinted or reproduced or utilised in any form or by any electronic, mechanical, or other means, now known or hereafter invented, including photocopying and recording, or in any information storage or retrieval system, without permission in writing from the publishers.

Trademark notice: Product or corporate names may be trademarks or registered trademarks, and are used only for identification and explanation without intent to infringe.

British Library Cataloguing in Publication Data
A catalogue record for this book is available from the British Library

ISBN: 978-1-032-41054-8 (Set)
ISBN: 978-1-032-42252-7 (Volume 29) (hbk)
ISBN: 978-1-032-42253-4 (Volume 29) (pbk)
ISBN: 978-1-003-36195-4 (Volume 29) (ebk)

DOI: 10.4324/9781003361954

Publisher's Note
The publisher has gone to great lengths to ensure the quality of this reprint but points out that some imperfections in the original copies may be apparent.

Disclaimer
The publisher has made every effort to trace copyright holders and would welcome correspondence from those they have been unable to trace.

GOVERNMENT
in West Africa

BY

W. E. F. WARD
C.M.G., M.A.

THIRD REVISED EDITION
including the Constitutions of
FRANCE and the U.S.S.R.

London
GEORGE ALLEN & UNWIN LTD
RUSKIN HOUSE MUSEUM STREET

FIRST PUBLISHED IN 1965
REVISED EDITION 1966
REPRINTED 1967
THIRD REVISED EDITION 1968
SECOND IMPRESSION 1969

This book is copyright under the Berne Convention. All rights reserved. Apart from any fair dealing for the purpose of private study, research, criticism or review, as permitted under the Copyright Act, 1956, no part of this publication may be reproduced, stored in retrieval system, or transmitted, in any form or by any means, electronic, electrical, chemical, mechanical, optical, photocopying, recording or otherwise, without the prior permission of the copyright owner. Enquiries should be addressed to the Publishers.

© *George Allen & Unwin Ltd.*, 1965, 1966, 1968

SBN 04 351018 3

PRINTED IN GREAT BRITAIN
BY PHOTOLITHOGRAPHY
UNWIN BROTHERS LIMITED
WOKING AND LONDON

PREFACE

THIS book is written primarily for Sixth Form students in West Africa who are studying the subject 'Government' for Advanced level examinations. But I hope it may be found useful by other readers who are interested in the practical working of modern government and in the constitutional history of West Africa.

The division into two parts is inherent in the nature of the subject. The constitutions of West Africa were drawn up by men who knew their Aristotle and their Locke, and the problems of civil government in West Africa are essentially the same as those which have been studied by political thinkers in Europe and America from the age of Socrates to our own day. A student cannot hope to understand the complicated constitutional struggles of the past fifty years in West Africa, or the constitutional problems with which the region is still faced, unless he is able to interpret the story in the light of some general principles of the art of government.

Some teachers may feel that here and there in discussing the art of government in Part One, I have gone into unnecessary, and indeed somewhat earthy detail on the practical difficulties and expedients involved in working a constitution or a political system. It seems to me essential to impress on students that all politics is the art of gaining and using power over one's fellow-men: that the politician is dealing with the stubborn facts of human nature: and that the most beautifully devised paper constitution will mean very little unless there are just and wise men to work it.

I have to thank the staff of the libraries of the Colonial and the Commonwealth Relations Offices for their help in digging up the Orders in Council, Acts of Parliament, Royal Instructions, Ordinances and Gazette notices which are the materials for any study of West African constitutional history. The librarian of the United States Information Service in London, the director-general of the Liberian Information Service in Monrovia, and the information officers in London of the High Commissions of Ghana, Sierra Leone and the Federal Government of Nigeria have all been most kind and helpful in answering my queries. I am grateful to Mr Simon Fraser for guiding my ignorant feet when I strayed in legal difficulties. None of these gentlemen of course is responsible for any of the statements or opinions in the book; the full responsibility for these is mine.

CONTENTS

		page
PREFACE		7
BIBLIOGRAPHY		10

PART ONE: PRINCIPLES OF GOVERNMENT

I	*What is Politics?*	13
II	*Democracy*	19
III	*Constitutions*	25
IV	*Power and Sovereignty*	38
V	*The Rule of Law*	50
VI	*Representative Government*	63
VII	*Party Systems*	85
VIII	*Presidential and Cabinet Government*	108
IX	*Some Problems of Parliament*	121
X	*Federal and Unitary Government*	133

PART TWO: POLITICAL INSTITUTIONS OF WEST AFRICAN STATES   145

XI	*Constitutional History Before 1945*	147
XII	*Partial Self-Government*	160
XIII	*Towards Independence*	176
XIV	*Ghana and Nigeria Since Independence*	215
XV	*The Organization of Government*	221
XVI	*Liberia*	255
XVII	*The French Constitution*	267
XVIII	*The Constitution of the Soviet Union*	277
	INDEX	287

BIBLIOGRAPHY

AWOLOWO, O., *Path to Nigeria Freedom*, London, Faber, 1947.

BIRCH, A. H., *Representative and Responsible Government*, London, Allen & Unwin, 1964.

BOURRET, F. M., *Ghana—The Road to Independence*, Oxford University Press, 1960.

ELIAS, T. O., *Ghana and Sierra Leone*, London, Stevens, 1962.

EZERA, K., *Constitutional Development of Nigeria*, Cambridge University Press, 1960.

FOSTER, MICHAEL B., *Masters of Political Thought*—Plato to Machiavelli, London, Harrap, 1947.

FYFE, CHRISTOPHER, *The History of Sierra Leone*, London, Oxford University Press, 1962.

HUBERICH, C. H., *The Political and Legislative History of Liberia*, London, New York, Central Book Co., 1947.

JENNINGS, IVOR, *The Law and the Constitution*, University of London Press, 1952.

JONES, W. T., *Masters of Political Thought*—Machiavelli to Bentham, London, Harrap, 1942.

LANCASTER, LANE W., *Masters of Political Thought*—Hegel to Dewey, London, Harrap, 1959.

MACKINTOSH, J. P., *The British Cabinet*, London, Stevens, 1962.

NKRUMAH, KWAME, *Ghana*, London, Nelson, 1957.

PHILLIPS, O. H., *Leading Cases in Constitutional Law*, London, Sweet & Maxwell, 1957.

RICHARDSON, NATHANIEL R., *Liberia's Past and Present*, London, Diplomatic Press, 1959.

STEWART, MICHAEL, *Modern Forms of Government*, London, Allen & Unwin, 1961.

STRONG, C. F., *Modern Political Constitutions*, London, Sidgwick & Jackson, 1952.

WADE, E. C. S., and G. G. PHILLIPS, *Constitutional Law*, London, Longmans, 1955.

WHEARE, J., *The Nigerian Legislative Council*, London, Faber, 1950.

WHEARE, K. C., *Modern Constitutions*, Oxford University Press, 1951.

WIGHT, MARTIN, *The Gold Coast Legislative Council*, London, Faber, 1947.

YANCY, ERNEST J., *The Republic of Liberia*, London, Allen & Unwin, 1959.

PART ONE

Principles of Government

CHAPTER I

What is Politics?

Beginnings of the study in ancient Greece: polis *means 'the city'. The Greek city-state: fundamental questions asked by Greek thinkers. Renaissance Europe, absolute monarchy v popular government: prestige of seventeenth-century England. Rousseau and the Social Contract. Compare Aristotle's view of 'the good life' and the purpose of the state.*
Paine and the rights of man: the French and American revolutions: nationalism.
Africa today still mainly influenced by Western political thought. Influences from Asia: (i) Islam, (ii) Mahatma Gandhi. African influence as yet only slight.

THE aim of the politician is to gain and use power over his fellow men. The art of using political power is one of the most difficult of the arts. However wise and experienced we may be, it is often difficult to decide what is the best thing to do. We may have three or four choices, each with its advantages and disadvantages. Then, when we have made up our mind which is the best, we are faced with another difficulty. Can we persuade—or compel—our people to choose it? And if not, what are we to do?

As in other arts, to become really successful we need natural gifts; but we can make better use of our gifts by studying where our predecessors succeeded and where they failed, and trying to find out the reason why. This study is called politics, or political science: it tries to discover the general principles on which government can be carried on successfully.

Politics, politician, policy: what is the meaning of the word *polit* which we see embedded in all these three words? This question takes us back to the beginning of our study, nearly 2,500 years ago. The Greek word *polis* means a city: but not such a huge city as Accra or Ibadan. Very early in their history, the Greeks ceased to live in small country villages. The people of several villages joined together into one city, and each city was an independent state. The city was small; the Greeks liked it to be so small that the voice of one man shouting in the market-place could be heard all over it. But it was a city-state. The people would go out and live on their farms at busy farming seasons, and they would go out too in order to make sacrifices at the old sacred places. But the city was their home. So when the Greeks began to think and talk and write about how a city-state or *polis* should be governed, they called that study *politics*.

Every Greek was a politician, and was proud of his *polis*. One Greek writer said that man was by nature a *politikos bios*, a creature who naturally took to city-life and politics. The city dweller, the *polite* man, looked down on the peoples of other countries who had not learnt, like the Greeks, to live in cities, and so remained simple villagers.

All this talk about the Greek city-states of 2,500 years ago may seem very remote from the affairs of a modern state of today, with an area of tens of thousands of square miles, and a population of several millions. Size and numbers certainly change the problems of government in some respects; for example, the small Greek city-states had no need to invent systems of representative government, or to divide powers between regional governments and federal. But the fundamental principles are the same today as they were then; and it was the Greeks who first asked themselves what these fundamental principles were. They asked themselves such questions as these: Why must we have a government at all? If (as they agreed) we must have a government, who should control it: should it be the wise, or the rich, or every citizen whether rich or poor, wise or foolish? If all citizens have a right to share in controlling the government, how can we prevent foolish or selfish citizens from causing disaster? How are the foolish and the selfish to be made wiser and unselfish; what sort of education should be given, and how much control should the government exercise over education? Should the government prohibit books, music or drama which it thinks bad for its citizens? Should a citizen be free to make as much money as he likes and do what he likes with it, or should the government take steps to prevent people from becoming insufferably rich? These questions, and others like them, are still occupying the attention of governments all over the world in one form or another; and the answers which Greek writers gave to them are worth our consideration.

In the course of time the small independent city-states passed away. The Roman empire succeeded them; and that empire in turn was broken up by the barbarians from the north who founded the nations of western Europe. But the ideas of Greece and Rome were not permanently forgotten. Greek literature was translated into Arabic, and in the twelfth century, the Muslims of North Africa and Spain passed on their knowledge of Greek political ideas to scholars in Italy and France, so that they were once more studied all over western Europe.

During the middle ages, most western European countries had systems of government which gave the ordinary people some share in public affairs. But for various reasons, the parliaments or national assemblies died, or at any rate lost their power, in Spain, Italy, and France. In the seventeenth century only England and Holland, both of them protected by the sea, retained any sort of popular government. France and Spain were ruled by absolute monarchs, and the general feeling in Europe was that popular government of the English or Dutch kind[1] was an old-fashioned and inefficient kind of government which would not be able to compete with the power and magnificence of an absolute monarch like Louis XIV of France. But when this was tested by war, England and Holland won, to the general surprise. People concluded that there must be some great virtue in the English system of government which made England so rich and powerful. French writers studied the English system, and studied the books which Englishmen had written about this sort of government. The French writer Rousseau (1712-1778) wrote a book called *The Social Contract*, basing himself on certain English writers of the seventeenth and eighteenth centuries and going right back to the beginning of things to ask the fundamental question, What is the State, and how does it come into being? This question had been asked by the Greek writer Aristotle (384-322 B.C.). Aristotle's answer has had great influence on political thought. He said that the State comes into being to provide for the bare needs of life, but that it continues in being 'for the sake of a good life'. By this he meant that every human community must provide itself with some form of government in the first place if it is to survive; but when it has done this, and organized itself into a State, the State machinery can, and should, do a great many things to make its citizens' life more worth living, which individual citizens could not do for themselves.

It is as well to pause a moment to consider this opinion of Aristotle. Nobody is likely to question the first part of his opinion. Even the smallest farming or fishing village in Africa, before the days of Western contact, needed some form of government. It must have someone to decide on peace or war: to decide when the yams are to be planted and harvested: when the lagoon is to be opened and closed for fishing: when the farm is to be moved to a fresh area of bush, or maybe the village itself moved to a new site: how disputes are to be settled and what fines or pacification fees are to be

---

[1] It was not democracy as we understand it today; it was very far indeed from the idea of 'One man, one vote'.

paid. And Aristotle's statement is much more obviously true when we consider a powerful and well-organised state like Ashanti or Dahomey or old Mali, which Ibn Batuta so much admired.

But what about Aristotle's second statement, that the State must see to it that its citizens are enabled to live 'a good life'? Most people would accept this principle, but the difficulty is in deciding how far in this direction the State should go, especially when the State is not rich enough to do all it would like to do, and has to choose. There has in the past been much dispute over this. In the first half of the nineteenth century for example, most English people thought that it was no part of the State's business to provide schools: schools should be provided by parents and by the Churches. It was not until 1872 that the State first provided primary schools, and thirty years later that it first provided secondary schools; and even then there were many Englishmen who protested strongly. We have moved far beyond this now. The whole of the modern theory of the welfare state is ultimately based on this saying of Aristotle. Modern States often provide not only such things as schools and hospitals, but also libraries, theatres, orchestras and opera and ballet companies, regarding these things as necessary parts of 'the good life', which the citizens could not provide on anything like the same scale without State aid.

To return to Rousseau: what use did he make of these ideas? Rousseau was writing at a time when France had no parliament. The king made laws, and he had complete executive power as well; for example, he could have a man arrested and imprisoned indefinitely without charge or trial. Rousseau reacted violently against such a state of things. He declared that the State came into being as the result of an agreement or contract, by which the individual citizens agreed to submit to its authority on condition that it governed wisely and justly, with 'the good life' of its citizens in view. He drew the conclusion that since government authority was based on an agreement, a Government which broke the conditions of the agreement had lost its right to authority, and so its citizens were justified in overthrowing it. As he looked round the world, Rousseau saw no Government that was completely carrying out its side of the agreement; the English Government seemed the best, but even that was far from perfect. 'Man,' said Rousseau, 'is born free; but everywhere we see him in chains.' One of Rousseau's contemporaries, the Englishman Tom Paine (1737-1809) wrote a book with a famous title, *The Rights of Man*; it had a large sale in America and France, as well as in England.

It would be going too far to say that the writings of Rousseau and Paine and others caused the American and French revolutions. But there can be no doubt that the Americans and the French were readier to use revolutionary methods against their rulers because Rousseau and Paine had taught them that their rulers had broken the social contract. When the Americans drew up their declaration of independence in 1776, they based it on the ideas of human rights and the social contract.

'We hold these truths to be self evident,' they said, 'that all men are created equal, that they are endowed by their Creator with certain unalienable rights, that among these are Life, Liberty, and the pursuit of Happiness. That to secure these rights, Governments are instituted among Men, deriving their just powers from the consent of the governed. That whenever any Form of Government becomes destructive of these ends, it is the Right of the People to alter or to abolish it, and to institute new Government, laying its foundations on such principles and organizing its powers in such form, as to them shall seem most likely to effect their Safety and Happiness.'

The influence of Rousseau and Paine is unmistakeable; but it is equally clear that these ideas are an elaboration of Aristotle's doctrine that the State continues in being in order to provide its citizens with a good life.

Largely as a result of the French Revolution, a new and still more revolutionary idea was launched: the idea that a nation has a right to be united under one government of its own choice. Germany and Italy at that time were divided into many small independent states, many of them ruled by absolute monarchs; the Austrian empire included Hungarians, Czechs, Serbs, Italians and other non-Germans; the whole of south-eastern Europe was ruled by the Sultan of Turkey. 'All Governments,' declared the French revolutionaries, 'are our enemies; all Peoples are our friends.' And so during the nineteenth and early twentieth centuries, one European people after another succeeded in establishing itself as an independent nation-state. It is this same idea that has brought colonialism to an end in Asia and Africa.

The political ideas under which West Africa now governs itself are thus mainly drawn from Europe: ideas first discussed in the Greek city-states, worked out largely by English experience, and given tremendous power by nationalism, which is the faith preached by the French revolutionaries that every people has a right to govern itself. The study of politics is based on the study of these ideas. We ask why it was that Aristotle or Rousseau or other writers thought out these ideas: why ideas that are hundreds of years old and invented to suit the needs of ancient Greece or of seventeenth-century

England or eighteenth-century France should be applied to modern Africa: what are the conditions in which these political ideas will work, and whether these conditions are found in Africa today.

We have said that the political ideas of modern Africa are mainly drawn from Europe. What about Asia? It is a fact of history that West Africa was colonised by Europeans, not by Asians; and the European colonial governments naturally brought in European ideas. Asia today, like Africa, is copying European political ideas, with presidents, parliaments, political parties, elections and so forth. There is so far but one rival to Western influence: Islam. Christianity, which—like Islam—arose in western Asia, draws a clear distinction between the Church and the State: 'Render to Caesar,' said Jesus, 'the things that are Caesar's: and to God, the things that are God's.' Christian thought has followed up this idea, and much labour has been spent in discussing what is to be done if Caesar does things which are hateful to God. In Islam there is no such distinction. All Muslim law, like the Quran itself, is derived from God. To a Muslim, Church and State are one.

One political idea from Asia is influencing modern Africa, and modern Europe; but it is an idea, not about exercising Government power, but about destroying it. When Mahatma Gandhi was trying to overthrow the British authority in India, he invented the system of civil disobedience. He hated the thought of fighting and bloodshed, and in any case he knew that the British Government in India was strong. His idea was that people should do something which, though in itself harmless, was illegal: what he himself did was to make salt from sea-water, which was against a law which gave the Government the sole right to make salt. He reckoned that if very large numbers of people followed his example, there would not be enough police to arrest them, magistrates to try them, or prisons to hold them. Thus, the whole machinery of government would come to a stop. It was essential to his system that nobody should resist the police: there was to be no fighting. He and his people would overthrow the Government, not by hating but by laughing at it. This Gandhian idea had a good deal of success against the British Government in India; Dr. Nkrumah tried it, again with some success, against the British Government in the Gold Coast; and more recently it has been tried in Europe.

It is only to be expected that foreign forms of government should gradually be modified in Africa under the influence of African ideas. But no extensive modifications have yet taken place. Here and there in West Africa we may notice an African idea which differs from the ideas of Europe; but it is still true that West Africa is so far governed mainly by ideas of European origin.

CHAPTER II

Democracy

Different senses of the word democracy. *Aristotle's sense. Can popular government be selfish? Modern misconceptions of democracy. Plato's view that good government depends on good men.*
Essentials of democratic government: (i) Government actions must be open to public criticism, and people must have power to change government. (ii) There must be an effective means of finding what the people want. (iii) Freedom of speech, writing and association, provided the law is observed. (iv) Impartial justice in the courts.
Political machinery for securing these essentials: (i) freely elected parliament; (ii) no intimidation of voters; (iii) life of parliament limited; (iv) Government responsible to parliament and the law; (v) free judiciary.

ALL of us nowadays say that we believe in democracy, and there is hardly a state in the world which has not a parliament, and a Government which claims to be supported by the people. But we use the word *democracy* in different senses, and it is important to discuss just what it ought to mean.

The word itself is Greek, and means 'government by the people'. Aristotle used it in a rather bad sense. He said that there were three ways in which a country might be governed. The supreme power might be in the hands of one man: or in the hands of a small group of men: or in the hands of the whole body of citizens. He went further, and said that much depended on the way in which supreme power was used. He knew from his experience that some people value power merely for what they can get out of it for themselves: a king can squeeze his people to provide himself and his court with luxury, a small ruling class can use the machinery of government to bring its members more wealth and power, and to keep down any awkward person who challenges their authority.

But Aristotle said that the whole body of citizens can use political power just as selfishly as a bad king or a narrow ruling class. He used the term *democracy* for a government in which the whole body of citizens shared power, but in which they used it for selfish purposes. If a citizen, Mr. A, votes for Mr. X in the hope that if Mr X gets into power he will appoint Mr A or his brother to a good post, or give them a profitable contract: or if Mr. B joins a political party in the hope that he may become a party secretary and drive about in a big car and enjoy exercising power—there, Aristotle would say, that is democracy.

But that is not what we today mean by democracy. We know that such things sometimes occur, but we would like to stop them.

All the same, some of our people have strange ideas of democracy. I was once travelling in a railway carriage in England which was marked 'No Smoking'. Three young men got in, and lighted cigarettes; and, encouraged by their example, two passengers who had not previously been smoking lighted up as well. I drew their attention to the 'No Smoking' notice. The young man to whom I spoke looked around, and replied, 'Five of us, two of you; that notice is cancelled. This is a democratic country.' That was his idea of democracy, but it was not mine; nor was it that of the guard of the train, whom I called. He said that regulations must be obeyed, and he soon had the cigarettes put out. Many people have a similar idea of democracy; they think that the majority can do as it likes, without caring for the feelings of the minority. They shout down minority speakers and refuse to listen to them. An example of this is the case which occurred in England a few years ago of a quarrel between an important town council and a club of fishermen. The town stood on the banks of a river, and the club had the right to fish along a stretch of the river below the town. The town council constructed a big new sewage plant, which turned the sewage into the river, where it killed the fish. The fishermen protested; the town replied that it had a perfect right to do what it had done. The fishermen thereupon brought an action against the town council. The council's only defence was that it would cost a great deal of money to purify the sewage before pouring it into the river. But the court held that the council had no right to destroy the fishing club's enjoyment in this way; the fishermen won their case, and the town council was compelled to purify its sewage.

Another idea commonly heard is that it is a democratic habit of mind to say, 'I am as good a man as you.' Now there is a sense in which this is true. The office messenger, or an illiterate labourer, may be far below the prime minister in official rank, and there are many more men qualified to fulfil the duties of the office messenger than those of the prime minister. But the messenger does fulfil a function; and how important his function is, his superiors will find out if he is ill or on holiday and they have to manage without him. And apart from his hours on duty, he is a husband and a father, he is a citizen with a vote; he is entitled to as much respect as the prime minister himself, and there will be something seriously wrong in any state which allows its prime minister to say, 'Oh, that is only my office messenger; he does not count.'

It is not a sign of a truly democratic society when one man says truculently to another, 'I am as good a man as you.' We should get much nearer to a true democracy when one man said courteously to the other, 'You are just as good a man as I am; I should like to know what you think.' But this suggests that democracy is not really a matter of political institutions at all, but of a habit of mind. Is this so?

This is a question to which much thought was given by the Greek thinker Plato (427-347 B.C.), the man who taught Aristotle. Plato was not particularly concerned with democracy as such, but he was deeply concerned with the question, What is the best type of government? He spent much time in discussing laws and political institutions; but he emphasised again and again that no government will be a good government unless it is controlled by good men. If Plato is right, no amount of care and skill in economic planning, settling party programmes, or drafting wise laws and constitutions will make a country a democracy. Unless the democratic spirit is widely present among the citizens, these political forms will be a useless sham. In the days before motor cars, it used to be said in England that a skilful lawyer could drive a coach-and-six through any Act of Parliament. A coach-and-six was a coach drawn by six horses; we might say, in modern terms, that a skilful lawyer could drive a three-ton lorry through any Act of Parliament. That is a picturesque way of saying that a skilful lawyer can usually find a way of enabling his client to do what he wants to do without breaking the letter of the law; there is nearly always some weakness in the wording of the law, some possibility which the draftsman and the parliament have overlooked. This is especially the case in the business world, where the law is complicated, and there is plenty of money available for paying lawyers' fees. A story is told of the great American financier J. P. Morgan. In 1890 the United States Congress passed a law against big business combines, and J. P. Morgan was threatened with prosecution under the new Act. He called on the President of the United States and said, 'Send your man to my man and they can fix it up.' By 'your man' he meant the Attorney-General; his idea was that the two lawyers should get together and find a way by which the letter of the law should be observed, but the great Mr Morgan should be enabled to carry on his business as before without being inconvenienced by having to obey its spirit. If such an attitude is widespread, democracy will not work. The law is no respecter of persons.

Plato's conclusion was similar. He said that the virtues of the

State depend on the virtues of the individual citizens; unless the citizens are wise and brave and just, their State cannot be. If we were to ask Plato how we are to secure democratic government (using the term 'democratic' in its modern sense), he would certainly reply that we must decide what qualities or virtues we wish our democratic government to possess, and must train our citizens so that they as individuals possess the same qualities.

If we leave the small Greek city-states and come to the large nation-states of today, what are the essentials of democratic government?

The first essential is that, generally speaking, all the Government's actions must be open to criticism by the people or the people's representatives; and if criticism is sufficiently severe, the people or its representatives must have the power of getting rid of the Government and of choosing a new one. We say 'generally speaking' because in practice it will not be possible for every one of the thousands of actions which the Government performs every day by one or other of its officials to be criticised in Parliament. But there must be some means whereby any single action, however small, can if necessary be brought to Parliament's notice and can be used as the ground for a serious criticism of the Government.

The second essential is that there must be an effective system of finding out what 'the people' want. This is difficult to achieve, and no democratic country has yet fully achieved it; all we have so far is a number of rough-and-ready, reasonably successful, compromises. There is not much difficulty in defining what we mean by 'the people'. All modern democracies would agree that we mean all adult men (with a few exceptions, such as lunatics, and—in Britain—members of the House of Lords). Most would include all adult women as well, though there are still some countries which do not allow women to vote.

The real difficulty comes in framing an electoral system which will enable people to express their ideas freely and elect members to represent them in Parliament, without falling into either of two opposite dangers. One danger is that, since people's opinions vary so much, Parliament will be divided into a large number of small groups: the groups will combine together in one way this week on Bill A, and next week will combine quite differently on Bill B. The Government will not know from one week to the next what its majority will be, and its life is likely to be a short one. The opposite danger is that Parliament will be divided into two great parties, each with its machinery, its powerful leaders, and its programme. As we shall see, the two-party system has much to recommend it; but there is always the danger that the ordinary voter may come to feel that he is unimportant. The party may send down at election time a candidate whom he dislikes, it may include in its programme some items which he dislikes. It is even possible that he may become so disgusted with incessant party warfare as to lose interest in politics altogether.

The third essential is that, provided he keeps within the law, everyone must feel completely free to say or to write what he thinks about the Government, whether for it or against it. He must be free to talk about it in private, to address public meetings, to write letters or articles in the Press, to publish pamphlets, to form political groups or parties. He must be able to do all this without fearing that he will be punished in any way: that he will be arrested and imprisoned, or that his brother will be dismissed from the Government service, or that his children will be refused a place in college. All this is, as we have said, provided that he keeps within the law. No Government can allow its citizens to form plans for overthrowing it by force. To kill the president or to overthrow the Government by force is treason; to stir up a crowd to assemble and shout and throw stones at members of parliament is sedition. Sedition and treason are crimes which the law will punish. Similarly, Cabinet Ministers are as much entitled as any other citizen to protection from libel and slander.[1] A citizen is entitled to say that he thinks a Minister's action unwise, and he may go further and say that all the Minister's actions are so unwise that he is not fit for his job. But he is not entitled to make defamatory statements about the Minister's private affairs, or about the Minister's private motives for his public actions.

We have spoken about the law and the protection which it gives. We shall say more later on about the law. All we need say here is that a fourth essential, not merely of democratic government, but of all good government of any kind, is a system of law and justice which the citizens feel they can trust. If two citizens go to law, they must feel sure that the Court will not favour A because he is richer than B, or higher in rank, or is a member of the Government party whereas B is a member of the Opposition, or for any other natural advantage which A may have over B: the Court will judge the case solely on its merits. Similarly, if the State is involved against one of its citizens, the citizen should be able to feel confident that he will be given a fair hearing, and that the Court will not start with a prejudice against him. We shall discuss this further when we speak of the Rule of Law.

---

[1] Slander is a statement by word of mouth which brings the person of whom it is made into hatred, ridicule, or contempt. Libel is a similar statement made in more permanent form, as in writing or in a picture.

These then are the four essentials of good democratic government. The Government must be prepared to face criticism, and to give way to a successor if the people desire, and all adult citizens must be able to make their desires known. Any citizen must feel free to criticise the Government without fear. And the Government and its citizens must feel that they can trust the law courts to administer justice without fear or favour.

We have set out four essentials of good democratic government. The essential political machinery needed to secure them is as follows. (1) There should be a parliament, freely elected by all adult citizens. (2) Proper arrangements (such as a secret ballot) must be made so that citizens can record their votes without fear. (3) A limit must be set to the life of the parliament, so that if the voters wish, they may elect a new parliament with a different policy. (4) The Government must use its powers in accordance with parliament's wishes and the law of the land; and if it fails to do so, parliament must have the power to call it to account. (5) The judges must be free to do their duty without fear, either of the Government, or of the parliament, or of wealthy and powerful citizens; and they must be trusted to administer justice fairly, whether between the Government and its citizens, or between one citizen and another.

It is easy to state these requirements; it is not so easy to provide and maintain them. Therein lies the difficulty of the art of government.

CHAPTER III

Constitutions

The United States constitution: how it describes the machinery of government. The Bill of Rights. Constitutions depending on an Act of the British parliament.
Amending a constitution: why this is usually difficult. How far is it true that Britain has no written constitution? The 1688 Bill of Rights; the 1911 Parliament Act.
South Africa's method of amending its constitution: increasing the size of the Senate to provide the necessary two-thirds majority.
Constitutional conventions: their uses: how they are enforced. Examples: appointment of prime minister in Britain, his right to ask for a dissolution; appointment to the public service commission in Ghana. Constitutional conventions as a means of changing the constitution.
What is an unconstitutional action? The Supreme Court's function of interpreting the constitution. Unconstitutional action in a country without a written constitution.

ONE means which is often used to lay down certain principles on which a country is to be governed is a document called a constitution. It is usual for a constitution to describe the machinery of government and the principles on which the machinery is intended to work. The most famous constitution in the world is that of the United States of America, which was written in 1787, after the thirteen British colonies had won their war of independence and had to decide how they were to govern themselves as a free country. As originally drafted, it consisted of a preamble and seven articles; and it is worth our while to look at it for a while, as a type of constitutional documents in general.

The preamble is very short, but is interesting because it shows clearly the political ideas in the minds of the constitution-makers:

'We, the people of the United States, in order to form a more perfect Union, establish justice, insure domestic tranquillity, provide for the common defence, promote the general welfare, and secure the blessings of liberty to ourselves and our posterity, do ordain and establish this Constitution for the United States of America.'

This preamble to the Constitution should be read in conjunction with the declaration of independence which the same statesmen had drawn up eleven years before; we have quoted a few lines from it in Chapter One.

The seven articles vary greatly in length. The longest is Article I, which describes the legislative department: how the Senate and the House of Representatives are to be elected and how they are to sit and carry out their duties: what their powers are to be, and what limitations are placed upon their powers. The next longest article is Article II, which deals similarly with the executive: that is, with the election and powers of the President and Vice-President. Article III deals with the judiciary; Article IV with the relation of the States to each other; Article V says how the Constitution may be amended; Article VI deals with national debts; and Article VII describes how the Constitution is to be brought into force. Article I is more than half of the total document, Article II takes a quarter; the remaining articles between them make up the other quarter.

All these articles describe the machinery of government. They take it for granted that the Government of the United States would preserve the rights of man, of which Tom Paine had written. But there was a strong section of the American people and its statesmen who were not prepared to take this for granted, and some of them went so far as to say that their States would not accept the Constitution unless it was enlarged so as to include a guarantee of human rights. The Government accepted their arguments; and only four years after the Constitution had come into effect, a series of amendments was passed to secure these human rights. The first Amendment, for example, guarantees freedom of religion, of free speech, of the press, and of assembly. The fourth Amendment guarantees that people's houses may not be searched, or their papers and property seized, without a legal warrant. The fifth and sixth Amendments guarantee that a citizen may not be punished without 'due process of law'; and 'due process of law' means a speedy and public trial by jury, with the charge against him openly stated, with the hostile witnesses appearing in court before him and his own witnesses compelled, if necessary, to give evidence. It has happened in some European countries that a person may be arrested and kept in prison for weeks or months without trial; he is told of no charge, he has no idea who has given information against him, and he fears that even if he is ever brought to trial his friends may be afraid to come into court and give evidence in his favour. All this would be impossible in the United States; it is contrary to the Sixth Amendment; it is unconstitutional. The Fifth Amendment moreover says that no person 'shall be compelled in any criminal case to be a witness against himself'. This prevents 'brain-washing', or brutal interrogation by the police before trial with the purpose of forcing the prisoner to make a confession which can be used as evidence against him.

We shall spend some time on the American Constitution because it is the oldest and the most famous written constitution in the world, and has served as a model for many others.

Some countries which are members of the Commonwealth have a written constitution which is based originally on an Act of the British Parliament: originally, we say, because it may have been amended since first enacted. Canada is one such country; its constitution was enacted by the British North America Act, passed by the British Parliament in 1867. The Commonwealth countries in Africa—Ghana, Nigeria, and others in all parts of Africa—are other examples; so is the Republic of South Africa, which was once a member of the Commonwealth. The South African constitution was originally based on the South Africa Act, passed in 1909; Ghana's constitution on the Ghana Independence Act of 1957.

Amending the Constitution

One critical question in any written constitution is, How is the constitution to be amended? No constitution is perfect, and amendments are sure to be needed sooner or later. More than 3,500 amendments have been proposed to the American Constitution, but only twenty-three of them have taken effect. The Canadian constitution has been amended several times. The difficulty is, that once a constitution has been adopted, it is for the lawyers to say precisely what it means; and lawyers have their own ways of interpreting documents. An article in the constitution may not suit the different circumstances of modern times. A group of politicians may argue, 'If the makers of our constitution had been able to foresee the circumstances of today, they would have worded this article differently; can we not stretch the old wording to cover our new needs?' But the lawyers will reply, 'Nobody can tell what the makers of our constitution would have said if things had been different. But we do know what they actually did say; and the wording of this article cannot possibly be held to cover what you propose. What you propose may be desirable; but it is unconstitutional.'

All written constitutions therefore tend to be somewhat rigid: that is, not easily altered. And they usually are made more rigid by the deliberate intention of the constitution-makers. Constitutions are important, often almost sacred, documents; they often represent weeks and months of negotiation between parties of different opinions, and they might not have been agreed to at all if it was thought that they could easily be altered. The Ghana constitution illustrates this. The Convention People's Party had held power in Ghana since internal self-government began in 1951, and it planned a unitary government for independent Ghana, with a strong central Government. The Opposition demanded a federal form of government, with a two-chamber parliament; and it wanted this to be defined in a written constitution which would be made difficult to amend. The constitution which both parties finally accepted was a compromise; in most respects the form of government was to be as proposed by the C.P.P. Government, but there were some concessions to the Opposition's wishes, and the constitution was made more difficult to alter than the C.P.P. had wished. The C.P.P. proposed that the constitution could be amended by a two-thirds majority of the members of Parliament who were in their places and took part in the vote: thus, if there were 105 members, but for any reason 24 were absent from Parliament when an amendment to the constitution was to be discussed, the amendment would be carried by 54 to 27. But this was not accepted, and the constitution as finally adopted said that it could be amended only by a two-thirds majority of all members, whether present or absent. Thus, in a Parliament of 105 members, 70 votes would be needed to carry the amendment, instead of only 54.

It is for such reasons as this that written constitutions are commonly made difficult to amend. The American Constitution cannot be amended unless there is in effect an overwhelming demand among the people. There are two ways in which amendments may be proposed: two-thirds of the House of Representatives may join with two-thirds of the Senate in proposing one, or the legislatures of two-thirds of the States may require Congress to call a special convention. When an amendment has been proposed, it must be ratified by three-fourths of the States (34 States out of fifty) before it becomes a valid part of the Constitution. It is easy to understand why only 23 Amendments have succeeded in making their way into the Constitution.

The British 'unwritten' constitution

It is commonly said that Britain itself has no written constitution; but that is not entirely true. Certainly, there is no one document corresponding to the American Constitution, to the British North America Act or to the Ghana Independence Act. Still more important, there is no law which is more difficult for Parliament to alter than ordinary laws; there is nothing that requires a two-thirds majority of Parliament, or the approval of three-fourths of the county councils, or confirmation by a special vote taken among the whole electorate, or any other extraordinary precaution.

On the other hand, there are many laws in force which lay down how this or that part of government is to be carried on. Of course, like any other law in Britain, they may in theory be changed at any time if Parliament so desires; but many of them have sunk so deep into the minds of Englishmen that it is impossible to imagine any free British Parliament wishing to change them. In 1688, for example, it was provided that the King cannot suspend laws without Parliament's consent: that subjects have a right to petition the King, and may not be punished for doing so: that excessive bail ought not to be required, nor excessive fines imposed, nor cruel and unusual punishments inflicted: that members of Parliament should be freely elected, and nothing said in Parliament should be questioned outside Parliament: that taxes could be levied only with Parliament's consent—and so on. This long and important law is called the Bill of Rights. As is usually the way in England, it was not an abstract declaration of the Rights of Man, but it was the settlement of a long fight between the Parliament and the King. The fight had ended with the defeat of King James II; his daughter Mary and her husband William were crowned queen and king, and the Bill of Rights laid down some of the conditions which the victorious Parliament imposed, and which the new queen and king accepted. Twelve years later, in 1700, another Act laid down that persons who held paid office under the king might not sit as members of the House of Commons, and that judges should hold office as long as they did their duty properly; their salaries should be fixed, and they should not be dismissed unless both Houses of Parliament voted for their dismissal. These provisions have a clear constitutional importance. One easy way by which the king might control Parliament would have been for him to bribe members by appointing them to jobs with large salaries but few or no duties. One way in which he might have exercised power over the people would have been to dismiss good judges and appoint and bribe bad ones. Both these tricks were now made impossible.

There have been more recent laws which have affected constitutional practice. 'All laws have to be passed by both Houses of Parliament and approved by the Queen'; this is a statement which is still largely true, and used to be completely true. In theory, the Queen still has the right to refuse her consent to a law which is submitted to her by Parliament. But it is more than 250 years since such a thing has happened, and for this reason alone it is unthinkable that the Queen should now try to exercise her right. There is another reason, even stronger. George III (1760-1820) was the last king of England to have a policy of his own. Since his time, it has always been understood that the Crown is above politics; the Queen acts on the advice of her Minister. Thus, there can be no question of her refusing her consent, for that would mean that her Ministers were refusing their consent to a Bill for which they were mainly, if not wholly, responsible—which would be absurd.[1]

Still, even though the Queen's consent to a Bill is invariably given, it is still necessary. The consent of the House of Commons too is always necessary. But since 1911 the consent of the House of Lords has not always been necessary. For some time before 1911 there had been friction between the House of Commons and the House of Lords. The Liberal Government had a strong majority in the Commons; the House of Lords was mainly Conservative. In 1909, the House of Lords took the strong step of rejecting the annual Finance Bill; and the Liberal Government determined that this behaviour must be stopped. It introduced a law which provided: (1) The Government might present a Bill for the royal assent without the agreement of the Lords, if the Speaker of the House of Commons certified that it was a money Bill (that is, contained no proposals other than financial proposals) and the Lords had not passed it within a month of receiving it; (2) if a Bill were not a money Bill, but a Bill to make changes in the law, and the Lords rejected it in three successive sessions of Parliament after the Commons passed it in each session, the Government might present the Bill for the royal assent without the Lords' agreement—provided two years had elapsed between the first debate on the Bill in the Commons and its final passing for the third time; (3) Parliament should last for only five years, instead of seven, as previously.

The effect of the new law would be to take away the Lords' power of rejecting a money Bill, leaving them with the power only of delaying the Bill for a month. A Bill other than a money Bill, which the Commons were determined to pass into law, could no longer be blocked by the Lords: it could only be delayed for two years. Could the House of Lords be expected to consent to a Bill which so drastically reduced its powers? Political feeling ran high, and the House of Lords was strongly inclined to reject the Bill. But the Prime Minister spoke to the King (George V) and let it be known that His Majesty had agreed, if necessary, to appoint enough new peers (pledged to support the Bill) to outweigh the hostile vote in the existing House of Lords. Faced with this threat, the Lords

---

[1] Ministers are not always wholly responsible. It is true that most Bills are introduced by the Government. But private members do still introduce Bills; and for a private member's Bill the Government cannot be said to be wholly responsible. But no private member's Bill could possibly pass through Parliament unless the Government gave it time and support; so Ministers are mainly responsible even for Bills originally introduced by private members.

CONSTITUTIONS 31

gave way and accepted the Bill, which became law as the Parliament Act of 1911. In 1949 the Act was amended so as to restrict the delaying power of the Lords still further.

There are two points to notice in this affair of the Parliament Act. The first is that it does lay down the powers of the House of Lords, which had never before been laid down by law, but only by custom. To that extent, it serves the same purpose as a written Constitution. The second point is that the law was passed in exactly the same way as any other law. True, the House of Lords was reluctant to pass it, and yielded only to a threat; but it did yield, and did pass the Bill so that it became law in the usual way. The threat that the King would create enough peers to ensure the passing of the Bill was an unusual one, but it was quite legal. No one has ever doubted that the Queen has power, if she chooses, to make every man in England a peer. The Parliament Act of 1911 was not the first law which had been accepted by the House of Lords only under such a threat.

These two Acts of 1911 and 1949 are modern examples which show, like the Bill of Rights, that it is not entirely true to say that Britain has no written Constitution.

How South Africa amended its constitution

Another interesting example of the way in which the rigidity of a Constitution (in this case a written Constitution) may be overcome is the means by which the South African Government contrived to remove Coloured voters from the general list, and place them on a separate voters' list. The South African Constitution was laid down by the British Government in the South Africa Act of 1909, which set up the Union of South Africa and gave it self-government. In the Cape Province, Bantu and Coloured voters had the same rights as white voters, but the Cape and the British Government failed to get Natal, the Orange Free State, and the Transvaal to agree to this liberal arrangement for the Union Parliament. The Cape was plainly on the defensive; and to make sure that its Bantu and Coloured voters could not easily be deprived of their votes by the Union Parliament, the South Africa Act provided that such a measure could only be passed by a two-thirds majority of the two Houses, sitting jointly. On this condition the Cape, which had threatened to stay out of the Union if its Bantu and Coloured voters were to be deprived of their votes, agreed to come in.

In 1936, the South African Government passed the Native Representation Act, which restricted the voting rights of the Bantu; it did not comply with the requirement of the two-thirds majority of a joint session, and the legal arguments by which it justified itself over this were not tested in the courts. But when in 1951 the Government tried to treat the Coloured voters as it had treated the Bantu fifteen years before, four voters brought an action against it, claiming that the Government's Bill, the Separate Representation of Voters Bill, was invalid because it should have been passed in the manner laid down in the South Africa Act of 1909—that is, by a two-thirds majority of both Houses sitting jointly. The Supreme Court of South Africa upheld the claim, and ruled that the law was invalid; and since the Government knew that it could not get its two-thirds majority, it had for the time to drop the idea.

But it found a way out of the difficulty in 1955. It increased the numbers of the upper House, the Senate, from 48 to 89. Most of the new Senators supported the Government, so the Government now had its two-thirds majority in the joint session; and it quickly used it, not only to carry through the Separate Representation of Voters Bill, but to repeal the obnoxious sections of the South Africa Act.[2] The courts held that there was nothing in the South Africa Act which would require a two-thirds majority of a joint session for a proposal to increase the size of the Senate. This device of increasing the size of the Senate, in order to overcome a hostile vote which is blocking the Government's way, is similar to the United Kingdom's device of overcoming a hostile House of Lords by the creation of new peers.

Constitutional Conventions

No written Constitution can possibly provide rules to cover every detail of the business of government; and if such a thing were possible, no business could be done because everybody would be too busy consulting the shelf full of books of rules. In government, as in all walks of life, much has to be left to the good sense and the good will of those who have dealings with each other. The written rules of the Constitution are supplemented by many unwritten agreements or understandings as to the way in which the written rules are to be understood and applied. (In a country like Britain, where the Constitution is largely unwritten, these unwritten understandings are even more important; but they are important everywhere.) These unwritten understandings are called the conventions of the constitution. Not only do they help the machinery to work smoothly, but

[2] It may seem strange that the South African Parliament should repeal part of an Act of the United Kingdom Parliament. But in 1931, the United Kingdom Parliament passed an Act called the Statute of Westminster, which laid it down clearly that the United Kingdom, Canada, Australia, New Zealand, and South Africa were equal members of the Commonwealth. It followed from this that none of the five Parliaments could henceforth control any other; and so South Africa claimed the power to control its own Constitution.

they help the constitution to adapt itself easily to changing needs. Without constitutional conventions, a country with a written constitution would be like a snake, which has to crack its old skin and grow a new one. The constitutional conventions help the constitution to grow and stretch like the skin of a mammal.

Constitutional conventions can always be enforced if necessary. If a convention were to be broken, there would certainly be much trouble and unpleasantness, and possibly a complete stoppage of government business. Everybody knows this; so if the convention requires you to do something which you would rather not do, you nevertheless obey the convention and do it. It is better to do it now without unpleasantness than to wait until you are forced to do it.

One important example of a constitutional convention in Britain is the appointment of the prime minister. In theory, the Queen may appoint anyone she chooses. But in fact, she is bound—by convention—to appoint the man who can command the support of the House of Commons. The party system helps her to know who this man is. If the Government has been defeated in Parliament, and resigns, the outgoing prime minister will advise Her Majesty to send for the leader of the Opposition and invite him to form a Government. The convention is enforced by the fact that his party will support him, but will support nobody else, and without the support of the majority of the House of Commons, the day-to-day work of government cannot be carried on. In 1951, for example, the Convention People's Party in the Gold Coast won thirty-four seats in the elections, while its opponents won four.[3] The leader of the C.P.P., Dr. Nkrumah, was in prison during the elections. But by the conventions of British parliamentary government, the Governor of the Gold Coast, Sir Charles Arden-Clarke, did the only possible thing in inviting Dr Nkrumah straight from prison to form a Government.

Another important convention of the British constitution is that the prime minister can ask the Queen to dissolve parliament whenever he chooses, and the Queen is bound to do as he asks. Behind this is the convention that the Queen must be above party politics. If the Queen did refuse to dissolve parliament when the prime minister asked her to, the prime minister would at once resign, and it would be extremely difficult for the Queen to find someone else able to form a Government with the support of the Commons. Her Majesty would immediately be involved in party negotiations and

---

[3] Besides these 38 elected members, there were 37 members elected by territorial and state councils; but the party allegiance of these 37 indirectly elected members is not clear.

involved in party politics, which is the thing that she must always avoid.

This particular convention is of the greatest importance in British politics, for it helps to keep Parliament in order. By law, the members of the House of Commons must not sit longer than five years; then there must be a dissolution and a fresh election. But there is no law which compels the Commons to sit for the full five years; on the contrary, as we have seen, the prime minister can bring about a dissolution when he pleases. Since no one is compelled to take up politics as a career, we may assume that members of parliament stand for election and take their seats because they enjoy the work of parliament. An election turns every member out of his seat, and gives him a great deal of hard work and worry and expense with the risk that he may be defeated and never return; it is an unpleasant experience, to be avoided as long as possible. Consequently, if the prime minister feels that his party is becoming uneasy and restive, and inclined to break into small groups, he can nearly always restore discipline with the threat of a dissolution. Similarly, when the parliament's five years of life is nearing its end, the Opposition is forced by this convention to behave sensibly and moderately. For, if one of the Opposition leaders, a man who is certain to be in the cabinet if his party wins the election, utters some reckless and irresponsible criticism, he may find that the prime minister takes him up on it, and says in effect, 'Very well; if that is the policy of the right honourable gentleman's party, I am sure that the country will prefer my policy. Parliament will be dissolved, and I am ready to fight an election on that issue.' No such convention existed in France in the nineteen-thirties. Parliament had a life of four years, and the prime minister had no power to have it dissolved until the four years were up. This was one of the main reasons why the members were divided into many small groups. If the Government were overthrown, there could not be a general election (unless of course the fall of the Government happened to coincide with the end of the four-year life of the parliament), and so members had no special reason to keep the Government in office. In fact, they had every reason to overthrow it; for members who held no office in the old Government might hope to be given office in the new. Under this system, the average life of a French Government was eighteen months. In 1934, the prime minister, M. Doumergue, tried to persuade France to adopt this convention; but the French parliament would not hear of it, and his Government fell.

Many other important features of the British system of government are matters of convention, not of law. It is by convention that we say that the Queen can do no wrong, though her Ministers may:

that the Cabinet has collective responsibility: that the civil service takes no part in politics, and that a Minister is not allowed to justify himself against parliamentary criticism by saying, 'The mistake was not mine; I was misled by Mr X, an officer in my Ministry.' We shall hear more of these conventions when we discuss cabinet government.

An interesting example of a constitutional convention in West Africa arose in Ghana in 1957 on the eve of independence. One of the fears expressed by the Opposition party was that when Ghana became independent, the C.P.P. Government would staff the whole civil service with its own members. There was in existence a Public Service Commission, whose duty it was to advise the Government on appointments to the public service; the Opposition feared that the C.P.P. would begin by filling the Public Service Commission with its own members, so that the Commission thereafter would appoint only C.P.P. members. To remove this fear, Dr Nkrumah promised that before appointing anyone to be a member of the Public Service Commission, he would consult the Leader of the Opposition; and he said that he hoped this would become a constitutional convention with all future prime ministers.

We have said that one use of constitutional conventions is to help a constitution to adapt itself to new conditions without violent change. Perhaps the most conspicuous example of this is the way in which the British Cabinet system developed. In the seventeenth century, the Minister was the king's servant, and had the unpleasant task of defending the king's policy against an often critical parliament. The Ministers developed the habit of consulting together and facing parliament with a policy jointly devised. Then the party system—itself purely a matter of convention—developed, and it became first convenient, and then necessary, for the king to choose all his Ministers from the majority party. Thus, the Ministers gradually changed from being responsible to the king, and became primarily responsible instead to parliament. But parliament itself was changing. In 1832 the first Reform Act was passed, which began the process of making parliament more truly representative of the people. The more parliament came to represent the people, the plainer did it become that all Ministers must stick together and accept collective responsibility for their policy.

This kind of development is still going on. There is still no law to say that a Minister must be a member of either House of Parliament, but by convention he must be. On the other hand, this convention itself is modified by another convention. It sometimes happens that a Minister has the misfortune to lose his seat in a general election, although his party is returned to power. He is not compelled to resign his post. Usually some member of his party who has been returned with a large majority will resign his seat to make way for the Minister; there will be a bye-election, and the Minister will again enter parliament. For the few weeks that this takes, convention allows the Minister to continue in office, though for the time being he is not a member of parliament. Again, a convention has been established in recent years that the prime minister must be a member of the House of Commons; a peer cannot now be prime minister.

Interpreting the constitution

Who is to say whether an action is unconstitutional? A Government's political opponents will often accuse it of acting unconstitutionally, using the word quite loosely. It often happens in the British parliament, for example, that a long and complicated Bill is being discussed, and the Government moves and carries a resolution fixing the time at which the discussion will be closed and the vote taken. Whenever this happens, the Opposition is indignant; it says that the Government is allowing insufficient time and is acting unconstitutionally. This happens, whichever party is in power; and no Government troubles itself over that accusation.

But things are different when there is a written Constitution. If the Government is accused of acting unconstitutionally then, it has its reply ready: 'Show us which article of the Constitution we are violating, and justify your claim that what we are doing is a violation.' This at once becomes a matter for the lawyers, and it is pretty sure to end up in the Supreme Court and to be settled by the Court's decision. We have seen, for example, that the Supreme Court of South Africa decided that the Separate Representation of Voters Act was invalid, because it had not been passed in the way prescribed by South Africa's constitution, the South Africa Act of 1909.

This duty of interpreting the constitution is one of the most important functions of the Supreme Court in every country which possesses a written constitution. Legal interpretation may be a very important means of helping the constitution to develop. In America for instance, the powers of the federal Government have been very greatly extended—much more than the Founding Fathers could have anticipated—by a series of legal interpretations of Section 8(3) of the constitution, which says,

'The Congress shall have power to regulate commerce with foreign nations, and among the several States, and with the Indian tribes.'

Since the clause was drafted, railways and motor cars have been invented: also aircraft, electricity power lines, and pipe-lines for oil and natural gas. All these things cross State boundaries; and so they become matters for the federal Congress, not for State legislatures. By this series of legal interpretations, the Federal Government has been strengthened in relation to the States; and so the constitution has in fact, though not in theory, been modified.

For practical purposes, there is no authority higher than the Supreme Court; and if the Supreme Court's interpretation of the constitution is unwelcome to you, there is nothing you can do about it. But even judges of the Supreme Court are fallible human beings, influenced by the general opinions fashionable in their day. Thus, the same constitution may be interpreted in different ways in different generations. The Supreme Court of the United States once held that laws passed in certain states to fix minimum wages and maximum hours of work were unconstitutional, because they infringed the basic right of 'freedom of contract'. But a later generation of judges reversed the decision. President Franklin D. Roosevelt (1933-45), who took office as President at a time of great economic distress, tried to remedy matters by a large programme of Government action which he called a 'New Deal'. Several of the measures he proposed were barred by the Supreme Court as unconstitutional. The President of the United States has great powers, and it was a time of great emergency; but he had to accept the Court's judgment. There was no higher authority to which he could appeal, and he had no power to dismiss the judges, or to appoint a batch of new judges to out-vote those who opposed his plans, or to act in defiance of the Court's judgment. The only power he had over the Supreme Court was to appoint new judges to fill vacancies when they occurred. Luckily for the President, some of the hostile judges were old men near retirement; and when one or two vacancies occurred he was able to fill them by judges more favourable to his plans, and get the Supreme Court to reverse its earlier decisions.

In matters not covered by a written constitution, a Government could properly be charged with acting unconstitutionally if it ignored an established constitutional convention. In Britain for example, it would certainly be unconstitutional if a Government was beaten in the House of Commons on a formal vote of confidence but refused to resign. So would it be in Ghana if, when Ghana had an Opposition party in parliament,[4] the Government filled vacancies on the Public Services Commission without consulting the leader of the Opposition.

---

[4] Ghana is now a one-party state, so that this particular case could no longer arise.

CHAPTER IV

Power and Sovereignty

Where does power lie, and what is its origin? Emergence of strong states out of mediaeval European disorder: sixteenth- and seventeenth-century thinkers conclude, (i) the king must have overwhelming power, (ii) the people on the whole must wish him to have it. This overwhelming power is called sovereignty.
Thomas Hobbes and his Leviathan: *his theory of sovereignty as the escape from the evils of the state of nature. Sovereignty must be absolute. Hobbes and the 'covenant'. Hobbes's thought conditioned by his experience of the civil war.*
John Locke: his thought conditioned by his experience of the 1688 revolution. His view of the state of nature and the social contract compared with Hobbes's. Peoples have lived without much political organization, and have voluntarily organized themselves into a state. States may be founded by force; but ultimately, government must rest on the consent of the governed. How far do these opinions correspond to facts?
Montesquieu and the separation of powers: his imperfect analysis of the English constitution of his own day. Influence of Montesquieu illustrated from the United States constitution: checks and balances. The separation of powers in other countries: in modern Britain the independence of the judiciary the only sign of this separation.

THE word *government* comes from a Latin word meaning the steering of a ship. The rudder and the tiller or steering-wheel are only a very small part of the ship, but they control the direction in which the whole ship moves. Similarly, the people forming the Government total only a small proportion of the whole body of citizens, but they control the action of the state.

How is this control exercised? This is a question which has occupied political thinkers all through European history; and in every century, men have based their thought on the political conditions they found existing.

One of the essential steps in the development of modern Europe was the emergence, out of the feudal disorder of the middle ages, of states with strong central Governments. England was the first, then came Spain and later still, France; and it was in these three countries that the idea of nationality first developed.

POWER AND SOVEREIGNTY 39

Political thinkers in the sixteenth and seventeenth centuries reflected on this development. They noted the painful struggles that the kings of England, Spain and France had with their nobles and with their parliaments, and they were struck by two features of the process. The first was that the king could never have established himself without overwhelming power. Henry VII of England, for example (1485-1509), would allow none of his nobles to possess artillery; and since no castle could stand against the king's big guns, his commands had to be obeyed. The second striking fact was that, although the nobles might regret losing their power, the great majority of the people were delighted to have one strong government to rule and protect them.

From these reflections, political thinkers drew two conclusions. First: in every state there must be someone, or some group of people, who possess overwhelming power. Second: this power may be misused, but there must have been a moment at which the mass of the people were glad to support it, even if they dislike the way in which it is being misused at present. This overwhelming power is called *sovereignty,* and the individual or group which holds it is called the *sovereign.*

This theory of sovereignty, which was first worked out in the sixteenth century, is clearly explained by the Englishman Thomas Hobbes (1588-1679), who published his famous book *Leviathan* in 1651. It was in the middle of the English Civil War; King Charles I had been beheaded two years earlier, and in *Leviathan's* year, Oliver Cromwell defeated the young king Charles II and forced him to take refuge across the sea. Hobbes was disgusted at the cruelty and wastage of civil war, and sought a strong sovereign power as the only way out. He writes as if he thought the sovereign must be an individual—either a king or someone like Oliver Cromwell, who ruled as strongly as any king. The sovereign's power, he says, must be absolute, and although the sovereign may allow someone to exercise power on his behalf, the sovereign power can never be shared; the sovereign's rights are 'incommunicable and inseparable'.

Until men have such a sovereign to rule over them, says Hobbes, their lives must be 'solitary, poor, nasty, brutish, and short'. Hobbes is so impressed with the evils of this disorder, that he cannot imagine anyone preferring it to the order which is imposed by a strong government. He takes it for granted, therefore, that all existing governments must have been originally founded by a group of men who voluntarily give up their natural right of self-defence, and who 'confer all their power and strength upon one man, or upon one assembly of men, that may reduce all their wills, by plurality of voices, unto one will'. It is as if they all make a covenant with one another,

'in such manner, as if every man should say to every man, "I authorise and give up my right of governing myself to this man, or to this assembly of men; on this condition, that thou give up thy right to him, and authorise all his actions in like manner." '

In this Hobbesian 'covenant' we see the beginning of the idea of the Social Contract, which was discussed at length by Rousseau.[1]

This theory of sovereignty has had a great influence on later political thought. Hobbes grants that sovereign power need not be held by one man; it may be held by an assembly. In modern times we should go further, and say that sovereign power may be held by a partnership. In modern Britain, for example, there is nothing which the Queen and Parliament together are incapable of doing. They have released named individuals from legal penalties which they had incurred; they have given independence to various British colonies; and similarly, they could, if they chose, make a treaty with Burma or Peru whereby London and the county of Kent ceased to be British and became Burmese or Peruvian territory. It was proposed a few years ago that the Mediterranean island of Malta should become legally part of Britain, and in 1940 the Churchill Government proposed to France that Britain and France should join into one country. Neither of these latter schemes came to anything; but nobody doubted that the Queen and Parliament had power to do them.

John Locke (1632-1704) was a schoolboy at the time of Charles I's execution, and he based his thinking on the politics of the England in which he lived: an England in which king Charles II was playing a skilful game against his parliaments. The king was determined to make himself an absolute monarch like his relative, king Louis XIV of France. He took French money, and would have liked to have French troops to enable him to crush the House of Commons. Locke's sympathies were on the side of parliament, and he took a genial and optimistic view of human nature in general. Hobbes thought that most men were incapable of governing themselves; Locke's view was quite the opposite. It was natural for Locke to sympathise with the Revolution of 1688, and to evolve a political theory which helped to justify it. Locke's theory, like Hobbes's, is based on the idea of the social contract, or (as Hobbes called it) the covenant. But the contract as Locke sees it is very different from that of Hobbes.

[1] See page 16.

POWER AND SOVEREIGNTY 41

'The natural liberty of man,' says Locke, 'is to be free from any superior power on earth, and not to be under the will or legislative authority of man, but to have only the law of nature for his rule.'

Locke looked at history and saw that there have been groups of people who have lived without much political organization—like the early Greek villagers before they organized themselves into cities, or like the primitive Anglo-Saxon clans out of whom the English people have grown, or like the early Dutch settlers in South Africa, who disliked all governments and trekked away into the interior to escape from government and find freedom. Similarly, Locke points out that there are cases in history of men who have voluntarily organized themselves into a political society. He quotes the beginnings of Rome and Venice, both of which cities were established by wanderers. Other examples are the establishment of the United States and of the Swiss Confederation. There are two clear examples in the history of Ghana: Okomfo Anokye's work at the end of the seventeenth century in bringing about the establishment of the Ashanti state, and the establishment of the Fante Confederacy in 1873. Africa is full of recent examples. There was no such thing as a Nigerian nation, for example, before the British came. During the British period, the feeling of Nigerian nationhood grew, and when the British rule ended, the many different peoples of Nigeria decided to hold together as one independent nation-state.

Locke realises of course that most states are established by force. England was hammered into a nation by the Norman kings from 1066 onwards; the kingdom of Mali was built up through the fighting of Mari Djata and his successors; the Turks came out of central Asia and conquered for themselves a kingdom in Asia Minor and Europe. But Locke emphasizes that conquest by itself gives no right; all government must rest on the consent of the governed. Government exists for the general convenience of those living under it; and if they find themselves worse off, instead of better, they have a right to change their government—by lawful constitutional means if possible, but if necessary, by force.

'Whensoever therefore the Legislative shall transgress this fundamental rule of society, and (either by ambition, fear, folly or corruption) endeavour to grasp themselves, or put into the hands of any other, an absolute power over the lives, liberties and estates of the people; by this breach of trust they forfeit the power the people had put into their hands for quite contrary ends; and it devolves to the people, who have a right to resume their original liberty, and by the establishment of the new Legislative (such as they shall think fit) provide for their own safety and security, which is the end for which they are in society.'

This is the use that Locke makes of his contract theory; and it is a very natural doctrine for one who lived through the 1688 revolution and sympathised with the revolutionaries.

Locke's view that all government must rest on consent can be defended from human experience. A Government may be originally established by force, but it cannot very long continue in power unless it receives some support from its subjects. The English disliked being conquered by the Normans in 1066 and being ruled by Norman kings instead of by their own English kings. But the Norman kings had very little trouble from their English subjects. On the whole, the English supported the Norman kings because their strong rule was far better than civil war among the Norman nobles. Again, though Africa today regards colonialism as evil, there was a time, sixty or seventy years ago, when many African peoples welcomed the establishment of British rule because it rescued them from tribal warfare and slave raiding and other discomforts of 'the state of nature'. Similarly, we may say that the Government rests on the consent at least of the majority of its people in every country where a citizen is free to criticize his government openly and to convert others to his way of thinking if he can, and where elections are free so that the majority vote can compel the Government to resign. It should be emphasized that both elements are necessary: both freedom to criticize, and freedom to change the government. There is a story of Frederick the Great of Prussia (1740-86) that he saw in the street a piece of paper stuck on a wall, so high that it could not easily be read. He made one of his officers take it down and bring it to him, and he found that it was a bitter attack on his Government. He had it put back on the wall, but much lower, so that every passer-by could easily read it. 'My people and I,' he said, 'have come to a good arrangement: they are to say what they please, and I am to do what I please.' That is not good enough.

Frederick the Great could do what he pleased. Hobbes and Locke have taught us that in each state there must be some man or group of men who is sovereign: that is, can do as he pleases. Locke modifies this by saying that if the sovereign uses his power contrary to the purposes for which it was given him, the people may take it back again; but even Locke does not deny that sovereign power must exist. In Britain, as we have seen, it belongs to the Queen in Parliament: that is, to the partnership between the Queen and the Parliament.

In every political society, even in the simplest, there must somewhere be this sovereignty: there must be someone who has the power (no doubt after holding the customary consultations) to give a decision which must be obeyed. In a large and complicated state, decisions of different types may perhaps be taken by different people. A civil servant may feel unable to decide a question on his own authority; he must consult his superior. In American slang, this way of referring to someone else for a decision is called 'passing the buck'. President Eisenhower of the United States used to have a card on his desk saying, 'The buck stays here.' The ultimate decision and responsibility must be his. Within the wide limits of the Presidential authority he was sovereign.

The fact that there are any limits to the Presidential authority is due largely to the teaching of the Frenchman Montesquieu (1689-1755). When Locke was a young man, the French Government, under its absolute king, had been at the height of its power; in those days France had not only been the leader of Europe in all the arts, but also in military power. She had been feared as well as admired. But in Montesquieu's day, fifty years later, the French Government was becoming weaker. England, Holland and Prussia had risen up as strong military powers, and French resources had been wasted in long years of unsuccessful warfare. Montesquieu, himself a Frenchman, spent two years in England trying to discover what were the features of the British system of government which enabled Britain to combine an efficient system of administration with a high degree of personal freedom. He thought he had discovered the secret in the separation of powers, and the system of checks and balances which prevented any one of the powers in the state from dominating the others.

Separation of Powers

Governments have three kinds of powers or functions: legislative, executive, and judicial—of making laws, of administering the laws, of hearing and judging disputes according to the laws. The legislative power belongs mainly to parliament (and similar bodies such as local authorities), the executive to the civil service and local government service, the judicial to the judges and magistrates. In Montesquieu's day, the Government was not nearly so closely concerned with the daily life of its citizens as it is today, and when Montesquieu speaks of the executive power, he is thinking of such matters as making war and signing a peace treaty, maintaining internal order, and negotiating with foreign countries.

It seemed to Montesquieu that in Britain the three powers were kept separately from one another, and that this was the secret of the success of the British government.

'When the legislative and executive powers are united in the same person, or in the same body of magistrates, there can be no liberty . . . Again, there is no liberty if the judiciary power be not separated from the legislative and executive. Were it joined with the legislative, the life and liberty of the subject would be exposed to arbitrary control, for the judge would then be legislator. Were it joined to the executive, the judge might behave with violence and oppression. There would be an end of everything were the same men or the same body (whether of nobles or of the people) to exercise all three powers.'

What Montesquieu means is that, if the judges were members of parliament, they would be subject to party passion, and their interpretation of the law would be coloured by their recollection of the debates in which they had taken part. In the criminals they tried, or in the plaintiffs and defendants who appeared before them, they would see party friends or party opponents. At present, a judge always takes the line, 'I am here to judge according to the law. I know nothing of what parliament intended, I know only what it has said. You may be right when you say that parliament never intended the law to have this effect, but as I understand the law, it does have this effect, and I am bound by it. I cannot change the law; only parliament can do that.' If the judge were a member of parliament, he could not take this line; and however hard he tried, he would never be able to escape the suspicion that his judgments were coloured by his political feeling. A man who has lost his case would say—as he will never dream of saying today—'Of course, as soon as I saw that X was to hear the case, I knew I had no chance. He is a Conservative, and so was my opponent; and of course the two Conservatives stuck together, and I, being a Liberal, was bound to be in the wrong.'

Again, if the judge were a cabinet minister, or a member of the civil service, it would be difficult for him to keep 'Government policy' from influencing his judgments. This is a danger which is much greater now than it would have been when Montesquieu wrote. There are large numbers of disputes nowadays between individual citizens and Government departments, as well as the cases in which the Crown prosecutes a citizen for breach of the laws. In 1951, for example, a poor labourer brought an action against the Ministry of Health in England. He had been treated in a Government hospital; he came out of hospital with his condition worse instead of better, and he claimed that the hospital authorities had been careless in their treatment. His first action failed, but the court of appeals reversed the judgment, and he won his case. Now if the judges had been members of the civil service, they would have seen the official files and the minutes on them. Their colleagues in the service would have brought pressure to bear on them: 'You mustn't let us down; we must stick together. Even if there was carelessness somewhere in this hospital, the man will not be able to prove it. It will be very unpleasant for the surgeon and the nurses to have to go into the witness box, and the public will gain the impression that things are much worse than they really are. The best thing will be for you to dismiss the case with the minimum of fuss and publicity.' And if the judges' professional conscience led them to resist this pressure, they might be told in solemn tones by the Permanent Secretary, or even by the Minister, 'It is not in the public interest that the work of the Department should be exposed to public criticism in this way.' With their official careers to think of, only very strong men would be able to resist such pressure. But, luckily for the plaintiff in this case, the judges in Britain do not have to think of their official careers; they are quite independent of the executive, and no such pressure can possibly be brought to bear on them.

Montesquieu lays great emphasis on the independence of the judiciary; he lays rather less on the separation of the legislative and executive powers. He grants that the executive must have some share in the process of legislation, even if only a veto. But he does not think that parliament ought to share in the executive power, which, he says, 'ought to be in the hands of a monarch, because this branch of government, having need of despatch, is better administered by one than by many'. He admired the British constitution as he understood it, because the executive was in the hands of the King and his ministers, the judiciary was quite independent both of King and of parliament, and the parliament's business was to pass laws and vote taxes.

Montesquieu's analysis of the British constitution was not entirely correct, even in his own day. He was correct as regards the judiciary. One consequence of the 1688 revolution was that the judges were declared independent, and their salaries placed beyond the control of parliament[2] and of the executive. As regards the executive, he was not far wrong. The king appointed his Ministers, and there was yet no law or convention to make him choose them from either House of parliament, though in practice, he found it convenient to

[2] Parliament passed an Act which gave up its right to vote money every year for judges' salaries, and so to have an opportunity every year of discussing whether to increase the sum or reduce it. Strictly speaking, parliament could repeal this Act and change the system at any time; but the convention is now so well established that it is unthinkable that parliament should break it.

do so. Moreover, as the king could appoint his Ministers, so he could dismiss them; and although the Ministers naturally consulted together, each gave the king his individual advice, and the king was not bound to act on it.

But the principle was already well established that the House of Commons alone could provide money; and it would not provide money unless it was generally satisfied with what the Government was doing. Thus, the executive was already responsible to the legislature for the broad policy, if not yet for every detail. Before Montesquieu's book appeared, the leadership in the Government had passed from the House of Lords to the House of Commons. After 1714, the king never attended debates in the House of Lords. And a more important change was coming about. King George I (1714-27) was a German, who spoke the English language badly and understood little of English affairs. He knew that the Whig party had made the revolution of 1688 and the Whig party again had brought him to the British throne. He could not possibly offend the Whig party, and so he had to allow it to organize the Government much as it wished. Under Sir Robert Walpole, who was his chief minister for over twenty years, the cabinet system began to develop: the ministers ceased to give the king their individual advice and acted collectively, and they worked in the closest possible co-operation with the majority in the House of Commons. In 1713, the House resolved that it would consider no proposals for expenditure unless they came from the Government; this made the Government directly responsible to Parliament for all State expenditure. Parliament would vote no money for longer than a year at a time; and since there is hardly anything that the Government can do without spending money, every action of the executive becomes liable to scrutiny by the legislature.

In such ways as these, the legislature was already becoming, even in Montesquieu's day, partly responsible for the work of the executive: it might have no powers to act, but it could allow, or forbid, the executive to act—and it could require the executive to explain why it had not taken action which parliament had approved.

On the other hand, the executive was becoming partly responsible for legislation. As the business of state expanded, more and more legislation was needed; and a bigger and bigger proportion of the new laws were introduced by the Government. Here again, the executive had no power of making laws; but it controlled the majority of the House of Commons, and that majority was willing to vote the laws which the executive proposed to it.

Thus, even during Montesquieu's lifetime, the legislative and executive powers of government were coming to be exercised, not by parliament and Ministers apart from each other, but by parliament and Ministers in collaboration. Today, as we shall see when we discuss cabinet government, that collaboration is still closer. Only the judiciary is completely free from both executive and legislature; and even that freedom is not beyond all danger.³ It is only fair to Montesquieu to say that as far as the legislative and executive powers are concerned, he is more insistent that they should co-operate closely together than that they should be strictly separate. Looking at the British parliament, he says,

'Here, then, is the fundamental constitution of the government we are treating of. The legislative body is composed of two parts which check one another by the mutual privilege of veto. They are both restrained by the executive as the executive, in turn, is restrained by them. These three powers should naturally form a state of repose or inaction. But as there is a necessity for movement in the course of human affairs, they are forced to move, but still in concert.'

The essential is that neither should dominate the other; there must be a system of checks and balances to ensure that they cannot move unless 'in concert'.

Montesquieu's work had great influence. The British went on developing their methods of government without paying much attention to a Frenchman's analysis of what they were doing. But abroad, the doctrine of the separation of powers and of checks and balances was carefully studied. In some European countries, new constitutions were introduced and parliaments established in imitation of the British system as described by Montesquieu. Sometimes the new and inexperienced parliaments were a thorough nuisance; they made long speeches and criticized the government without being able to do any constructive work in partnership with the executive. In Germany, for example, the new constitution had to be revised so as to enable the executive to get on with its work without being too much hindered by parliament. In Germany, and in some other countries, the doctrine of separation of powers was applied so as to set up an executive largely free from parliamentary control.

But it is in the United States that the doctrine has had most influence. Besides their respect for Montesquieu, the Americans had another reason for adopting the doctrine. In colonial days, the American colonies were governed under the terms of grants or charters made by the king. Those charters were issued at a time when the executive power belonged to the king, and when no one doubted his right to organize the government in his new American

---

³ See the discussion of administrative courts on pages 57-60.

lands as he pleased. It was usual for the charters to provide for a legislative assembly, but to put the executive power in the hands of a governor appointed by the king. The Americans did not much object to this arrangement, which on the whole resembled the system in England itself. Like Montesquieu, they admired the British system of government; like him, they did not realize that at the time of their war of independence, the executive power was already passing from the king to the cabinet. By putting their new Constitution in writing, they perpetuated what they conceived to be the British constitution of their day.

Under the American Constitution, the executive power belongs to the President, and every officer in the United States, whether in the armed forces or in the civil service, draws his authority from the President. He appoints the members of his cabinet; each of them is in charge of a Government department, and is personally responsible to the President, but not to Congress. There is no collective responsibility. The President is commander-in-chief, and can declare war and make peace, though his peace treaties require to be approved by a two-thirds majority in the Senate. The President is elected for four years, and the members of his cabinet resign when he goes out of office.

Congress, the legislative body, consists of two Houses, the upper House or Senate and the lower House, the House of Representatives. The members of the cabinet may not sit or vote in either House. The executive has no power of introducing a Bill into Congress; the President may send Congress a message recommending it to make such-and-such a law, but he cannot make Congress act on his recommendation. The President is elected on a party vote for four years, and the House of Representatives is elected on a party vote for two years; so it often happens that half-way through his term of office, the President finds himself faced with a hostile House of Representatives. Every two years, moreover, one-third of the Senate has to be elected, also on a party vote; so it may happen that the Senate too is hostile to the President. The President has no power of dissolving Congress.

Executive and legislature in the United States are thus severely independent, and each has a check on the powers of the other. The legislature for example can check misgovernment by the executive; it can refuse to vote taxes. The executive can check unwise legislation by Congress; the President can veto its Bills. The royal veto on a Bill has not been exercised in England since 1707, but the President of the United States frequently vetoes Bills today. On the other hand, Congress can force a Bill into law in spite of the President's veto, if there is a two-thirds majority in both Houses in favour of doing so. Congress did this twenty times between 1933 and 1952.

The American judiciary is independent both of the executive and of Congress. The Supreme Court has a powerful check on the powers of both: it can declare any Bill, or any executive action, to be unconstitutional. On the other hand, Congress and President have checks on the judiciary: the Congress establishes courts and draws up rules for court procedure, and the President appoints the judges, though he cannot dismiss a judge or interfere with his salary.

We shall discuss later on the differences between presidential government of the American type and cabinet government of the British type.[4] Here we are discussing the general question of power and sovereignty, and the theory of the separation of powers. All we need add at this point is that the doctrine of the separation of powers, which has had so much influence in the United States, and somewhat less influence in some other countries, has had little or no influence in Britain, except for the care taken to keep the judiciary independent of Government or parliamentary control. In Britain there are none of the careful checks and balances which the American Constitution provides to ensure that the different branches of government cannot dominate each other.

[4] See Chapter Eight.

CHAPTER V

The Rule of Law

The sovereign may be legally absolute, but his power is limited by moral force: he must obey the law.
First meaning of the rule of law: all state authority must be used in accordance with the law; arbitrary power is not allowed. But there are qualifications to this: (i) What is the law of the land? In Britain, we have common law, statute law, statutory regulations and by-laws. (ii) Arbitrary acts are not allowed, but discretionary acts must be: parliament lays down the limits of discretion to be allowed to a Minister. (iii) Citizens' personal liberty must be secure. The writ of habeas corpus. But emergency legislation may sometimes be necessary.
Second meaning of the rule of law: all men are subject to the same law. But this is qualified by the fact that not all law is dispensed in the ordinary courts; nowadays some of it is dispensed in administrative tribunals. How can administrative tribunals comply with the rule of law? Their advantages in certain types of case.
Third meaning of the rule of law: 'This is a free country.' The belief in human rights. What will preserve human rights? They cannot be preserved merely by paper constitutions.

BOTH Hobbes and Locke assume that as long as a political society endures, its sovereign must be absolute. But this doctrine of absolute or sovereign power is modified by another fundamental constitutional doctrine: the Rule of Law. Legally, the sovereign may be able to do whatever he pleases; but the doctrine of the Rule of Law means that the sovereign's legal power is limited by a moral force. The sovereign is bound to exercise his power in accordance with the law of the land; if he acts contrary to the law, he is destroying the fabric of society, and (as Locke would say) throwing his people back into the state of nature. The rule of law, as we shall see, means more than this; but it certainly means that the sovereign is morally bound to rule according to the law.

FIRST MEANING OF THE RULE OF LAW

The first meaning is the one we have already mentioned. All who bear any part of the State's authority must use it in accordance with the laws of the land. There must be no such thing as arbitrary power: that is, power which is used simply at the discretion of the officer using it, without any regard to the law. Nobody is allowed to say, 'I do not care what the law on the matter may be; this man is a nuisance, and he shall be imprisoned.' Nobody is allowed to say, 'The State needs this piece of land, so we will take it. We will talk of paying compensation afterwards; if the owner is reasonable, we may pay him a fair sum, but if he makes unnecessary difficulty, we will pay him nothing at all, just as a warning to other property-owners.' These are examples of arbitrary power.

Why should such arbitrary power not be allowed? Because every citizen is entitled to know his rights and his duties. We expect everyone to know what the law requires him to do. If we prosecute a man for failing to render an income-tax return, or to take out a licence for his car or his radio, we shall not allow him to escape punishment by pleading, 'I did not know that I had to do this.' We shall reply, 'Then you ought to have known; if you did not know what the law was, you should have asked.' Similarly, we as government officials ought not to escape punishment if we violate a citizen's legal rights —for example, by punishing him for an action which is not an offence against the law, or by taking away his property without sufficient compensation, or by spending his money in ways which his representatives in parliament have not authorized. If arbitrary government like this were allowed, we should be ignoring all that Locke and Rousseau have taught us.

First qualification
There are three qualifications to be made to this. One is the meaning of the phrase 'the law of the land'. If we wish to know whether what we are doing is permitted by the law, there are three kinds of law we have to consider. First, there is the common law. The common law in Britain and America is the law which was originally based on the law and custom which was common to all the Anglo-Saxon tribes. The common law develops as cases and judgments accumulate; a judge gives his decision in the case before him on the precedent of decisions given in similar cases. Common law is case law, law based on recorded judgments. In *The Merchant of Venice*, Shylock's case against Antonio is clear: Antonio has signed a bond, and the bond is forfeit; why should not Shylock claim the penalty? But it is plain that Shylock is seeking, not mere justice, but revenge; and so Antonio's friends urge the Duke to stretch the law:

> 'To do a great right, do a little wrong,
> And curb this cruel devil of his will.'

But Portia, though she is Antonio's counsel, will not have it. The law must not be stretched, it must be obeyed. If the Duke gives a decision contrary to the law.

> ' 'Twill be recorded for a precedent;
> And many an error, by the same example
> Will rush into the State. It cannot be.'

That is case law. Britain has no criminal code. Many of the most serious crimes, such as burglary, forgery, and embezzlement, are not the subject of any statute or Act of Parliament. They are crimes at common law.

Next comes the statute law, the law which is contained in Acts of Parliament. The Road Traffic Acts, for example create offences of varying gravity, each with its appropriate penalty. There are very many Acts which describe offences and the penalties attached to them.

But there is also a third kind of law, the statutory regulation. Parliament often gives a Minister the power to make regulations and to lay down penalties for breaking them.[1] Similar powers are given to local government authorities, or to a railway company. It is under such regulations that we find ourselves forbidden to throw down litter or to pick flowers in a public park; to enter a railway carriage while it is moving; to smoke or sing or play a musical instrument in a public library; to park a car so as to obstruct the traffic, or to drive the wrong way down a one-way street.

There are thus these three kinds of law: common law, statute law, and the by-law or statutory regulation. The citizen is expected to know the law and obey it; and similarly, the official is expected to use his authority in obedience to the law. The statutory regulation gives the official or the Minister no chance of governing arbitrarily. For one thing, the regulation must be published and made accessible to the public. For another thing, parliament is careful to limit the powers which it delegates to the Minister. The regulations are made in accordance with the terms of a statute (which is why they are called statutory regulations) or Act of Parliament; and the statute will lay down in general terms the subjects on which the Minister is empowered to issue regulations, and the maximum penalty which the courts may inflict for any breach. Further, it is usual for the regulations to be laid before parliament

---

[1] This is sometimes described in another way: it is said that parliament delegates some of its legislative power to the Minister; and his regulations are described as delegated legislation.

for approval before they are brought into force, so that parliament has a chance of disallowing any regulation which it thinks bad.

Second qualification

The second qualification is that we must distinguish between an arbitrary act and a discretionary act. Arbitrary acts are bad, but some discretionary acts are inevitable. Governments must have certain general powers to take administrative action, and within limits, what action they take and when they take it must be left to their discretion. Let us suppose for example that the Ghana Government wishes to extend its internal air services. It is clearly in the public interest that it should do so, and it would be unreasonable to require the Government to come to parliament for a special Bill every time it wishes to acquire land for a new airfield. The Government will ask parliament to pass a general Act which lays down the conditions on which land may be acquired for such purposes; and —under the rule of law—it will act in accordance with the terms of the Act. Now if a man living on the outskirts of Peki or Enchi or Salaga is notified that under this Act the Government intends to acquire his land for the construction of an airfield, he may very likely grumble, 'Why should this happen to me, and not to my neighbour, or to someone living on the other side of the town?' But he cannot accuse the Government of acting arbitrarily. The Government is acting within its legal powers and is following the procedure laid down in the law. Whether the Government should decide to build the airfield this year, and not five years hence, and on this side of the town and not on the other side—these are matters for the Government to decide in its discretion according to the advice of its experts. Again, someone in Nigeria may make a living by ferrying people across a river, and the more traffic there is, the better the living that he will make. But the day may come when the Government decides that his ferry should be replaced by a bridge. It must have discretion to choose the exact site of the bridge and the timing of the construction according to the public interest and its programme of public works. The ferryman cannot accuse the Government of acting arbitrarily. The Government can reply, 'But you must have known that a bridge would be built here sooner or later. You cannot blame us for building it now. We should have built it years ago if we had been able to, and you should think yourself lucky that your ferry has been allowed to run for so long.'

Another frequent series of discretionary acts arises out of modern town planning and traffic requirements. Houses and land are acquired for the purpose of building a trunk road. Governments must have discretion in such matters, and the rule of law is satisfied if no one's property is acquired without his having an opportunity to protest, and without his receiving fair compensation. It is usual for such actions to be taken only after long discussion and public inquiry. Sometimes things happen in the opposite way. A farmer may find that because a new road has been made near his land, one of his fields which was of little agricultural value becomes very valuable as a piece of building land. He may decide to build a restaurant or a petrol filling station on it; but when he applies for permission he may find that the Government uses its discretion to refuse permission. This sort of discretionary act is inevitable; it is quite different from an arbitrary act.

Third qualification

One of the fundamental purposes of the rule of law is to ensure that the citizens' personal freedom shall be preserved from arbitrary interference. Locke taught us that men have natural rights of life, liberty, and property. One of the causes, both of the English revolution of 1688 and of the French revolution a century later, was that the kings claimed to override the law in the interests of the State. The King of France maintained his power of arresting and imprisoning men who inconvenienced his government, without having them tried for any offence against the law. In England, this power had been dropped before 1688; Charles I (1625-49) had used it, but his successors had not dared to.

In Britain, with its largely unwritten constitution, this particular freedom is maintained by an institution called by the Latin name *habeas corpus*. This Latin phrase means, 'You are to produce the body'; it is the opening of a legal document which is addressed by the king (or by the courts of justice, in the king's name) to the keeper of a prison. The document orders the keeper, 'You are to produce the body of X, whom you have in your prison, before the courts, and explain why you are holding him there.' This document, or writ, was used in cases where a man's friends complained that he was being held in prison, but had not been tried for any offence. The courts held in general that such imprisonment was wrong: if a man was accused of wrong-doing, let him be tried, and unless the accusation was very serious (such as murder) he ought to be released from prison on bail until his trial. As early as 1344, there is a case where the keeper of the Tower of London answered that he had the prisoner in his keeping because the king had given special orders to that effect. But the king's courts would not accept this as a sufficient answer, and they let the man out on bail. In 1679, parliament passed the Habeas Corpus Act, which secured that every citizen who is arrested or imprisoned for any crime (except treason and certain other serious crimes) is entitled of right to have this writ issued, and to be released from prison on bail until his trial. The courts may be in vacation, but any judge may—in fact, must—issue it even during vacation time; and a judge who neglects to issue the writ, or a gaoler who neglects to reply to it, incurs a heavy penalty. Prisoners who, because of the seriousness of their charge, were not entitled to the writ of habeas corpus must be given speedy trial. If you are in prison as the result of a court sentence, you may perhaps think your conviction unjust or your sentence excessive. But your remedy is not in habeas corpus. That is only for people in prison but not yet tried.

It so happens that one of the leading cases concerning habeas corpus comes from Nigeria. Chief Eleko Eshugbayi was deposed in 1928, and was arrested and deported, in accordance with the law then in force. He applied to a judge for a writ of habeas corpus; the judge heard his application and refused it, on the grounds that everything had been done according to law. The chief then applied to a second judge. This judge refused to listen to him, saying that he could not interfere with his colleague's decision. The chief appealed to the Supreme Court of Nigeria, which dismissed his appeal. The chief then appealed still higher, to the judicial committee of the privy council in London. This court rejected his first claim that his case had not been properly investigated; it held that the judge who heard him had gone into the matter thoroughly. But it gave judgment in favour of the chief on his second point. It said that even if one judge had refused to issue a habeas corpus, the chief had the right to apply to every judge in Nigeria, one after the other, and each of them was bound to consider his application afresh. Thus, it is settled law that in Britain, if one judge refuses my application for a habeas corpus, I am entitled to have my application heard by one judge after another, in the hope that one of them will disagree with his colleagues and grant me my release on bail.

This institution of habeas corpus, which so effectively protects a British citizen from being kept in prison without a trial, has been taken over into America and into West Africa. The Liberian constitution, for example, provides,

'That all prisoners shall be bailable by sufficient sureties, unless, for capital offences, when the proof is evident, or presumptions great; and the privilege and benefit of the writ of habeas corpus shall be enjoyed in this Republic, in the most free, easy, cheap, expeditious and ample manner: and shall not be suspended by the legislature, except upon the most urgent and pressing occasions, and for a limited time, not exceeding twelve months.'

We should say, then, that in normal times, any Government which claims the power to arrest and imprison people without trial is breaking the principle of the rule of law. But, as the quotation from the Liberian constitution shows, any Government may sometimes claim that the times are not normal. We recognize that in times of emergency it may be necessary to curtail such fundamental liberties as speedy and open trial. During the 1939-45 war, the British parliament passed an Act empowering the Government to make defence regulations; and under the Act, the Government made a regulation giving it power to arrest and imprison without trial. But even here, parliament did what it could to protect the freedom of the individual. It laid down five classes of people who might be treated in this way. The Home Secretary appointed an advisory committee, to whom persons arrested under the regulation could appeal. Every month, the Home Secretary was required to report to parliament how many people he had detained under the regulation, and in how many cases he had not accepted the advice of his committee. All these defence regulations were of course repealed as soon as possible after the end of the war. In times of public danger, any Government may be forced to take such temporary powers and to abandon the rule of law for a time.

When the emergency is over and normal times return, it is part of the rule of law that no man shall be arrested, imprisoned and punished except for an offence against the law. The Government has no power to arrest a man because he has criticized its policy in speech or in writing. In political, as in other trials, a man must be accused of some specific crime (such as sedition or treason) which is known to the law; he must be brought before the ordinary courts as soon as possible, and if convicted, must be punished according to the law. In political, as in other trials, moreover, a man is presumed innocent until he is proved guilty: it is for the prosecution to prove his guilt, not for the prisoner to prove his innocence. The rule of law requires that an accused person should be tried according to the law which was in force at the time when his alleged offence was committed. It would be unjust if I were arrested and charged with an offence, and when I protested, 'But I did this three months ago, and there was no law against it,' the court replied, 'No, there wasn't then, but there is now; the new law came into force last week.' Similarly, it would be unjust if I were sentenced to five years imprisonment, when at the time of my offence the maximum penalty was a £25 fine.

Again, it is no crime in Britain to be suspected of intending to commit an offence. The law can take no account of a man's thoughts until they have resulted in speech or action. A friend of mine may be charged on good evidence with conspiracy or sedition, and the police may think that I am likely to be involved in his crime. But unless they can find evidence against me, the rule of law forbids them to arrest me. They cannot convict me without evidence, they cannot even put me on trial without evidence; and if they arrest and imprison me without evidence, and merely on suspicion, I shall be entitled to bring an action against the police for wrongful arrest and imprisonment. That is part of the rule of law.

SECOND MEANING OF THE RULE OF LAW

All men are subject to the same law. No one is so great that he can claim to be above the law, and wrongs committed by public officers will be tried in the ordinary courts. The prime minister may be in a hurry to get to the House of Commons to attend an important debate; but if in his hurry his car causes an accident, he or his driver will be prosecuted and fined just like any other citizen. In the eyes of the law, all men are equal: rich or poor, educated or uneducated, high or low. If the town council digs a hole in the road and leaves it unlighted at night, so that I fall into it and break a leg, it is the ordinary courts that will settle the case. The central or the local Government cannot have the case tried in a special court with a bias in its favour. I have quoted a case in which a club of poor fishermen successfully sued a large and wealthy town council for spoiling their sport. Some people might think that the interests of a large and important town were more important than those of a handful of humble fishermen. But, under the rule of law, the courts held that the interests of the few are as important in the eyes of the law as those of the many: the town council had no right to interfere with the pleasures of the poor.

Qualification of this meaning

There is one important qualification to this meaning of the rule of law. We have said that the rule of law requires that disputes should always be heard by the ordinary courts. But nowadays there are many cases which are not heard by the ordinary courts, but by some kind of specialized court set up by an Act of Parliament. Not only are there many such cases, and many such courts, but there is a tendency for their numbers to increase. What are we to say then about the rule of law in this respect?

Let us first look at some examples. They are taken from England, a country which has always been jealous of giving too much power to the executive and has upheld the independence of the judiciary. If there are so many such examples in England, there are probably more still in countries which have a tradition of entrusting great powers to the executive.

There are, first of all, many cases concerning the ownership and use of land. If a new road or bridge or reservoir is to be built, the Government has powers to compel owners to sell it the land that is needed. This raises two questions: is it really necessary for my land to be taken, and what price should I receive? Then again, there are laws which restrict my right to use my land as I like. I may wish to convert my house into a shop or a factory; but I am not allowed to do so without permission. I must apply for permission, and my neighbours must be given an opportunity to say what they think of my proposal; and if permission is refused, I may wish to appeal to a higher authority. All such cases as these are heard, not by the ordinary courts, but by a special Lands Tribunal.

Another example concerns public transport. No one is allowed to start a new bus service or a new air line without permission. If I wish to start such a service, I have to show that there is need for it, and my competitors must have an opportunity of objecting. Air lines, buses, and railways must apply for permission before increasing their fares, and they must show good reason why the increase is necessary. There is a Transport Tribunal to consider these matters.

These and other special tribunals must handle large numbers of cases which would otherwise have to be handled by the courts of law. Why have these special tribunals been established, and what are their advantages and disadvantages?

In the first place, we notice that the issues they try are not, as a rule, strictly legal issues. I admit that the Government has legal power to compel me to sell it my land, or to refuse me permission to instal high-speed machinery in my dwelling-house, to the annoyance of my neighbours. I quarrel with the Government because it proposes to pay me much less compensation than would be fair: or because I think it ridiculous for my neighbours to claim that the noise will hurt them. I want to be allowed to run a bus from my village into the market town on market day. The bus company objects that it is already running two buses inwards in the morning, and two outwards in the evening; but I can bring seventeen witnesses who will say that those buses are inconveniently timed for the needs of our village. These are not questions of law; they are questions of fact or opinion. The law is clear, and is admitted by both sides. We do not need a lawyer, but a technical assessor, to answer such questions as these: will my extra market bus cut seriously into the revenue of the bus company and cause them to curtail their existing service? Will the machinery I wish to instal in my house be a serious nuisance to my neighbours? What is a fair price for this land which I am being compelled to sell? This suggests that a special tribunal may have an advantage over the ordinary courts of law in deciding such technical questions.

Next: the special tribunal is likely to be quicker in working than the law courts. The courts are overloaded with work, and there may easily be two years between the day when a case is put down on the list and the day when it comes to be heard. But if the Government wants its new road, or the railways want permission to increase their fares, they need to have a quick decision. Speed, then, is another advantage.

On the other hand, there are dangers which have to be watched: notably the danger that the executive should contrive to be judge and jury in its own case. Specialized administrative tribunals could easily be worked so as to destroy the rule of law over a large part of the national life. If the rule of law is to be maintained, certain conditions must be laid down under which special tribunals shall work. (a) Before any action is taken which will affect my rights, I must be given proper notice and an opportunity of putting my view. (b) I must be allowed to choose whether I will put my own case or be represented by a lawyer. (c) I must have an opportunity of hearing and criticizing the views put forward by the other side. (d) the membership of the tribunal must be such as to inspire confidence; it must seem impartial, and free from the influence of the Government department concerned.[2] (e) Like a law court, the tribunal must follow recognized procedure and must show a reasonable regard for precedents. (f) There must be a right of appeal to the ordinary courts on a point of law.[3] (g) The tribunal's decision should be supported by reasons, if I ask for them.

[2] For example, I should not feel confident if the lands tribunal before which I pleaded my claim for compensation consisted of two officials, one from the Treasury and one from the Ministry of Works. However amiable personally, they would find it hard to award me a fair price because both of them are permanently engaged in keeping down Government expenditure. As a matter of fact, this could not happen in England. The president of the lands tribunal must be an experienced lawyer, and the members must be lawyers, or surveyors, or others experienced in land valuation.

[3] Thus, if the tribunal admitted the grounds of my claim but awarded me only £3,000 compensation instead of the £4,000 I asked for, I could not reasonably claim a right of appeal to the ordinary courts. But if the tribunal said, 'You have asked for £4,000, basing your claim on sections 15 and 16 of the Act. But section 16 does not apply in your case, so we have awarded you compensation on the basis of section 15 only; and under the terms of section 15 we can award you only £3,000,'—in that case I should want to appeal, on the grounds that the tribunal was wrong in law when it said that section 16 did not apply.

To sum this up: provided the special tribunals are seen to act justly and in accordance with the spirit of law, we can say that the rule of law is maintained. What we have to guard against is a tribunal whose decision is dictated to it by a Minister before ever the case begins.

THIRD MEANING OF THE RULE OF LAW

The third meaning is that which enables us to say proudly, 'This is a free country'. What do we mean by this? We mean that our fundamental personal freedom is safe. We are free to come and go as we choose: to buy a house in Lagos, to change our mind and move to Ibadan or Katsina, to take a holiday at Jos or on a cruising liner. No one has the right to forbid us to stay where we choose or to go where we choose unless he can show legal powers which we can challenge in the courts.

We are free to say what we like, to write it down, to discuss with anyone we choose, provided of course that we do not injure other people's rights. We may express our views by writing articles in the Press, or by speaking in the market-place or over the radio. No matter how unusual our views are, we have a right to express them and try and convert others to them, again provided that in doing so we do not injure other people's rights. If any one wishes to stop us, he must show a reason which we can challenge in the courts. We are free to choose our friends where we will. If someone gives us a piece of kindly advice: 'If I were you, I would not see too much of that man. The Government dislike him very much, and I think he will soon find himself in trouble. You had better keep away from him.'—we are able to reply, 'He and I have been friends ever since we were at college together. I have nothing to do with his politics, and I have no need to be afraid of the Government.'

And suppose the police do take notice of us: what then? We know that there are certain safeguards of our freedom. If a policeman arrests us, he must either produce his warrant from the magistrate for doing so, or must tell us his reasons for arresting us without a warrant—and unless his reasons are satisfactory, he may find himself in trouble in the courts. We know that when we are formally charged, we are not compelled to make any statement to the police, and are entitled to send for our lawyer to protect our interests. We know that it is not for us to prove our innocence, but for the prosecution to prove our guilt. In some countries, modern techniques of interrogation or 'brain-washing' by the police can make most accused persons say anything the police want them to say; but in a free country that sort of thing cannot happen.[4]

In some countries, these personal freedoms of speech, person, property, and association are guaranteed by the constitution. But experience seems to show that a constitutional guarantee is not always worth very much. Whether these freedoms are guaranteed by a written constitution, or merely by custom and tradition, the important thing is that they should be real and effective.

The idea that there are such fundamental rights as these, which every human being possesses, developed slowly. Aristotle said that there were some races who were naturally suitable for slavery. The Greek and Roman civilizations were built on slavery, and slavery has existed over most of the world. When slavery itself is abolished, the mental attitudes which it encourages have a way of surviving. People seem to feel it necessary to comfort themselves by saying how much better they are than some other group of people. And so we have the world-wide problem of group-feeling: one group despising, or maybe hating, another. Everywhere there have been honourable exceptions, men who have refused to regard themselves as belonging exclusively to one group, and have recognized their kinship with people outside. But too often, even today, the feeling exists that 'We' are good, wise and righteous; 'They' are evil, foolish or dangerous; we must watch 'Them' carefully to see that they do not threaten our way of life. And where such a feeling exists, it seems to be almost instinctive that we should try to weaken the other group by refusing it privileges which we ourselves possess. In every country there are groups who feel themselves in danger from others, and whose natural reaction is to cry, 'Keep them down!'

It was during the seventeenth and eighteenth centuries in Europe that the belief began to grow that God—or 'Nature'—intended all men and women to possess certain fundamental rights. The idea can be seen in Hobbes, and it becomes still plainer in Locke and Thomas Paine. From their reading of Locke, Paine, and Rousseau, those who drafted and agreed to the American Declaration of Independence in 1776 regarded the rights of man as 'self-evident':

'We hold these truths to be self-evident, that all men are created equal, that they are endowed by their Creator with certain unalien-

---

[4] There were one or two cases in England in 1962 and 1963 where prisoners prosecuted police officers for ill-treating them while they were being questioned at the police station. Much public indignation was aroused; there was an inquiry, and several police officers resigned or were dismissed, including some of high rank. This sort of thing can happen anywhere; the important thing is that if it happens, those responsible should be punished for it.

able Rights, that among these are Life, Liberty and the pursuit of Happiness. . . .'

This American doctrine has swept the world. In the last twenty years, the United Nations has put out a Declaration and a Convention of Human Rights, and most Governments have accepted them.

And yet we know that there are still countries in which these fundamental human rights are not safe: countries in which it is unfortunate to be of the wrong colour, or the wrong political party, or the wrong religion, or the wrong caste, or the wrong class. Human rights, fundamental freedoms, the rule of law, will not be preserved by written declarations. What then can preserve them?

This question brings us right back to Plato. Plato argued that a just State will be one which is peopled by just men. Human rights and the rule of law will exist only as long as the great majority of citizens believe in them so strongly that they are willing to take trouble and run risks for them. It has been said that 'the price of liberty is perpetual vigilance'. Each of us is awake when his own liberty is threatened; most of us are inclined to close our eyes when the threat is to our neighbour's liberty. It has been said, too, that a people gets the Government it deserves. We ourselves are responsible for the rule of law. If we break the law in all sorts of petty ways and aim merely at living an easy life and keeping out of trouble, we are behaving like slaves, and we shall deserve a Government which will treat us as slaves. If we wish for justice and freedom, we must cultivate the virtues that justice and freedom require.

CHAPTER VI

Representative Government

'What concerns everybody should be approved by everybody.' How are we to find out what people desire? Despotic government, common in history, does not trouble to find out; it governs people (at the best) according to the king's idea of what is good for them. A good despotic government may be very effective. On the other hand, a pure democracy of the type often found in Africa works well as long as customary law is in force, but it is ineffective in modern conditions. So far, no system has been found which combines high efficiency with great responsiveness to popular desires; we have to compromise.

The idea of representative government is the English compromise. Its essential conditions: (i) a representative parliament, (ii) freedom of parliamentary discussion, (iii) Government bound to accept the decision of parliament.

Representative parliament involves: (i) free elections; (ii) proper register of electors; (iii) proper constituencies; (iv) a real choice of candidates and programmes; (v) a politically educated electorate; (vi) frequent elections.

Freedom of parliamentary discussion involves: (i) parliamentary privilege; (ii) adequate information; (iii) freedom from Government interference, either by corruption or intimidation.

Binding parliamentary decision involves the power of the purse. Function of the parliamentary opposition. Cabinet ministers need not be members of parliament for representative system to work successfully.

EVERY Government in the world today would claim that it governs its people in their own interests: it gives them the treatment that is good for them. Nearly every Government would go further, and would claim that it governs in the way its people desire. It has been said that one mark of a truly democratic Government is that it is able to go further still, and to claim, 'We trust our people to know what is good for them; and if they tell us to change our policy, we do so.' There are perhaps not very many Governments today that could justifiably make this last claim.

However, the fact that nearly every Government claims to govern its people in the way they desire shows that to govern thus is widely regarded as a mark of good government. A maxim of the Roman lawyers used to be, 'What concerns everybody should be approved by everybody'; and this is generally accepted as the ideal. It is of course, like all ideals, impossible to achieve completely in an imperfect world. No action of a Government can please everybody. But a good Government gets as near to the ideal as it can: it gives everybody the opportunity of expressing his opinion, and it tries to act so as to win the approval of as many as possible.

This at once raises an important practical problem: How are we to find out what people desire?

The problem hardly existed in the Greek city-states. They were so small that when a man shouted in the market-place he could be heard on the city wall; and in cities like Athens, which had a democratic form of government, all the adult male citizens (that is the free men, not counting the slaves) could attend the city assembly, and could speak and vote. It was a simple matter for the rulers to find how opinion was divided on a given proposal. Rome too was originally a small city-state; but when she grew to be an empire, Rome met the problem that faces all modern states. There were too many citizens in the Roman empire, there are too many in Britain or Nigeria, for it to be possible that each of them should claim the right to take part personally in the central legislative assembly. In Britain and Nigeria, and in all modern states except a few of the very smallest such as Monaco, there is the additional difficulty that most of the citizens live too far away from the assembly building to be able to exercise the right, even if they had it.

Rome never solved this problem. There were many causes for the downfall of the Roman empire, but one of them was that its central legislative assembly, the Senate, did not develop. The Senate which was suitable for a small poor city-state was utterly unsuitable for a large wealthy empire. In the last three hundred years or more of its existence, the Roman empire was a despotism; the emperor chose whomever he pleased to be his officers and advisers, and the Senate merely ratified his decisions. Such a despotism has been the usual type of government in most parts of the world. The king looks for faithful and capable men to command his armies, run his treasury, administer justice, and organize the administration. Within certain limits, he is free to choose anyone he likes, but here and there he will find a local chief or noble who is so powerful that he cannot safely be ignored. Having got his men together, he will consult them, and if he is a wise man he will listen carefully to their advice, even if he decides not to take it. If the king is a wise man and strong, this form of government may be very efficient in bringing peace and prosperity. The trouble comes when the king is weak or foolish. But even in its best days, such a government is ineffective in finding out what its people desire. There are usually village councils of some kind, and there is usually a system by which any subject, however humble, can bring a complaint direct to the king. But there is no effective link between the village council and the king's council of nobles.

In some parts of Africa, there has been developed a whole pyramid of councils. The family council sends the head of the family to speak for it as a member of the village council; the village headman speaks for his village in the divisional chief's council; and so upwards to the highest council of all. There is a great deal to be said for a pure democracy of this kind. Everyone has a chance to say what he thinks, and his opinion plays its part in deciding the action that is finally taken at the top. The system works perfectly as long as the state is living by customary law and is not being affected by great economic changes: when everybody knows what he ought to do and how much he ought to receive, and when decisions are few and simple—Is this a case for war, or shall we try one more embassy? What shall we say to these people who are asking us to give them land to settle on? But the system breaks down under modern conditions: when councils have to make new decisions very quickly, when new economic opportunities are breaking up the old customs. It is a beautiful system for its own day, when there is always time to adjourn the council so that its members may think things over and discuss them with their own people. But it will not do for people who have to make decisions in a hurry.

Here then are two types of government: the first, a government which may be effective and strong and prosperous, but which on the whole gives people what it thinks good for them, and not necessarily what they desire: the second, a government which is based throughout on the idea that people should have what they desire, but which under modern conditions cannot be quick and efficient. So far, the world has not seen a government which is equally successful in both respects.

The idea of representative government was developed in England —we may say roughly between 1250 and 1650—as a compromise between these two ideals. Like all compromises, it is far from perfect; but it is the best attempt so far made, and the idea has been copied all over the world.

We need not discuss the reasons for England's good fortune. They were partly historical, partly geographical. In France, Spain and Italy there were assemblies which at one time were developing towards something like the English parliament. But everywhere on the Continent, the kings proved stronger than the assemblies, and they broke the assemblies' power and set up absolute monarchies.

Only in England did the assembly prove stronger than the king, and reduce the king to the position of a constitutional monarch.

What are the characteristics of representative government of the English type which make it a workable (and reasonably successful) compromise between the aims of efficiency and of carrying out the people's desire?

For representative government to be workable, three conditions must be fulfilled; and each of the three will not be fulfilled unless a number of precautions are taken.

Three Essential Conditions
1. The parliament must be as truly representative as it can be of all sections of the people.
2. The members of parliament must be able to discuss with complete frankness, and the Government must leave them free to decide as they choose.
3. The parliament's decision must be binding on the Government.

There is a great deal involved in these three conditions, and we shall discuss them separately.

A TRULY REPRESENTATIVE PARLIAMENT

We have said that the parliament must represent all sections of the people as truly as it can. We do not claim that the British parliament, or any other existing parliament, is completely successful in this. Among several million voters, there are more shades of opinion than any assembly of a few hundred men can hope to represent adequately.

First requirement: free elections

The first requirement is that the voters shall have an opportunity of choosing the people they wish to represent them. This implies that they have freedom of choice. It must be open to anybody to offer himself as a candidate, and the voter must feel free to vote for A or B or C with no fear of the consequences. This means that he must vote secretly, with no one watching to see how he votes. In Britain and most countries where the voters can all read, the vote is made by secret ballot. The names of all the candidates are printed on a slip of paper. The voter reports to the clerk in charge, who ticks his name and address in the list to make sure that he has not voted already, and gives him the voting slip. The voter takes his slip into a part of the room which is shut off by partitions from everyone else; he makes a cross against the name of the candidate he chooses, folds the paper so that no one can see how he has voted, and drops the folded paper into the slit of the locked ballot box. He is warned that if he writes his name, or makes any other mark on the paper whatever except the cross, his vote will not count. This system of the secret ballot allows the voter to choose his candidate in perfect freedom. It is surprising that it was not adopted in Britain until 1872. Until then, voting was in public. First of all, the electors voted by a show of hands. There was usually so much noise and disorder that it was impossible to be sure who had won on the show of hands, and one or other of the candidates would demand a poll: this meant that clerks would sit at tables writing down the electors' names in columns, and each elector would ask to have his name put down for Mr A or Mr B or Mr C. This system meant that each man's vote would be recorded, so that before voting he had to consider what his landlord or employer would think. The secret ballot was a great improvement.

A modified, and somewhat less secret, form of ballot is used in some countries where many voters are illiterate. The candidates are designated by symbols—a cock, an elephant, and such—and the illiterate voter puts his paper in a box marked with the symbol of his choice. This is plainly an inferior system, for it is possible for a policeman or party representative to sit by the box and memorize the list of those who vote in it. It may be a necessary system for the time being, but it should be replaced by the fully secret ballot as soon as possible.

It sometimes happens that the Government interferes with freedom of elections by issuing only one list of candidates. Only candidates approved by the Government are allowed to stand for election, and each voter, instead of being free to choose between A and B, is free to choose A or nobody. There are other ways in which a Government can interfere with elections: for example, by 'losing' a box of voting papers from a district which is known to be opposed to the Government. Another method is what is known as 'gerrymandering': that is, re-drawing the boundaries of the electoral districts so as to lessen the value of opposition votes. There may, for example, be three electoral districts of equal size, two of which are safe to return a Government candidate and the third is safe to return an Opposition candidate. If the third district is divided between the other two, its voters may find that their votes merely increase the size of the anti-Government minority in those two districts, without endangering the Government position: thus, instead of two Government and one Opposition candidates, the whole mass of electors now return two candidates only, both of them Government. It is plain that any such tricks as these make the elected parliament less truly representative of the people.

It is all very well having a long list of candidates to choose from; but there is a danger in having too long a list. If there were twenty candidates standing for one seat, it would be possible for the winning candidate to have only one-fifth of the votes, the rest being scattered among the other candidates. The winner could not be said to represent the people. To limit the numbers of candidates to those who have a reasonable chance of winning the seat, it is usual to provide that candidates must deposit a sum of money when they announce their candidature, to be forfeited if they do not win a minimum percentage of the votes.

Second requirement: proper electoral roll

In modern times, people move about much more than they used, and arrangements must be made for keeping the list of electors—the electoral roll—up to date: adding the names of new electors and deleting those of electors who have died or left the district. This is usually the responsibility of the local authority; but the voter himself is ultimately responsible for claiming his right to vote. If literate, he receives a form every year to fill in; if illiterate, he may have to go to the local government office to record his claim. The electoral roll is printed and is available for public inspection. Here again, it is necessary that everyone who is entitled to vote should have his claim admitted; and on the other hand, that there shall be no trickery such as stuffing the roll with the names of voters who do not exist and putting up people to vote on their behalf. One of the most effective means by which Negroes in some Southern States of America were denied their civil rights for so long was keeping their names off the electoral roll. Being thus unable to vote, they were unable to make their voice heard, not only in Congressional and Presidential elections, but in local elections.

Who is entitled to vote? This is a question which has aroused great political feeling. In modern Africa, we have heard a great deal of the slogan, 'One man, one vote'; it has been regarded as especially important in some multi-racial countries in Africa, where Africans have accused the European and Asian communities of denying them votes in order to keep them in political subjection. If we ignore these multi-racial countries for the moment, and consider the theory of representative government, we shall find that representative government has in the past worked quite well when the franchise has been restricted, and that the practice of 'One man, one vote' is even younger in Britain than the secret ballot. Until 1832 there were only a million electors in Britain: those who owned freehold land in the country, and a small handful of people in the towns. In 1832, the vote was given to the richer tenants and leaseholders in the country, and to all the richer householders in the towns. In 1867, the vote was given to all householders in the towns; in 1884 to all householders in the country. But no women yet had the vote; nor did men who lodged in someone else's house instead of holding a house of their own. By two Acts in 1918 and 1927, the vote was given to all men and women. But although after 1927 everyone had a vote, Britain had not yet reached the position 'One man, one vote'; for some people had two votes. Business men no longer had two votes, one for the place where they lived and the other for the place where they worked; but university graduates still had two votes, one for their home and one for their university. It was not until 1948 that the university vote was abolished, and Britain became completely a land of 'one man—and one woman— one vote'. There are still some countries where women cannot vote.

The theory behind all this restriction of the franchise was that people should not have the vote unless they know how to use it. The weakness of the restriction was that in practice you were not asked whether you knew how to vote, but whether you lived in a house of such-and-such a value. There is a good deal to be said for the idea that people who do not understand politics should not take part in it by voting. In the nineteenth century, a good many people in England were quite content to leave politics to people whom they regarded as better fitted than themselves. Even today, there is a proportion of electors at every general election who do not trouble to vote—ten or fifteen per cent. But today it would be impossible in Britain to try and restrict the franchise. It would be impossible to test people's understanding of the questions involved before deciding whether or not to allow them to vote; even if they do not understand the questions in detail, people often have strong views on them; and no one would be prepared to allow other people to govern the country without consulting him in an election. This intense political consciousness is not yet found in every country; but it will come.

There was an interesting experiment in Kenya in 1956. A law was passed which gave Africans a restricted franchise. Seven qualifications were laid down, some educational, some economic: for example, one was that a man should have passed through an intermediate school course, and another was that he should be earning at least £120 a year. The vote would be given to anyone who satisfied any one of these conditions, and a man who satisfied more than one might be given additional votes. The system did not work, because it was applied only to Africans, and the African leaders naturally would not tolerate it. But it is an interesting attempt to ensure that votes should be in the hands of those best fitted to use them. Had some such system been adopted in Britain in 1918, and copied in other countries, we might perhaps today have had better Governments and parliaments. But we have chosen the other road, and it is now too late to turn back.

In Australia, a voter is compelled by law to record his vote; he can be punished if he stays at home. But no law can compel a man to vote wisely and usefully.

Representative government can work well on a restricted franchise: there may be special reasons for insisting on 'One man, one vote' in a given country at a given time, but we cannot say that this maxim is generally essential to the theory of representative government. The essential thing is that the government shall be carried on according to the wishes of the people, as expressed by the people's representatives. But politics is only to a very small extent concerned with ends; it is almost entirely concerned with means. All of us want peace, law and order, prosperity, freedom: these are the ends of government. The questions begin when we ask how we are to achieve these things, and whether we can have them all: should we have a one-party state, or many parties? should we draw our revenue from direct or indirect taxes? should we import cotton cloth from abroad because it is cheaper and better than our own, or should we put a heavy customs duty to keep out foreign cloth and encourage our own cotton industry? Questions like these are concerned with means, and they are the questions which occupy the minds of Governments. Even in a relatively well educated country like Britain, much more so in a country where a large proportion of the electors is illiterate, there are many electors who do not understand such matters. They vote, but they do not understand what they are voting for; the Government is not carried on according to their wishes, because—as far as political means are concerned—they have no wishes.

In one African country, there was a political party which came to power with the slogan, 'One Country, One People!' Many of the voters were illiterate, and knew no English. For them, the party leaders reduced their slogan to a simpler form: 'O.C.,O.P.' It was customary for a speaker to challenge his illiterate audience with a shout of 'Oh-See?' and for the audience to shout back, 'Oh-Pee!' Now, that may be an essential part of the process of political education. But while the process is in that early stage, we cannot claim that representative government has yet been fully achieved. Representative government is fully achieved when voter X says, 'For such-and-such reasons I am in favour of an import duty on foreign cotton goods, so I shall vote for Mr A, who supports that policy', and voter Y can give his reasons for supporting Mr B, who is against the import duty. But, as we have said, representative government can work satisfactorily even when imperfect: when only some of the people have political views which their representatives can express in parliament, while the rest of the people are content to leave the details of government to others.

We should say a word about the special problem of elections in a multi-racial state like Kenya or Cyprus or Malaysia. Minority groups, such as the Europeans in Kenya and the Turks in Cyprus, are often anxious lest their own special interests should be ignored by the majority. To protect their interests, they sometimes suggest that a proportion of the seats in parliament and in local government bodies, and perhaps a proportion of the posts in civil service, should be reserved for them. It is sometimes suggested that elections should be held on the basis of a communal roll of electors: that is, instead of the names of all electors (of whatever race) being put on one list (a common roll), they should be put in separate lists: one list for Greeks and another for Turks. Then Greek electors could vote for Greek candidates, and Turks for Turkish.

These suggestions raise questions which we have not space to discuss at length. First, how far is it true to say that the Turks in Cyprus, or the Europeans in Kenya, have special interests? One Turk may be a senior Government official, another a business man, a third a doctor, a fourth a poor farmer: is it true that these four have a common interest as Turks which is stronger than the common interest which the Turkish doctor has with his Greek medical colleague? What is it that the minority group fears?

The usual answer which the minority makes is, 'We fear that the majority will exclude us from political power. If we stand for election to parliament, we shall never be elected; the best posts in the civil service and in commerce will be given to people of the majority; if our children wish to succeed, they will have to cut themselves off from our group and identify themselves with the majority.'

Assuming that there is some justification for this fear, how far will the system of reserving parliamentary seats and voting on a communal roll help to lessen it? The reserved seats will always be a minority; all they can do is to give minority spokesmen a chance of expressing minority views. They can never enforce their views by their votes. The usual argument in favour of the communal roll is that if elections are held on a common roll, no minority candidate will ever be elected: Greeks will never vote for a Turk, Africans will never vote for a European. How far this is true is a matter of opinion. If it is true, then the minority have a legitimate fear: the Turks have a common interest as Turks as well as their common professional interests with their Greek colleagues.

The usual argument against the communal roll is that although it may safeguard minority interests, it ensures that there will always be a minority interest. All multi-racial states must look forward to a day when race will no longer matter: a day when the best man will be chosen, no matter whether he is Greek or Turk, African or European: a day when people will think of themselves merely as Cypriots or as Kenyans. But as long as the communal roll exists, racial groups are encouraged to think of themselves as separate. The communal roll prevents the groups from growing together. In this, as in so many other matters, if we wish our system of government to work well, we must think less of our differences and more of the things we have in common.

Third requirement: proper constituencies

No completely satisfactory system has yet been devised of dividing a country into constituencies. The pattern of settlement varies greatly. One part of a country will be rural, another urban: one part of a town will be all offices, another all factories, another all quiet residential streets: one rural area will be closely settled with farmers and villages, another will be thinly peopled with shepherds and cattle-keepers. Ideally, the country should be so divided into constituencies that each section of the community is fairly represented in parliament. But this is difficult to achieve in practice.

The usual system is to arrange constituencies of roughly equal population, each returning one member to parliament. This has the obvious superficial fairness that each group of 60,000 or 70,000 people, or whatever the figure may be, has equal representation. But it has disadvantages. The area of a constituency is almost sure to include different kinds of settlement. It may be a factory area with a minority of well-to-do managers and professional people, or a small town with a minority rural population, or a mainly residential area with a minority group engaged in light industry. The system has the disadvantage that in every case the minority group can never make its views heard. It is true that to some extent constituencies balance one another: a Conservative minority here is balanced by a Labour minority there. It is true also that while there are some 'safe' seats on either side, there are others which are more evenly balanced, so that a small swing of votes may turn the majority into a minority. But this introduces us to the second disadvantage of the system.

In Britain and America, and very likely in other countries as well, it has been found that most voters are faithful to their party, whatever its political fortunes may be. An American says, 'I always vote the Republican ticket'; an Englishman says, 'I always vote Labour'

—and others are equally faithful Democrats and Conservatives. But there is a minority which votes now for one side, now for the other. This 'floating vote' (as it is called) may amount to ten per cent or so of the total electorate. The system of single-member constituencies gives a great importance to this small floating vote. Let us imagine a constituency of 70,000 electors, of whom 80 per cent turn out to vote. This means a total of 56,000 votes recorded. The seat is held, let us say, by the Unity party with 33,000 votes; the Federal party got only 23,000. A comfortable Unity majority of 10,000. Now suppose there is a floating vote of ten per cent, that is, of 5,600 voters; and in the next election these voters change sides. This will reduce the Unity vote to 27,400 and bring the Federal vote up to 28,600. The Unity member loses his seat, and the constituency is now represented by a Federal member with a shaky majority of 1,200. If this kind of change happens in several constituencies, it will very likely bring about a change of Government. Thus, in the British House of Commons of some 600 seats (representing the same number of constituencies), a Government majority of eighty is reckoned comfortable: but a Government with such a comfortable majority will be overthrown by a swing in some fifty constituencies, one in twelve. And there are many more than fifty constituencies where such a swing is possible.

Thus, one result of the system is that a comparatively small swing in public opinion—a minority of the votes in a minority of the constituencies—may bring about a big change in the composition of the parliament. This is not altogether a bad thing by any means: for it tends to ensure that Governments have a working majority, which is a great help to the efficient working of the parliamentary system. But if we look at it from the point of view of the question we are now considering—how are we to ensure that parliament accurately represents the wishes of the electors?—it is a defect. A small change in the opinion of the electors may make a very big change in the composition of the parliament; the pendulum swings violently. After every general election in Britain, the defeated party is careful to point out that its triumphant rival has a big majority of the seats in parliament, but only a tiny majority—or even sometimes an actual minority—of the votes cast in the whole country.

Various schemes have been devised to remedy this defect, to ensure that the proportion of the different parties in parliament corresponds more nearly to the proportion of the votes they obtain. One scheme was that constituencies should not necessarily be geographical, but voluntary. Candidates would not represent a group of people all living in one place, but a group of people scattered all over the country. A candidate would require a fixed minimum number of votes to be elected, and there would be a central office to put candidates and electors in touch. The attractiveness of this scheme is that the Unity minorities in a group of 'safe' Federal constituencies might combine together and put one Unity member into parliament, whereas at present the votes of the minority in a 'safe' constituency are useless.

Nowadays we do not hear much about voluntary constituencies. Most of the reform schemes that are advocated depend on the general principle of the transferable vote. Under the present system, the voter is told to place his mark against the one name he chooses; there may be half a dozen candidates, but he is allowed to make only one mark on his paper. Let us suppose that there are three candidates, A, B, and C. It is very likely that A will be elected with 17,000 votes, while B gets 16,000 and C 15,000. Then A is said to represent the electors, whereas in fact nearly two-thirds of the electors said they would rather have someone else. Under the system of the transferable vote, each voter would mark his paper to show his order of preference. A candidate would be declared elected if he obtained a majority of the votes; in this constituency of 48,000 votes, he would need 24,001. On this first count, A with his 17,000 votes is not yet elected. The clerks now go through the papers again and examine the second preferences. As no candidate obtained a clear majority on the first count, they add the second preferences to the first preferences until one obtains the majority.

There are other systems which use the principle of the transferable vote. One of them replaces the single-member constituency by a large constituency with two or three members. The electors have as many votes as there are members to be elected, and mark their papers in order of preference. Again, second and later preference votes are used as they may be needed until the required number of candidates is elected.

Systems like these undoubtedly provide a parliament whose composition shows much more accurately the wishes of the electors than the British system of the single non-transferable vote. They have their advocates in Britain, and as an experiment, university members were elected on a transferable vote system until university representation was abolished in 1948. But it does not seem likely that the British will abandon their present method of voting. The violent swing of the pendulum in British general elections does have the advantage of providing a Government usually with a working majority; and the two main parties in British politics find this a great advantage. A party would rather spend a few years in opposition, and then return to real power, than find itself forming a

Government with a majority too small to be workable. This is a case in which it seems that two virtues are irreconcilable. It is good to have a parliament which accurately reflects public opinion; it is good also to have a Government with a working majority. But it seems as if we must choose between them; we cannot have both. So far, the British people prefer the working majority.

Fourth requirement: a real choice of candidates and programmes
A vote is a means by which a man shows which of two choices he prefers. If there is no choice, there is nothing to vote for. It is true that in Russia, for example, you can, in theory, show by refusing to vote that you disapprove of the official list of candidates or of the official programme. But in practice, so much pressure is put on the Russian electors to support them, that it is unwise to refuse to vote in favour of the Government's candidates. If we wish to have a Government which genuinely represents the people's wishes, we must give the people a free choice between A, B and C, who represent different parties and different policies. One of the advantages of a party system is that it provides such a choice. If there are two or more parties asking for our votes, their candidates will have to explain to us what they have to offer. It is the speeches and posters and pamphlets of the parties and their candidates which educate the electors in the political questions that have to be decided. It is natural that many electors think of their own selfish needs or of the particular needs of their district, and their first question to a candidate is, What will he do for them? But it is part of the candidate's business to teach the electors to think of wider matters than these. There are few questions in politics in which all the right is clearly on one side, and most political decisions have to be a compromise between advantages and disadvantages. If there is a choice of candidates and programmes, the electors are able to make their own decision.

Even in England, where the party system is strong, it sometimes happens that there is only one candidate for a seat, and the clerk in charge of the election (the 'returning officer') can declare him elected unopposed. When it happens, it is usually because the candidate is a distinguished statesman or a distinguished citizen of the constituency, and the other parties decide not to oppose him, either as a compliment to him or because they think opposition will be futile. They may say, 'He is a great man; he will be very useful in parliament, and anyway we cannot hope to beat him on his own ground, so why spend the money and effort for a few hundred useless votes?' But unopposed candidatures are not common in England.

Fifth requirement: political education

Speeches and posters and pamphlets, we have said, are useful in helping the electors to understand the questions the Government has to consider. Representative government cannot succeed unless the electors—or at least a good proportion of them—have this understanding. To educate the electors is one of the great problems in modern states. In ancient Greece it was easy. Everyone could attend the assembly and listen to the speeches, and every young man did so and looked forward to the time when he himself would be taking part in the debates. Today, Governments and parliaments are too remote from us. It is very easy for us to be immersed in our business and pleasure. Many people do in fact neglect their duty of being well-informed on political matters: not merely the young and thoughtless, but older and well educated people who should know better. Many people's political ideas are little more than prejudices. It is important that there should be means by which people can learn the ins and outs of political questions: brains trusts and talks on the radio, newspaper articles, and books, as well as the party materials we have already mentioned. The means should be provided, even if too few of the electors are ready to use them.

Sixth requirement: frequent elections

When we have elected a good parliament, we have put our fate in its hands. The electors do not govern; parliament governs. But if the country is to be governed according to the wishes of the electors, the Government must be required to come to the electors again every few years. This gives the electors the chance of re-electing the Government for another term of office, or of electing a different Government in its place. Also, it gives the electors in each constituency the chance of changing their member if they wish, even if they do not wish to change their party allegiance. Parliaments should be elected for a period of not more than a few years: the House of Commons in Britain for not more than five years, the American House of Representatives for two years and the Senate for six. Frequent elections remind the Government that it is responsible, through parliament, to the people; and they remind each candidate that he 's responsible to those who elected him last time and who may, or may not, elect him again.

DISCUSSION AND DECISION IN PARLIAMENT

We have laid down six conditions which must be reasonably well fulfilled if a good parliament is to be assembled. But the best of parliaments can be of little use unless its discussions are well-informed and frank, and its decisions are taken freely and influence the Government's actions. This again requires certain conditions.

First requirement: parliamentary privilege

Privilege is a legal term. It means the right to say something that would ordinarily involve legal consequences. All parliaments must criticize the Government, or individual Ministers: it is one of their most important functions. They could never do their work properly if a member of parliament must pause before speaking, and reflect, 'How can I say what needs saying without bringing on my head an action for slander?' It must be one of the fundamental rights of a parliament that anything said in it is privileged: that is, cannot be challenged in the courts or by anyone outside. The English House of Commons fought for its privileges very early in its history. In January 1642, King Charles I entered the House to arrest five members whose speeches had especially angered him. He did not find them, for they had been warned and had escaped; but as he withdrew from the hall, the angry mutter of 'Privilege! privilege!' rose around him. Eight months later, the Civil War began.

Parliamentary privilege is maintained very carefully in Britain today. Newspapers print accounts of what goes on in parliament (until the latter part of the eighteenth century, parliamentary privilege would not allow them even to do this), but they have to be very careful how they comment. The House of Commons has a standing committee on privileges, and it often happens that a newspaper article is passed to the committee, for the committee to consider whether it constitutes a breach of privilege. The House has powers of arrest, and a journalist or editor who committed a serious breach of privilege could find the consequences serious.

Like all privileges, this privilege of parliament has to be used with discretion. There was a time in the eighteenth century when parliament insisted on its privilege so much that it was in danger of becoming a tyrant. Nowadays, it often happens that the committee on privileges reports that a newspaper article submitted to it does constitute a technical breach of privilege, but that the breach is so small that parliament would make itself ridiculous if it took official notice of it. The mere fact that the article has come to the committee's notice will be enough to warn the editor that he must be more careful. Much must always depend on the good sense and good taste of members. A great deal of thought and hard work through the centuries has gone into the work of laying down parliamentary procedure so as to make its work effective, and the House itself is the sternest critic of any of its members who oversteps the limits of good taste.

But parliamentary privilege must be preserved if parliament is to do its work properly. Any Government which takes it upon itself to suspend the parliamentary privilege of an individual member or of a group of members is repeating the mistake which King Charles I made in 1642. It may not lead to civil war, but it will lead to the end of efficient representative government.

Second requirement: adequate information

If a Government finds parliament a nuisance, there is a more subtle way in which it can weaken the effectiveness of parliament. It can withhold information. It is essential that members of parliament should be able to get at the facts and figures they need if they are to attack the Government, or defend it: to investigate complaints: to understand the problem which a proposed law hopes to solve. The effectiveness of any parliamentary government will depend very largely on the way in which the Government cooperates with its supporters and its opponents in supplying them with the information they need to do their work.

There are various means by which parliament obtains its information. First, there is the parliamentary question. The working day of the House of Commons begins with question-time. Any member is entitled to put a question to a Minister, and he need give no reason why he is putting it. There must of course be some order and regularity in the procedure. His question must be submitted in writing, and the clerks of the House will make sure that his question is in order: for example, that he is addressing the right Minister, and that his question relates to something for which that Minister is responsible. A member would be in order, for example, in asking the Secretary for Commonwealth Relations how many British teachers are employed in Sierra Leone, for that is a matter which may well concern a member who is interested in Commonwealth education, and it is reasonable to expect the Minister to be able to get the figures through the British High Commissioner in Freetown. But the member would not be in order if he asked why the Sierra Leone Government did this or did not do that, for Sierra Leone is an independent country, and no British Minister has any responsibility for what Sierra Leone does or does not do. The clerks would stop any such question: it could not be asked.

Questions to Ministers cover an immense range of subjects, and the information they seek is sometimes very detailed. One of the problems of parliamentary procedure is to keep question-time from growing too long. This is especially true in the case of supplementary questions. The original question must always be in writing; but if the Minister's reply does not seem immediately conclusive, any member of the House—not merely the original questioner—is entitled to follow it up by supplementary questions on the spot. 'Arising out of that, Sir,' they cry, 'may I ask. . . .' The Speaker of the House often reminds members that the more supplementary questions they ask, the fewer of the original questions will be answered on the floor of the House, and that question-time must not be used for a debate. The sputter of supplementary questions is often closed by the original questioner saying, 'In view of the Minister's unsatisfactory answer, I beg to give notice that I shall raise this matter on the adjournment.'

It is more satisfactory to the questioner if his question can be answered in public so that his fellow-members who are interested may hear. It often happens that question-time ends with many questions left unanswered; the Minister will answer these in writing. Sometimes the answer to a question contains a mass of figures or details; in such a case it is usual for the Minister, with the leave of the House, to circulate the answer in the written record of the House's proceedings. But every question is answered.

What, every question, without exception? Well, there must always be the possibility of an exception. No Minister would reveal the details of confidential negotiations with another Government; no Minister would answer a question such as 'If so-and-so happens, what will the Government do?' The Chancellor of the Exchequer (the Finance Minister) will never answer a question on what changes in taxation he intends to make in his new Budget, and the Home Secretary, who has to advise the Queen whether or not to commute the death sentence on a convicted murder, will not say what advice he intends to give. To the 'If—' question, the Minister will reply briefly, 'That is a hypothetical question.' What he means is, 'You ask me what I would do if so-and-so happens. I cannot possibly say until I know the circumstances; the thing might happen in half-a-dozen different ways, and a great deal will depend on how it happens.' There are polite formulas for replying to the last two questions, but they both amount to 'Wait and see; you will know in good time.' As to the question on confidential matters or matters affecting national security, the Prime Minister will have the support of the Leader of the Opposition in refusing to give an answer at the moment; but he will be pressed to give an answer as soon as possible, and the House will not let him forget the matter. Here again, the House uses its good sense and discretion; but it is very jealous of its right to be told all it needs to know. Since the clerks of the House will stop all questions that are not in order, every question that is put is one that deserves an answer; and if it is not to receive one, the House will insist on a convincing reason why.

We have mentioned the adjournment debate.¹ There is a useful convention in the British House of Commons, by which the last afternoon of the week's work is given to a series of half-hour debates on any matter the House wishes to discuss. These debates take place on the motion that 'The House do now adjourn.' A member wishing to raise a matter on the adjournment must give due notice, in order that the Minister concerned may look up the facts and prepare his answer. There is time for the member's speech of criticism, the Minister's reply, and maybe one or two very short supplementary speeches. The great advantage of the adjournment debate is that it gives the Minister the opportunity of making a longer and more detailed reply than he can possibly make in question-time.

Then of course there is a mass of correspondence between members and Ministers: queries which members do not feel should take up the time of the House, but which nevertheless they want answered. And moreover, since it is only human for a Government to seek to justify itself, there are great numbers of Government papers: reports of Commissions, despatches from abroad, summaries of correspondence with foreign Governments, statistics and so forth, which are laid before parliament for its information. In all these ways, parliament acquires the information that it must have if it is to do its work.

Third requirement: freedom from Government interference

Thus we have elected a good parliament. It represents the electors reasonably accurately. It is understood that members are free to say what they like, and to ask any question they like with the certainty of having a reply. Its members are well informed; they have all the knowledge they need to carry out their responsibilities. There is one other thing needed to enable their debates and decisions to be useful: they must be honest, made with only the public interest in mind, not a member's private interest.

The English Civil War and the Revolution settled it that the king could not hope to compel parliament to do as he wished. But in the latter part of the eighteenth century, King George III tried to bribe parliament to do as he wished. Bribery was no new thing. Sir Robert Walpole, who was prime minister from 1721 to 1742, used to say, 'Every man has his price.' Although as early as 1700, a law had been passed to prevent men from sitting as members of parliament if they held paid employment under the Crown, it had been ineffective. In the reign of George II (1727-1760) it was reckoned that two hundred members of parliament were being paid by the Crown, and in 1742 another law was passed to stop the practice. But George III

¹ See page 79.

did much more: he formed a party in parliament which was openly called 'the King's Friends', and he formed it by bribery. The King's Friends might not themselves hold a salaried post, but members of their families might; or they might be paid for voting as the king wished. George III was able to do this, because in his time the king had income of his own which was not closely controlled by parliament. But he was not content with using his own income; he found parliament ready to vote taxes which were spent in this kind of corruption.

We must not think that parliamentary corruption would be impossible nowadays. It would probably not be possible in Britain, for Britain has learned its lesson, and the House of Commons today would be intensely sensitive to the least suspicion of corruption. But it would be possible in a country where Ministers and members of parliament are inexperienced—where the lesson has not yet been learned. It is a danger to be watched for. It would of course be the ruin of representative government.

A few examples may show the care that is taken in Britain to avoid any suspicion of parliamentary corruption. It sometimes happens that a member of parliament speaks in a debate on some subject in which he has a financial interest. By the custom of the House, he must begin by mentioning the fact. If he does not do so, and the House learns of his interest, he will be severely censured. If a member is promoted to be a Minister, he must dispose of any financial interests which could possibly affect his official duties. There was recently, for instance, a Minister of Transport who was a director of a big firm of contractors. He immediately cut his connection with the firm, so as to avoid any suspicion that he might be making money for himself or for the firm by Government expenditure on roads and bridges. In matters of this sort, it is impossible to be too careful. This sensitiveness which the British parliament shows on the subject of corruption is not a sign of superior virtue. There is a proverb, 'The burnt child dreads the fire.' The British parliament burnt its fingers very badly over this matter of corruption in the eighteenth century, and it does not want to burn them again.

It would be possible, and equally disastrous, for a Government to influence the decisions of parliament not by rewarding members when they do what it wishes but by punishing them if they go against its wishes. It would ruin representative government, for example, if members of the Opposition found that their children or their relatives were systematically refused places in school and college, scholarships for study abroad, posts in the civil service, and other benefits which ought to be awarded impartially.

GOVERNMENT BOUND BY PARLIAMENTARY DECISION

There is not much that need be said under this heading. The most efficient and statesmanlike parliament will clearly be useless if the Government ignores its decisions, and means must be found of compelling Government to respect them.

The power of the purse

It has been found in many countries that the most effective means of making Government respect parliament's decisions is to make parliament solely responsible for voting taxes. That was how the kings of England were gradually brought to obey parliament. As long as the king had money of his own he could afford to do without parliament; and for a long time the king was able to do without a parliament as long as he was content to live quietly and at peace. It was when the king wanted extra money for troops or warships that he had to summon parliament and ask for it; and very early in its history, parliament formed the habit of refusing to vote taxes until the king had listened to its complaints and suggestions and agreed to the conditions which it laid down. It was not till the end of the eighteenth century that parliament got control of all the king's income, so that the king and his Ministers became completely dependent on parliament for all the expenses of government.

This power of the purse is retained by various devices. Parliament will never vote taxes for more than a year at a time, and there are various laws—one example is the Army Act, which authorizes the Government to keep and pay an army—which, like the taxes, have to be renewed every year. This device ensures that parliament must be summoned every year. If parliament were to grant taxes for a longer period—say five years—the Government would be free to govern more or less as it chose for that time. It is not a good thing for the executive ever to be free from the watchful eye of the legislature; it gets into bad habits. It might even begin to experiment in governing by decree, without the sanction of a parliamentary law. Governing by decree is a habit-forming drug; once governments begin it they find it hard to leave off. Annual parliaments, which keep control of the purse rigidly in their own hands, are the best safeguard against government by decree.

The power of the purse is a very real thing. Since every activity of the Government depends on money voted by parliament, every activity can be supervised under the terms of a financial resolution. If the Opposition is critical, for example, of the Government's policy in public health, it can force a debate when the estimates for the department of public health come before it. The Opposition can move a resolution that the estimates be reduced by some trifling sum—£5 or so—and can bring forward all its criticisms in favour of its resolution. The Government must reply; and if its reply is broadly satisfactory, the resolution will be withdrawn and the estimates passed intact. But if the reply is not satisfactory, parliament has in reserve the extreme power of refusing the estimate altogether. This extreme power is never used nowadays, because Government and Opposition alike have learned sense; they know that there must be a fair give-and-take in politics. But the power still exists. Normally of course the Government majority will be sufficient to defeat any Opposition resolution; but in extreme cases the Government may see a revolt within its own ranks. Such things have happened.

In all this discussion, we see the effect of the parliamentary Opposition. Where there is no parliamentary Opposition, as in a one-party state, the nature of parliamentary government is changed. Criticisms are made within the party, either in a private or a public meeting. The decision is taken, and the party as a whole must support it, both in parliament and outside. In Russia, criticism is sometimes very frank and forceful at party meetings; but once the party has taken its decision, criticism must cease. Whether this can be called representative government depends on the organization of the one party; it may be so organized as to give the people—or any rate the party leaders—all over the country an opportunity of making their views heard and considered at party headquarters; or it may concentrate all power in the hands of one man or a very few men at the top. In the latter case, it could not be called representative government.

Cabinet Ministers not necessarily members of parliament

An Englishman is under the temptation to think that for good representative government it is necessary that Cabinet Ministers should be members of parliament, liable to be censured individually or collectively by parliament and compelled to resign. That is the British way, and it works well. But the American example shows that representative government can work equally well when Cabinet Ministers are not even allowed to be members of parliament. We recall that the American Cabinet is appointed by the President and is responsible to him, not to Congress. The United States Congress, like the British parliament, has the power of the purse, and it finds it has enough control over the executive without the additional control which the British system gives. We shall discuss this further in the chapter on Cabinet and Presidential government.

Here we may leave this discussion of representative government.

It is not an easy art, and we have seen that many conditions have to be fulfilled if it is to work well. It needs some skill, but it needs, above all, what we have called the spirit of give-and-take: the spirit of co-operation. The system gives immense opportunities for obstructionism, if people want to demonstrate their power and serve their own ends. Short-sighted and selfish politicians can bring the whole system to a stand-still. It is a beautiful system when it works well; but as Plato said, good government requires good men.

CHAPTER VII

Party Systems

British and Americans are accustomed to two parties, but some countries have several, and others have only one.
Origins of the English two-party system: the historical origins help to explain its character. Democrats and Republicans in the United States. The day-to-day work of politics is concerned with means, not with ends. All agree that we want peace, prosperity, justice; differences of opinion come when we discuss how to obtain them. A political party is a group with common views on certain political means. Pure personal loyalties are not enough to establish a party. Advantages of a party system: (i) it compels the Government to listen to criticism which may be much needed; (ii) it is the most effective method of political education. But parties must be led by honest and unselfish men; the electors must not come to think that politics is a dirty game. Two-party system stronger than a system of many parties, which leads to unstable coalition governments.
One-party systems: in Russia, Nazi Germany and Fascist Italy. Fundamentally different conception of a party: in these states it is a disciplined group of revolutionaries, not (as in the West) a spontaneous group of people who think broadly alike on certain problems. One-party states in Africa, as in Ghana. Historical reasons for the one party arising in opposition to a colonial Government. A second reason for the one-party state in Africa: Africans like unanimity and tend to rally behind a majority leader. Third reason in African conditions: the need to create nation-states out of many different tribes never united until colonial days.
Disadvantages of the one-party state, even in Africa. (i) The Government will be criticized, and it is an advantage to have critics out in the open instead of underground. (ii) criticism need not be hostile and weakening, it may be constructive and strengthening. (iii) When all the urgent tasks are finished, differences of opinion will burst out, and it is better to have them expressed by a rival party than to have the bitterness of a party split. (iv) If critics of the Government are never allowed to try their hand, they will never learn any better.
The party system at work: in parliament and in the constituencies.

IT is difficult for an Englishman or an American, or for the citizen of any of the democratic countries of Western Europe, to imagine parliament without political parties: in Britain and America, two major parties, and in France and some other countries, several. But there have in recent years been several examples of parliaments in which—officially at any rate—there has been only one party. Nazi Germany was one, Fascist Italy was another; in Communist countries only the Communist party is allowed (at least when the Communist Government is fully in power; in the early stages some other parties are permitted to exist, as long as they follow the Communist party line). Since African countries became independent, some of them too have thought of having a parliament with only one party. Ghana is already a one-party state; and in January 1964 the Prime Minister of Uganda was reported as saying that Uganda could not afford the divisions which a two-party state must have. What is the reason for parties—one, two, or many?

Let us look again at the English parliament, with its seven hundred years of development. It was more than three hundred years before the English parliament began to develop parties. Until the seventeenth century, the parliament had only one policy: to stand up for the people against the king, and make the king grant the people's requests before it would grant him any money. It was like many a modern trade union, which has only one policy: to stand up for its members against the employer, and make the employer grant better pay and conditions. It was still more like an African legislative council in the colonial period, which had no responsibility for policy and could only criticize the policy which was laid down by the Governor and his officials. How could the English parliament, or the African legislative council, have any divisions? It needed all its united strength to stand up to the king, or the Governor. If its members began arguing among themselves, it would be dangerously weakened; the Government would play one group off against another. When British colonial officials complained that African members seemed to have no policy beyond that of opposing the Government, they were perhaps forgetting three hundred years of English parliamentary history.

We can perhaps see the beginnings of division in 1641, when parliament's opposition to King Charles I was growing more and more bitter. The civil war was growing very close, and members were already wondering, if it came to fighting, on which side they would be. To many of them, a king was still sacred, and they could not imagine fighting against him. In that year, the parliament passed a resolution called the Grand Remonstrance. It was carried only after a long debate and by a narrow majority. Members were clutching their swords; 'I thought,' said one of them, 'we all sat in the Valley of the Shadow of Death.'

But the true beginnings of the English parliamentary parties date from forty years later. The civil war had been fought; Charles I had been executed, Cromwell had made England a republic; and after his death, King Charles II had been brought back to reign over his kingdom. The new parliament was long faithful to the new king; but after a time many of the members found great cause for complaint. They disliked his foreign policy; he wanted to make England an ally of France. They disliked his religious policy; they thought that (like the French king) he would like to see England a Catholic country. They knew that he meant to govern as much as he could without a parliament. And they were much afraid because Charles had no children, and the next king would be his brother James, who was a Catholic. Probably most of the members of the parliament agreed in these feelings. But one section of them decided to take action. They brought in a Bill to exclude James from succeeding to the throne. The rest said no: this was going too far. They opposed the Bill, and it was defeated. In due course, James became king, and a very bad king he proved to be. In three years he had caused such trouble that there was a revolution, and he was exiled from the country. The party division which had begun over the Exclusion Bill was perpetuated by the revolution and the events which followed it. The parliament became divided into two main parties, and this two-fold division has remained ever since.

This bit of history gives us a clue to the basis of English parties. Many political questions, perhaps most, can be reduced to some such basic formula as this: 'We hold this much ground. We would like more. We might perhaps get more, but if we try for it, there is a risk that we may fail, and even a risk that we might lose some of what we have. On the other hand, if we stay quiet, no one will trouble us; we can hold what we have safely.' Now in such a position as this, there will always be some who say, 'Let us risk it'; and others will say, 'No, it is not worth the risk.' It is a matter of differences in temperament: the eager (the rash, if you like) against the cautious. It is sometimes a matter of differences in ideals: one party thinks that the important thing is to remedy the evils it sees, the other party replies, 'You may or may not succeed in remedying these evils; it is quite certain that in your efforts you will destroy those other good things.' There may be differences of economic interest involved as well. In the eighteenth century, the Tories were the party of the agricultural interest, attached to the exiled Stuart royal family, inclined to make an easy peace with France; the Whigs were allied with business and finance (and later on, with manufacturing), were devoted to the new royal family from Hanover in Germany, believed in fighting France and developing the empire in India and America. In the nineteenth century, the names changed. The Whigs became Liberals; they kept up their alliance with business and industry, they pushed for parliamentary reform and more democracy. The Tories became Conservatives; they remained attached to agriculture, were cautious over experiments in democracy, and (under the influence of Disraeli and Chamberlain) became supporters of the idea of a colonial empire, which the Liberals disliked. In the last fifty years, the Liberals have been replaced by the Labour or Socialist party, which is openly desirous of making many changes in Britain; the Conservatives remain a party which recognizes that changes must come, but wants them to be as gentle and painless as possible. No doubt there is much in this greatly compressed paragraph of history with which a keen party man would disagree; but the point is that in Britain, the Labour and Conservative parties do correspond to a natural division. How natural the division is can be seen from the difficulties which the small Liberal party of today finds in trying to make room for itself between the two main parties.

In the United States too, there are two main political parties, Democrat and Republican. They succeeded a group of earlier parties which were formed at the time of the War of Independence. The Democrat party was formed in 1828, the Republican in 1854. Originally, the two parties had clearly opposed policies. The Democrat party began as a party of workers and small farmers. Until the time of the American Civil War in 1860, it depended a good deal on the votes of the cotton-growers of the South. This meant that gradually it found itself forced to defend slavery, and the rights of the individual States against the Federal Government. The Republican party on the other hand was formed in 1854 to fight slavery. It was very strong among the business men of the North; and when the North won the Civil war and abolished slavery, the two parties hardened on these lines. The Republicans stood for business and industry and a strong Federal Government; the Democrats stood for agriculture, states' rights, and 'the Southern way of life'. As time went on, these divisions became less marked, and today it is not easy for a foreigner to see any clear division between the policies of the two parties. But the point is that when the parties came into existence, they were sharply divided over questions of policy.

In some countries there are several political parties. In Denmark, for example, there are four main parties; electors vote for a party, not for an individual candidate, and the seats in parliament are distributed among the four parties in proportion to the votes they have received. In France there are many parties.

We must never forget that politics is concerned with power, and that it deals almost entirely with means, not with ends. We are all agreed on what we want: peace, prosperity, justice, and so forth,

The question is, how are these ends to be achieved, and who is the best man, or the best group of men, to achieve them?

A political party is a group of people who have a policy which is different from the policy of other groups. Its members may be drawn together in the first place by a common temperament, or attitude of mind; or by opposition to some one great evil—as the Republican party of the United States came together in opposition to slavery. But having once formed, a party develops a steady line of policy of its own. The Labour party in Britain, for instance, originally formed from a feeling that both the Liberal and the Conservative parties were too much the party of the rich and of the employers. They might try to help the workers and the poor, but they could not possibly see things from the point of view of the workers and the poor. The workers and the poor must help themselves, and they must have their own party to represent them in parliament. That was how the party began; but it was not long before it developed a policy of its own. It declared that important public services like gas, electricity and the railways ought not to be run by private companies and make a profit for their shareholders; they ought to be nationalized and run for the benefit of the whole community. Accordingly, when the Labour party came to power, it nationalized these industries, and some others. In some other branches of policy, there has been less difference between the Labour and the Conservative parties. In foreign policy they have usually held together (except that the Labour party strongly opposed the Conservative Government's action at Suez in 1956); in colonial policy, the Labour party was at one time more ready than the Conservative to develop political institutions in the colonies, but since 1945 the Conservative party has moved just as fast as the Labour party would have done in giving the colonies self-government.

A separate policy is a necessity. It is not enough for a group of men to come together and say to the Government, in effect, 'Your ideas are sound; you are trying to do the right things. But if we were in power, though we should follow your policy, we should be more efficient than you are; and less corrupt.'

This is an important point, for it has a bearing on the question whether party divisions are a help or a hindrance to a country. If you have two or three or more groups of men, all striving for power but all intending to make the same use of power if they get it, then your country will certainly be weakened, as the Prime Minister of Uganda is reported to have said. It would be much better for those men to work together as one team, instead of pulling in rivalry against each other. But if you have two parties, each with its own policy and each containing good men who would be capable of running the Government, it may be a great advantage to the country. There are reasons for this.

Advantages of a genuine party system

In the first place, it is good for us all to be criticized. We all suffer from a tendency to think that we are doing very well, and to become slack and self-satisfied. Cabinet ministers and civil servants perhaps suffer from this tendency more than people in the business world. They have their system, and it is easy for them to slip into the belief that as long as they keep the papers moving from one desk to another, they are doing their job. It is good for them to be reminded that people are more important than papers: to have their mistakes pointed out to them: to be shown where their policy has produced results which they cannot have intended. But this could surely be done within the party? Yes: it can be done and in a one-party state it is done. But it makes all the difference if the criticism is made by a rival party, which can say, 'If you do not attend to what we are saying, you will find yourselves thrown out of power at the next election.' A critic inside the party can be ignored, and he often will be. The word will be passed down from party headquarters, 'Tell that man of yours not to make a nuisance of himself. We cannot allow him to make the Government (or the Party) look foolish or inefficient.' But a rival party cannot be treated like this. Thus, the first advantage of a good party system is that it makes the Government more careful and efficient; it keeps it from becoming self-satisfied and going to sleep.

The next advantage is that it is the most efficient means of political education. If a Government has no rival party, it will no doubt publish information leaflets to explain to the electors how wise and hard-working it is. But Government leaflets will tell us nothing about the Government's mistakes. After a time, the Government information leaflets will lose their value, for everyone will know that they are only one side of the story, and it is a matter of general experience that no one is perfect, and that all stories have two sides.

But a rival party will have its own newspapers and information leaflets, and its leaders will go up and down the country making speeches. They will give the electors their own side of the story; they will point out the weakness in the Government's case, and tell them all about the Government's mistakes. This in turn will make the Government leaders explain themselves. The electors will listen to the speeches and read the articles and leaflets put out by both sides; they will learn how complicated political questions are (if you listen to one side only, it all seems much simpler than it really is) and they will make up their minds which side seems to have the stronger case.

A warning is necessary here. If the party system is to be useful, it is necessary that the leaders and spokesmen on both sides should be honest and discreet, ready to give their opponents credit for the good they do. They must not abuse their opponents indiscriminately. No party is completely virtuous and wise, but none is completely wicked and foolish. A party spokesman who says, 'They are a dirty lot of crooks, and everything they do is wrong; vote for us instead!' is showing himself unworthy to govern his country. It is sometimes said, 'It is the business of the Opposition to oppose.' True: to oppose the Government whenever it goes wrong, and to show itself, if it can, a preferable alternative to the Government in power. But not to oppose the Government on a point where it has acted well, and where the Opposition would act in just the same way. Indiscriminate opposition is not only dishonest, it is bad political tactics. The electors will soon see through it, and they will become disgusted with both parties. They will begin to say, 'Politics is a dirty game; decent people had better keep out of it.' And that will be very bad for the country.

If this warning is heeded, and the parties are wisely and honestly led by men who are seeking their country's good and not merely their own selfish advantage, a two-party system can be a source of great strength to a country. A system of many parties also can be an advantage, though the more parties there are in a parliament, the weaker each party will be, and the more necessary it will be for two or more parties to combine together to form a government. A government which is formed thus by an alliance between parties is never as strong as a government which is formed by one party with a good working majority in the House. The reason is that different parties have different policies, and although two parties may agree on some points, they cannot agree on all. Let us suppose that a given party has a policy made up of four points which it wishes to carry through parliament: points A, B, C, D. If the party is strong enough to form a government by itself, it will probably carry all four points. If it is not strong enough for this, it has to form an alliance with another party, whose policy contains points A, B, C, but not D; instead of point D it has points E and F. The joint Government will carry the three points which the two parties have in common, and then disagreements will begin and the Government is likely to fall.

Another weakness of a multi-party government is that when the parties are trying to agree on terms, it is probable that there will be quarrels over appointment to the different Ministries. Perhaps each party has a very good man who specializes in foreign affairs. But there is only one Foreign Office, so only one of the two can be Foreign Secretary. What can we do for the other man; can we find him an important Ministry which will interest him and which will not disappoint someone else who was hoping to get it? And so it goes on. A two-party system is stronger, if it can be managed.

One-Party Systems

A good two-party system has great advantages, and we may wonder what reasons a country can have for foregoing these advantages and setting up a one-party State. We may divide the one-party States now existing into two groups: the group of the communist States, and that of the newly independent States in Africa and elsewhere which feel that they 'cannot afford the divisions' which result from two parties.

The one-party State began in Russia, the first country to have a communist Government. It was followed by Nazi Germany (1933-45) and by other countries as they came under communist rule. Nazi Germany was not communist, but there was much in its theory of the State which was the same as the theory of the State under communism.

The first reason for setting up a one-party State is that the communists (and the Nazi[1] party in Germany resembled them in this) have a completely different conception of a political party from that held in the Western countries. In the West, the parties are broadly agreed on the ends they desire; they disagree over the means of achieving them. All parties (except the communist party) agree that they want democracy—using the word in the sense in which we have described it in this book—a society in which men and women are free to develop their own interests: in which there shall be equal opportunities of education for all: in which people are free to own private property, to make money and to spend it. They accept Aristotle's statement that the State exists to make life worth living for its citizens. Because of this broad agreement, their differences arise over details, and often they are simply a matter of laying stress on two different aspects of the same truth. In the United States, for example, a strong Federal Government is needed, but State rights must be respected. The Republicans, as we have seen, tended in their early days to stress the strong Federal Government, the Democrats to stress State rights. In Britain, all are agreed that we should leave the individual citizen as much freedom as possible, and protect the workers and the poor against unfair treatment by the rich

[1] The word Nazi is a shortened form of the party's name; it was the National Socialist party: in German, National-Sozialistisch.

and the employers. The Conservatives tend to stress individual freedom, the Labour party tends to stress the poor man's need of protection.

But the communists accept nothing of all this. They believe in the policy laid down by Karl Marx, and as soon as they come to power they carry that policy into effect. The communists reject all the basic assumptions of the West. They are a revolutionary party, and want to break up Western society and replace it by a society ordered on Marxist lines. The workers must be given arms: they must seize political power by force; they must take control of all farms, factories, banks, businesses of all kinds. The State—as representing the workers—must be the only employer. Marx taught that after a time, when the State had performed its task of destroying the 'capitalist' society and replacing it by a communist society, the State would no longer be needed, and would 'wither away'. We have not yet seen that happen in any communist country.

Such a complete revolution cannot be carried out unless there is a well trained and well organized group of revolutionaries. This group is the Communist party. It must submit to severe training and discipline. Its members must submit their will and intelligence entirely to the party leaders. They must believe that the individual is of no account, the party is everything; they must carry out implicitly all orders which the party gives them; they must believe that whatever helps the party in its revolutionary struggle is good and true, and whatever hinders it is false and evil. A devoted member of the Communist party has much to teach us all in discipline and self-sacrifice.

But it is by no means everyone that is capable of such conduct. The party leaders choose their members with great care; it is a privilege to belong to the party, and a severe punishment to be expelled from it. From time to time the list of members is scrutinized, and those who have not maintained the required standard are expelled. The Communist party is kept fairly small; it is a group of picked and reliable political leaders. Communism is the only political belief which is allowed. It is a crime punishable with long imprisonment, or even with death, to start a rival party, or even to disagree with a party decision. Within the party, there may be free discussion until the party has made its decision; but the decision once made must not be questioned. But most of the people in a communist country are not members of the party; they are not regarded as worthy of the honour of membership.

Things are quite different in the West. In the West, we drift into a political party because we find that we share its general attitude to the political questions of the day. Even those of us who are not keen party politicians could probably say, if pressed, that they find themselves more in sympathy with this party or that. The hard, fierce, intolerant Communist party member has nothing but scorn for us Liberals or Socialists, Conservatives, Republicans or Democrats, Action Group or C.P.P. or N.C.N.C. members. Parties who do not believe in socialism, he believes, should be swept away because they are the enemies of the people; parties who do believe in socialism are even worse, because by encouraging the people to believe in the possibility of gradual reform they are fatally weakening the people's power of bringing about the only change that can be of any real help to it—the communist revolution.

The one party which is permitted in the communist State (or in Nazi Germany) is a totally different kind of organization from any of the ordinary parties in the West. They come together spontaneously from below; the one party is rigidly and ruthlessly organized from above. Western parties exist to bring about progress within a society; the one party exists to break society in pieces and reorganize it on a completely different basis. The question is sometimes asked, Which system is the better? The question, in that form, cannot be answered. It depends on what you want. If you accept the general basis of society and wish to make improvements, you had better stick to the Western system. If it is revolution that you want, if you believe that it does not matter what happens to the individual as long as the State, or the party, survives, then go for the one party. The one-party state will give you revolution and the all-powerful state; it is not designed for any other purpose.

African One-Party States

The idea of the one-party State in Africa may be influenced here and there by the communist ideal, but in the main, it comes from another source. We have said[2] that in its early history, the English parliament was united in its struggle against the king; and similarly, the legislative council in an African colony was united against the colonial Government. Party divisions at such a period would have been inappropriate, and a source of weakness. But social and economic conditions in a colony were not changed the moment the Union Jack was hauled down and the new flag of independence hoisted. Political responsibility was now entirely in African hands; but the colonial Government's work in such matters as education, health, communications was still far from finished. The new independent African Governments had their hands full with development schemes of all kinds: new schools, hospitals, harbours, airfields, power stations, rural water supplies, housing, community

[2] See page 86.

PARTY SYSTEMS 95

development, anti-erosion and anti-locust campaigns, land settlement schemes and so forth. Every one agreed that these things were needed. They must be pushed ahead as fast as money and staff could be obtained for them. Thus, there was no room for disagreement except on trivial details: the new Government must push ahead with these developments, and could count on general support as long as the people could see that it was producing results. How then could there be any true party divisions? A party system, to be useful, must reflect disagreements over policy, and if there is no disagreement, there can be no true party system. This was the weakness of the National Liberation Movement in Ghana in 1955 and 1956. The party called itself a national party, but it had very little hold on the south. Its strength was in Ashanti; it drew its support from two main sources: the traditional loyalty of the Ashanti people to the Asantehene and the discontent of Ashanti cocoa-growers at the price the Government allowed them for their cocoa. The party leaders had been in opposition to Dr Nkrumah and the Convention People's Party for years. But they had had no alternative policy to suggest; they appealed to the electors on the ground that anything the Nkrumah Government did, they would do better. The rise of feeling in Ashanti seemed to give them a new chance, and they adopted a policy of federation. They said that the C.P.P. Government was too centralized; Ghana should adopt a federal form of government so as to give more freedom to Ashanti and the North. They fought the 1956 election on this issue, but they won only 32 seats out of 104. Even in Ashanti and the North, their own territory, there was a strong C.P.P. opposition; the N.L.M. won 27 seats and the C.P.P. 19. In the south, the C.P.P. won 52 seats out of 57.[3] Federation as a policy was dead: could a national opposition party exist without a policy?

This, then, is one reason why some African states tend towards a one-party system: there is general agreement so far over policy. No matter which Government were in power, it would face the same tasks and would have to set about them in much the same way.

There is a second reason; and here we come upon a distinctively African contribution to political thought. There is a difference between African and European ideas of democracy. Not all African peoples had developed a democratic constitution, but some of them had developed a constitution which was very highly democratic. If there is a European group of 100 people, 51 of whom want one thing and 49 another, the group will do as the majority wish. The

[3] These figures do not quite add up: 52 and 19 make 71, not 72 C.P.P. seats. One member who was elected as an independent joined the C.P.P., making the total 72.

minority will shrug its shoulders. Some will give way with a good grace, some will even co-operate in carrying out a decision which they think wrong. But some will grumble, 'Well, they have rejected my advice; they will certainly get into trouble, and when they do, they can get themselves out of it; they need not ask me to help them.' But that is not African. If an African group is divided in the same way, the discussion will go on till the minority, one by one, come over and join the majority. When the chief thinks the discussion has gone on long enough, he will say that the general sense of the meeting is that this view should prevail. As soon as he has announced this, it is the duty of the remaining members of the minority to drop all opposition and swing whole-heartedly into support of the majority. It is a much better tradition than the European; its only disadvantage is that the discussion takes so much longer. An African group feels the need of complete unity much more strongly than a European group. Perhaps the feeling goes back to the days when an African village or family-group would be ruined if it were disunited: there was danger all around, danger from famine, wild animals, and above all from the spirits. It must hold together if it were to survive. At any rate, the feeling is there.

Now when this feeling persists into modern conditions, it is not surprising if a national leader and the party supporting him feel as if he is a great chief and the party are his elders. An election has been held, and the opposition party has been shown clearly that it is in a minority. Surely its duty now is to cease criticizing and back up the majority party and its national leader? This duty is all the plainer because most independent African countries are still short of men and women trained in the techniques needed in a modern state. It is a pity if a man who is competent to take a post refuses to take it and spends his time in criticizing the man who does.

There is a third reason which may move some African statesmen to propose a one-party system. One of the great problems of modern Africa is, how to develop the idea of nationality among the mass of the people who have not yet begun to feel it. The nation-states of modern Africa are the creations of colonialism. There were no Nigeria, Ghana, Kenya or Uganda before colonial times. There were Fulani, Yoruba, Ashanti, Fante, Baganda, Acholi, Kikuyu, Kipsigis and so on. And there are still village people in Africa who have hardly yet begun to think of themselves as members of a tribe, let alone as members of a nation. Many of the political parties in modern Africa were originally tribal associations, and some of their members still think of them as such. We all agree that our political parties ought to be national parties: or rather, that we should cease to think of ourselves first as members of a clan or a village or a tribe, and learn to think of ourselves as Nigerians or Kenyans. The party cry of the Sierra Leone party we have already mentioned, 'One Country, One People!' should be suitable for us all.

Thus, it is only natural if an African political leader becomes impatient with some of his rival political parties, and says, 'The majority of the nation has elected me as its leader. I am thinking of the nation as a whole. You, and you, and you are not thinking of the nation as a whole. You are thinking of your own people, the people who speak your language. You want to make sure that they get a fair share of the new schools and hospitals and roads and so forth, and a fair share of posts in the Government service. You can trust me for that. I want to lead a united nation forward into the future; you are looking backward into the past. I call on you to forget these old tribal rivalries: disband your tribal parties: let us go forward together.'

These are good reasons in Africa for thinking of a one-party state, reasons which have nothing to do with communism.

Even in Africa, however, the one-party state has disadvantages. First: however attractive in theory, it demands in practice a very high degree of devotion and discipline. If a Government deliberately decides to dispense with outside criticism, it is essential that Ministers and civil servants should be constantly criticizing themselves; and it is difficult for those who hold power to keep up to this pitch of alertness and humility. Second: although there may be no room at present for great differences of opinion on matters of policy, the time will come when such differences do occur. If only one party is legally permitted to exist, no machinery will be available by which those differences can be expressed. You can prevent people from openly criticizing, but you cannot prevent them from thinking and from muttering in secret. Most Governments have found it better to allow people to express their thoughts openly. At least, you then know what they are thinking; if you drive discontent underground, you do not know who your critics are, and what they are thinking. Once a Government starts on this road of suppressing criticism, it finds it hard to turn back. All politics has to take account of human nature, and it is part of our nature that we do not like being criticized. When statesmen and civil servants have ruled for many years without open criticism, they will not often be magnanimous enough to say that the time has now arrived when open criticism may be permitted.

The one-party state is sometimes advocated because the Government has too much important work to do to spend time in answering hostile criticism. But criticism need not be hostile; it may be friendly and helpful. You cannot tell what the criticism will be until you have listened to it.

Perhaps the greatest disadvantage of the one-party state is this. As we have said, the time will come when differences of opinion will arise over matters of policy. It may not come for many years; but it will certainly come; and the more effective the Government has been in finishing the urgent tasks on which everyone is agreed, the sooner disagreement will arise over what is next to be done. If there is only one party in existence, that disagreement will still express itself. But it will express itself through a split in the party, which is likely to cause much more pain and upheaval than a rivalry between two parties which has lasted for many years.

In colonial times, some Europeans used to say that Africans were not yet ready for self-government, for they had no political experience. Those who believed in preparing Africa for independence used to reply, 'Of course they have no political experience; and unless they are given self-government, they will never get any. They must be given the chance of learning by their own mistakes.' This same argument can be applied to the one-party state. A Government will often complain, with perfect truth, that its critics make such foolish and irresponsible criticisms that they are not worth listening to. But as long as there is a one-party state and critics are allowed no share of power, they will never learn any better. The most effective way of political education is for a Government to say to its critics, 'You say that we are governing badly. Very well; our time is up, and now it is your turn. You try your hand, and we shall see what a mess you will make of it!'

THE PARTY SYSTEM AT WORK

A Government's strength depends on its parliamentary majority. As long as it has a solid majority, a Government can do anything it likes; when its majority crumbles away, it becomes powerless. No matter how urgent and important may be the problems of home and foreign affairs, no Government can afford to relax its attention to the problem of maintaining its parliamentary majority.

The Party System in Parliament

Neither the American Congress nor the British parliament is a collection of the wisest and most virtuous men and women chosen by their fellow citizens to govern the country. It is a collection of people who accept the discipline, as well as the programme, of a political party, and have been chosen by the party organization as suitable candidates for election. There have in the past been independent members of parliament, but their day is over. Not only is a parliamentary election too expensive a business for an individual to undertake on his own resources, without assistance from party funds, but the electors prefer a candidate with a party allegiance. We discuss later on how the party system works in the constituencies; let us first see how it works in parliament.

There are many people who take a somewhat detached view of politics. They may on the whole prefer party A to party B, so that they vote for party A candidates and are glad if party A is able to form a government. But this does not mean that they support every point in the party's policy, and they may criticize freely some of the party's actions and proposals. But people like this do not get into parliament. A member of parliament must have convinced the electors (and the party workers in his constituency, of whom we shall hear more later) that he supports the party programme on all points, with few reservations, or none. It is with this assurance that he presents himself in the House; and there the party machine takes hold of him.

Each party employs a number of officials (themselves members of parliament) who are called Whips—the term is taken from the sport of fox-hunting, in which a Whip helps the huntsman to control the hounds. The party Whip has one important aim: to see that his party always has the greatest possible support when a vote is taken. This aim causes him to have various duties. He is a go-between between the party leaders and the ordinary or private member—the backbencher as he is often called, for a reason which is obvious. In the first place, he conveys to the back-bencher the wishes of his leaders. He warns him what business will be taken each day; on what points a vote is likely to be taken; which of these points are most important to the party's strategy; and (as far as he can) at what hour the important votes are likely to be taken. He sends all members of his party a printed slip of instructions. From his party's point of view, a member's main duty is to be in his place to vote for his party. He need never make a speech, he need not listen to the speeches of other members; but he must be there to vote. In the House of Commons at Westminster, there are smoking-rooms, restaurants, a library, and other rooms besides the debating chamber. In all of them there are electric bells which ring whenever the House is to take a vote. The chamber itself may be nearly empty, with only twenty or thirty members on each side; but when the bells ring, members come pouring back to vote. They do not know how they are to vote. They know what Bill the House is discussing, but they do not know whether it is discussing a clause which their party supports or an amendment proposed by the other party. It does not matter; the Whips are there to see that they vote with the party. The House takes its decision by 232 votes to 194, and quickly empties again until the next vote is taken.

There seems at first sight something ridiculous in this. If decisions are to be taken by hundreds of members who have not been listening to the debate, why have the debate at all? But the question is not as simple as this. In the first place, members of parliament have many other things to do than to sit listening to debates. They have a very heavy correspondence, for anyone with a grievance or an opinion thinks himself free to write to his member of parliament about it. They must meet their constituents, civil servants, and representatives of this or that interest who have information to give them or views to express. Since parliament's working day is often twelve hours long and sometimes much longer, they must have time to eat, and perhaps even to sleep. Much of parliament's work is done in committees, and many members who are seldom seen on the floor of the debating chamber put in hours and weeks of faithful toil in committee. Besides, parliament deals with such an enormous range of subjects that no one member could possibly take an interest in them all, much less understand them all. Every member must specialize to some extent, and it is not likely that a member who is specially interested in education and foreign affairs will be equally interested in land drainage or the problems of the iron and steel industry. We shall discuss later the question of parliamentary debates and their value.

There is a good deal of contact between the Whips on the two sides of the House. They belong to different parties, but to the same House; and they have an interest in seeing that the House gets through its work efficiently. They will be in touch with each other to arrange the time-table of business: which Bill will go through easily, which will arouse opposition? Can we get through this item of business by eight o'clock next Wednesday, so that we can make a start that night on the committee stage of the Bill on land drainage? Or have you so many members wanting to speak on the first item that land drainage must wait till Thursday? When the Leader of the Opposition at Westminster asks the Government spokesman to tell the House the order of business for next week, he is not asking on his own behalf. He knows that the order has been settled by the Government and Opposition whips in consultation, but he wants the back-benchers to have an opportunity to comment.

The private member's main duty is to vote; but many members desire to make their mark in debate. Another duty of the Whip is to find out each member's strong points and special interests, to pick the likely debaters and those likely to deserve promotion to ministerial rank. It is a duty very like that of the captain of a football or cricket club, who has to pick his first eleven and arrange the members of the team in the most suitable positions.

For we should be wrong if we thought that a debate which is attended by only a handful of members is a waste of time. There is always someone there to represent the Government and to listen to the points made in the speeches: even if the Government is represented only by one of its Whips. And both parties attach great importance to a big debate on some question of important policy. It is not that the Opposition has any hope of defeating the Government, though even that has occasionally happened. The Opposition knows that the Government has a nominal majority of, say, forty-seven, and the Whips will see to it that on such a great occasion the majority will not fall below forty, allowing for invalids and unavoidable absences. To both parties, the value of the debate is that it gives them a chance of explaining and defending their policies: the Opposition will be able to put itself forward as a good alternative government, and the Government will have a chance of confounding its critics by its sound arguments and debating skill. The more serious newspapers will report a big debate in considerable detail, and even the popular papers will pick out a few interesting points for their own style of treatment. Thus, if a big debate achieves nothing more, it gives both parties ample publicity with the electors, and it is worth while for both parties to make an effort to shine.

Great occasions like this are comparatively uncommon. The kind of debate which goes on all the time is the unspectacular discussion of the clauses of a Bill in committee. Very few Bills are quite uncontroversial. There are some Bills which the Opposition will welcome in principle, but which it will endeavour to improve in committee; there are others which it objects to violently, and which it endeavours in committee not so much to improve, as to render ineffective. This is where the aspiring member has a chance of doing good service to his party by speaking. The Government is often prepared to admit that the details of its Bill are imperfect, and to accept suggestions from either party for improving it. Here again, the back-bencher must consult his Whips to find out if clause 73, on which he wishes to propose an amendment, is one which the party leaders are prepared to see modified, or which they are determined to maintain in its present wording. This type of work gives a chance to the member who is making for himself a reputation as an authority on the subject which the Bill deals with.

One side of the Whip's functions, then, is to make sure that his back-benchers do what the party leaders want them to: speak, if necessary, in accordance with the party's policy, and above all, vote.

But this is only one side of his functions. If it were the only side, parliament would be less attractive a career than it is. There is no hard and fast line between the leaders and the led. Today's Minister or party leader was a back-bencher yesterday; and the back-bencher of today hopes for promotion tomorrow. The member of parliament has opinions of his own, and he is in touch with the party organization in his constituency, as well as with many individuals in his constituency who come to him with their troubles, although they may not be party men at all.⁴ If his party is in power, his party leaders will be too busy with the cares of office to keep as closely in touch with their constituents as the back-bencher can. He has not merely the right, but the duty, to pass on his views to the Whips, who will use them in forming their general estimate of opinion within the party. It is as important for the Whip to tell the party leaders what the party is thinking as it is for him to tell the private member what he is to do. The question is sometimes asked, whether party leaders control their party or are controlled by it. It will depend to some extent on the leader's personality and on external circumstances: some leaders can exert more control than others. But in general, both answers are true. A party chief can lead his party as long as he leads it in the way it is prepared to go and at a pace it is prepared to keep up. If he goes in the wrong direction or at the wrong pace, he is likely to meet trouble. It is the Whip's business to keep leaders and back-benchers in touch with each other and hold the parliamentary party together as a disciplined but contented team. Sometimes the Whip is assisted in this part of his business by a committee of back-benchers. Such committees often hold great influence; Ministers and party leaders discuss their proposals with them in detail, and when things have gone wrong, discuss the cause of the trouble and who is to blame.

Some writers bewail the growing strength of the party machine, and the decline of the independent member. But strong party discipline is essential if parliaments are to get through their enormous volume of business effectively. The day of the independent member may be over, but back-benchers still have some power. They still have the right to introduce Bills of their own, and if a private member's Bill receives sufficient back-bench support, the Government may take it up and provide enough time for it to be passed into law. The back-bencher can help to influence his party's policy in another way, besides telling his Whip or the party committee, 'I

⁴ It is a tradition—a constitutional convention, if you like—that a member, once elected, represents all the electors in his constituency: those who voted against him or did not trouble to vote at all, as well as those who voted for him.

have had 150 letters in the last fortnight on this point; I really think the party had better reconsider it.' What he can do is to put down a motion for the House to debate, drawing attention to some point of policy and inviting the House to agree with his views on it. Other back-benchers will add their names to his, and if the motion attracts a formidable body of supporters, the party leaders are sure to take notice of it. The motion will not be debated; it is intended merely as a warning to the party that there is strong back-bench feeling on the point, and it will be withdrawn, having served its purpose.

If all else fails, and if his feelings on the subject are strong enough, a back-bencher can vote against his party. But this is an extremely strong step, so strong that it is rarely taken. A member taking it puts his political career in danger. Not only will he be strongly condemned in the House, but he may find that he loses the support of the party organization in his constituency. Parliament will always honour a member who thus puts conscience before party; but it is only to be expected that keen party men on his own side, and the Whips in particular, will be too keenly aware of the damage he has done the party to think much about his conscience.

The Party System in the Constituencies

A modern, well organized political party is based on an organization which covers the whole country and has branches in all the parliamentary constituencies. Usually, the constituency branches send delegates to the national convention or conference of the party, which takes place once a year. The party organization (the 'machine', it is often called) may have separate sections for young people and for women: sometimes also for other special groups— the Labour Party in Britain has sections for teachers and for scientific workers, for example.

One reason why the independent candidate has almost vanished is that, although the Government provides the premises and the machinery for use on election day, and although strict limits are laid down by law on the expenditure which a candidate may properly make, electioneering is still an expensive business. During the weeks of an election campaign, a candidate must have committee rooms in which his supporters can meet him; he must have large quantities of posters and leaflets and other propaganda printed; he must pay a full-time election agent; he must hire halls for his meetings. And his expenses do not begin only with the announcement of the election. While parliament is still sitting, he must 'nurse the constituency'; that is, he must visit it often and make himself known, and must study the views and the needs of the voters. He will be expected to subscribe to local charities. It all costs a great deal of money and the party organization here has a great advantage over the private man. Everyone knows the broad outline of the party programme, and people are willing to subscribe money and turn out and work to get their party candidate returned. Party funds are needed to pay a candidate's election expenses.

Let us suppose that the organization of a party in one constituency is faced with the job of selecting a new candidate. Its old candidate perhaps has told it that he wishes to retire from politics at the next election; or he may have died; or he may have offended the party too deeply to be forgiven. There may be a local man who offers himself as a new candidate. If not, the local branch will ask the party headquarters to find them someone. The new man arrives. He is interviewed by the chairman and committee of the local branch. He is questioned on every aspect of his political faith. He passes this preliminary test, and is introduced to the rank and file members of the branch, and is again questioned. He is asked how he would vote on this question and on that; he is asked to pledge himself to support this and that cause, till it is hard for him to remember what he has or has not promised to do. On many points he will be provided by national party headquarters with notes on the party's accepted policy; but there will be many points of local interest on which headquarters can give him no guidance. Eventually, the local branch adopts him as its prospective candidate for the next election; in due course he fights the election and—we will suppose—is elected.

The local party organization has carried its man; but it does not sit down and rest until the next election draws near. Its keen supporters have a steady programme of activities which are meant to attract new members to the branch and to explain and defend the party's policy to the public. Now and again they will try and get a leading member of the party in parliament to come down and make them a speech, and they will expect their own member to keep in touch with them.

The member's duty to his constituents

When a group of people send someone to represent them at a meeting, there are two ways in which they may regard his duty. They may discuss the matters on the agenda paper of the meeting: make their own decision: and instruct their representative to announce their decision at the meeting and vote for it. They regard their representative as a delegate; they do not send him to use his own discretion, but merely as a mouthpiece to express their opinion. This system has an appeal in certain parts of Africa. In 1925 the Governor of the Gold Coast established a system of provincial councils of chiefs; and he invited the provincial councils to send representatives to the legislative council. But his scheme was unpopular, because people said that by African custom a chief had no authority to give his own opinion; he must consult his people, and give not his opinion, but theirs. At trade union conferences in Britain, the unions send their delegates with similar strict instructions.

But there is another way of regarding a representative's duty. In 1774 the city of Bristol elected two members to represent it in parliament. One of them announced that he would always vote in parliament according to the instructions he received from the Bristol electors. But the other member, Edmund Burke, disagreed with this view. He said that he would always consider carefully what the electors said, but he would not bind himself always to agree with them. He would always do his best to serve the electors:

'It is his duty to sacrifice his repose, his pleasures, his satisfactions to theirs; and above all, ever and in all cases to prefer their interest to his own. But his unbiassed opinion, his mature judgment, his enlightened conscience, he ought not to sacrifice to you. . . . Your representative owes you, not his industry only, but his judgment; and he betrays, instead of serving you, if he sacrifices it to your opinion. . . .'

Burke's eloquence amounts to this: that members of parliament who do their duty conscientiously will be much better informed than their constituents; they will listen to debates, they will read Government reports, they will attend committees and receive deputations on all kinds of matters. The views of their constituents therefore should be only one of many factors which determine their own views. They sit in parliament not only to represent their constituency but to discuss the affairs of the nation; and they will be false to their national duty if they come to the House with minds closed against any arguments and information they hear there, and determined to vote in obedience to the views of a constituency committee.

This view of Burke's has prevailed, and it has almost become a convention of the constitution that a member of parliament votes according to his own judgment, even if that is contrary to the wishes of his constituents. Moreover, a member of parliament regards himself as the representative of all his electors, of those who voted against him as well as those who voted for him.

But the convention is not solidly established. Modern conditions have modified the relationship between a member and his constituents. When Burke was member for Bristol, Bristol was two or three days journey from Westminster. Nowadays we have the newspapers, radio and television, and many other ways of acquiring information on all matters discussed in parliament. Keen party members in a constituency nowadays are much better informed than they could possibly have been in Burke's day, and their views must be given more weight. Local party organizations nowadays tend to keep a strict eye on their own member. He is allowed a good deal of latitude, but if he departs too far from the party line, he will find himself in trouble. A member who finds himself embarrassed will come down to his local party organization and explain his embarrassment. For example, if he has put his name to a motion critical of his party's policy, he will explain why he has done so. The local committee will probably pass a resolution of confidence in its member, and he will go back to parliament happy in its support. But there are limits beyond which the local committee will not go. In 1956, some Conservative back-benchers in Britain refused their support to the Conservative Government over the Suez affair. They were required by their constituency associations to explain themselves. Some were censured, one was told that his local association would not support him at the next election and would seek a better candidate.

This last case is an interesting illustration of the limitations which the party system of today sometimes puts on Burke's doctrine. The member, Mr Nigel Nicolson, did not obey his party's whip; he did not vote against his party, but abstained from voting in support of it when instructed to do so. The party association in his constituency, after hearing what he had to say, passed a vote of no-confidence in him by 298 to 92. Mr Nicolson considered that this vote did not truly represent the feeling among the Conservative voters in his constituency, and he refused to resign his seat. In fact, he did receive much local support, and for two years the local Conservative association was torn by disagreements. Then the national leaders of the party intervened. They said that the dispute was weakening the party, and must be healed. They suggested that all known Conservative voters in the constituency should be asked to record their views in writing: in other words, there should be a local referendum on the question whether or not they supported Mr Nicolson as their member. This was agreed to, and Mr Nicolson promised to abide by the result, whatever it might be. The vote was taken. The figures were: For Mr Nicolson, 3,671; Against him, 3,762; Abstained, 2,118. Mr Nicolson thus found himself in a minority of only 91 on a total vote of nearly 7,500; and we may surely take it that the two thousand who did not trouble to vote cannot have strong objections to Mr Nicolson. Nevertheless, as he had promised, Mr Nicolson resigned his seat in parliament; though it was agreed that, to save the expense and trouble of a bye-election, his resignation should not take effect until the next general election.

Even in normal times, when things are going smoothly, the member will be watched by his constituency association. It will read the official report of parliamentary proceedings to see how he spoke and voted. It will pass a resolution on policy and ask him to bring it to the notice of the party machine in parliament. The member today cannot have as much independence as Burke claimed, even though most thoughtful people would agree that Burke's view should still be the general policy, and that a member should not be merely a delegate of his local party organization.

All this may sound formidable. But these things all come down in the end to a question of personal relationships between the member and his local committee. Both must try and be sensible: for if it is bad for a member to have the reputation of being a difficult man, it is just as bad for a constituency association to have the reputation of being a difficult body to please. They must both have at heart the interests of the party. It is true that the constituency organization may tend to be more extreme in its views than the member. With his more intimate experience of parliamentary affairs, he may sometimes have to tell them, 'I fear it is not quite as easy as you think. I will try and find an opportunity of telling the Whip your views, but this is not the moment.' The member must educate his local committee in what is possible, just as the committee must educate him in what is desirable. The art of politics is in finding the best possible compromise between what we would like and what we can get.

CHAPTER VIII

Presidential and Cabinet Government

Is the head of the state to hold real power, or only formal and ceremonial power? If he holds real power, the system is called presidential government; if only ceremonial power, it is called cabinet government. (But some presidents nevertheless hold only ceremonial power.)
United States the type of presidential government, based on the theory of the separation of powers. The president is head of the executive. How the president is elected in the United States; and in Ghana. The president is not only head of the state, but head of his political party. Relationship between president and Congress; possibility of friction. Ghana as an example of a president who is always assured of parliamentary support; weakness of Ghanaian parliament and strength of the presidency. Ghana's constitution in some ways intermediate between American and British.
Cabinet Government: all Ministers must be members of parliament. Real power in the hands of the Prime Minister; he chooses the Ministers. He is leader of majority party in parliament. The shadow cabinet. Majority leader system copied in constitutions of Sierra Leone and Nigeria.
Cabinet collectively responsible to parliament. Qualifications of collective responsibility in modern times: individual Ministers may resign or be dismissed, but a Government with a working majority need not fear defeat on a motion of confidence. But cabinet must speak with one voice.
Parliament's power over Government is exercised through Government back-benchers and the fear of the electorate, not through voting power. But cabinet does not abuse its power over parliament; it is an accepted convention that opposition rights must be respected. Power of a Prime Minister with cabinet and parliamentary majority solid behind him is almost as great as that of president: in some respects greater.

EVERY State has some individual as its head: a King (or it may be a reigning Queen, as in Britain and in Holland) or a President. We need such a Head of State for formal and ceremonial purposes at least: someone to open Parliament, to appoint and receive ambassadors, to sign and approve Acts of Parliament, to make treaties, to appear on ceremonial occasions, while the band plays the national

PRESIDENTIAL AND CABINET GOVERNMENT 109

anthem and the guard of honour presents arms. We need this focus for our loyalty; we need someone to cheer.

Shall we allow the Head of our State to have, not merely these formal and ceremonial powers, but real power? That is a question on which states differ. Britain is the type of a country which has withdrawn all real executive power from its Head of State (the Queen); the United States is the type of country which allows its Head (the President) to hold real power. In modern times, most countries which have a king or a queen as their head have put the real executive power in the hands of a cabinet. Some presidents too have no more power than this: Ireland, Italy and Israel are examples. Other presidents follow the United States pattern in being the real holder of executive power: examples of this are France (under General de Gaulle; before his time there was a different constitution), Spain, and Ghana. This type of government, in which the Head of State holds the real executive power, is called presidential government; it is not a very accurate name, because as we have seen, many presidents do not hold real executive power. The system which is followed in Britain, Holland, Italy, and Israel is called cabinet government.

We have seen that the United States worked out its system of presidential government on the theory of the separation of powers. According to this theory, it would be wrong for the executive and the legislative powers of government to be in the same hands. The legislative power lay with Congress, so the executive power must be placed elsewhere; and the President was chosen to hold it. Under the old colonial system, the American people elected their own legislatures, but the king and parliament of England claimed the right to tax them. The colonial Governor represented the king's executive power, which was much greater in those days than it is now. In some respects, the United States Constitution reproduces the old colonial system, but with one great difference. Each State in the Union has its own Governor; but the Governor is no longer appointed from outside, he is elected by the people of the State. Similarly, the President has the powers which the colonial Governors tried to exercise; but he too is elected by the people, and his term of office is limited.

We have mentioned in Chapter IV the principal features of the American President's executive power. He can appoint any one he likes to be a member of his cabinet, except—an important exception—a member of Congress. It does sometimes happen that he invites a member of Congress to take office; but if the Congressman accepts, he will of course have to resign his seat in Congress, and most men would rather keep their seat there. The men (and women) chosen need not have any political experience, and in fact most of them do not have. They need not be from the President's own party; it may happen that the President will appoint someone from the other side. Most members of the cabinet are business men; and when the President's term of office is over and his cabinet has to resign, they will go back to the business world again.

Electing the President

Different countries have different ways of electing their president. When the United States began to elect its presidents, it did not want the president to be too dependent on Congress; so it would not allow Congress to elect the president. Instead of that, it set up a system of indirect election. In each State, the State legislature was to choose a number of men (the number was to be in proportion to the State's population) for the sole purpose of choosing the best man in the nation to be president. But very soon, political parties appeared, and the election of president became a purely party matter. We need not discuss the details of presidential elections. Several candidates may be nominated by each party in different parts of the country, but eventually a national party convention reduces its candidates to one. The presidential election campaign then opens. In each state the people vote, not to elect their president, but to elect the members of the State's electoral college. But since the voting is on strictly party lines, each candidate for the electoral college is openly pledged to vote for his party's national candidate for the presidency. Moreover, it is a convention of the constitution that all the votes in the State's electoral college are given for the candidate who wins a majority of the popular vote. Thus, in 1964, the State of New York had forty-three electoral votes, while Wyoming had three. If the Republican candidate had a majority of only one vote over his rival Democrat in the New York elections, he would be given all forty-three of the State's votes for the presidency. Thus it is more important to win a small majority in a large State like New York than to win a sweeping majority in Wyoming.

Not all countries have adopted such complicated ways of choosing their president. In Ghana, for instance, candidates for election to the Assembly (the parliament) declare which candidate they will support for the presidency; and the presidential candidate of the party which wins a majority in the Assembly is declared to be elected President.

President and Parliament

But whichever means may be chosen of electing a president, the fact remains that he is elected as a party man. As president he is

Head of State, and must show himself in many respects above party; but he is nevertheless a party leader, and he may find many of his Government's proposals opposed for party reasons. In the United States, this is particularly difficult, for the president is elected for four years, while the House of Representatives is elected for only two. It may easily happen that half-way through his term, the president finds himself faced by a hostile House of Representatives. The Ghana Constitution avoids this difficulty, for president and assembly are elected together and they finish together; if the president dissolves the assembly, he must resign.

Under the theory of the separation of powers, it is the business of the president and his cabinet to administer the country, but it is the business of Congress to make the laws and provide the money to enable them to do so. It is one of the chief functions of Congress to criticize the administration, so although the executive and the legislature ought to work smoothly together, there is plenty of opportunity for them to pull in different ways. The president and his cabinet cannot make laws. All they can do is to consult with committee chairmen and party leaders in Congress, and prepare Bills which a sympathetic member is ready to introduce there. But a Bill introduced in this way has no priority over a Bill introduced by a private member. The president may recommend a Bill to Congress, but Congress is not bound to take any notice of his recommendation. It may leave his Bill utterly neglected because it thinks no law is needed on the subject; or it may prefer to introduce a Bill of its own in preference to the Bill recommended by the president. In either case, the president is helpless.

There is a similar possibility of friction over finance. The president and his administration draw up a budget, but the money has to be provided by Congress. This means that a series of appropriation bills has to be introduced and passed there; and the executive has no more power over an appropriation bill than it has over any other bill. The sum of money which Congress votes for a head of the administration's budget may be larger or smaller than the administration wishes, and it may be subdivided into items and granted under conditions which greatly limit its usefulness from the administration's point of view. Neither the president nor any member of the executive may come into the Congress to argue the case. The president can send messages, and the executive can have private meetings with party leaders in the Congress; but Congress acts as it thinks fit. The president can veto a bill, but he cannot veto individual clauses of a bill. Congress often votes a much smaller sum of money than the president has asked it for; and much time is wasted in negotiations.

There are special reasons for this in the United States. One reason is that a member of the House of Representatives (in which all financial proposals must be made) is much more concerned with his local affairs than a British member of parliament. He is much more expected to see that his constituency gets a good share of Government expenditure: roads, water resources, harbour improvements—federal expenditure of all kinds. A congressman will not be popular if he devotes his mind to higher things such as national policy, and neglects to provide his home district with this kind of 'pork', as they call it. Moreover, party discipline is not as strict as it is in the British parliament. The local party organization is much more interested in having a member who will bring home the 'pork' than one who will loyally support the party's national policy; and it will not allow the national party leaders to interfere too much with its member's freedom. This is perhaps a relic of an earlier age in American politics, and there are leaders in America who would like to change it to suit the needs of the modern world; but they will not find the change easy.

This frequent lack of harmony between the president with his cabinet and the legislature is a defect in the American constitution which has arisen largely because of the development of party spirit. It is the price that the United States has to pay for its strict adherence to the doctrine of the separation of powers; and it is a price that many Americans think well worth paying. In the United States, as in Britain, there is much agreement between the parties on the main issues of policy. Thus, the long negotiations between the executive and the legislature tend to be limited to questions of secondary importance.

But all presidential government need not be affected in this way. The constitution of Ghana has shown how precautions can be taken to ensure that president and legislature remain in sympathy with one another. In Ghana, as in the United States, the president appoints the members of his cabinet, and he may dismiss them; and it is the president who assigns his department to each. But whereas in the United States a cabinet minister cannot sit in parliament, in Ghana he not only can but must. The President must choose his Ministers from the members of parliament, and if a Minister is so unfortunate as to lose his seat in parliament, he must resign his post. This arrangement gives Ministers the great advantage that they can speak in parliament to explain and defend the Government's policy. On the other hand, Ministers are not responsible to parliament. Parliament may disapprove of a Minister, but if the president supports him, he need not resign. His position is strong, because the parliament's power over finance is limited. The budget estimates are drawn up by the executive and laid before parliament for its approval; but parliament is not allowed to move any amendment. It must pass the estimates as a whole, or reject them. In Britain, parliament could show its disapproval of the Government's policy by moving a reduction in a departmental estimate; and if the motion were carried, either the Minister concerned would resign, or else the whole cabinet—almost certainly the whole cabinet. In the United States too, as we have seen, the legislature has unlimited power to amend the budget. The president of Ghana has another power which is greater than that of the American president. He can assent to a bill, or reject it, or assent to part of it; and parliament has no power, such as the American parliament has, of over-riding the presidential veto.

This constitution of Ghana[1] is still young; Osagyefo President Nkrumah and his Convention People's Party are in full power, with all the reputation they have gained through obtaining the country's independence. It will be easier to judge it fifty years hence, when perhaps political parties may be more evenly balanced and there may be two strong rival candidates for the presidency. But it does seem to concentrate, like the United States constitution, great power in the hands of the executive without necessarily involving the friction between executive and legislature which is so marked in the United States. In this respect it seems to lie between the American and the British forms of government: that is, between presidential and cabinet government. To cabinet government we must now turn.

CABINET GOVERNMENT

The most conspicuous difference between the American and the British systems is that whereas an American Minister cannot be a member of parliament, in Britain he must be. There is but one qualification to this: it may sometimes happen that in a general election, the Government as a whole is returned to power for another term, but a particular Minister loses his seat. Strictly speaking, he should then resign his post. But nowadays he is given some latitude. Usually, someone from his party who has won a safe seat will resign it in order to give the Minister another chance; and for the week or two that this takes, the Minister will continue in office.

The next big difference is that although in theory Ministers are

---

[1] I use the term 'constitution' here to refer not only to the document so-called, but to the various Acts, such as the Presidential Elections Act and the Presidential Affairs Act, both of 1960, which elaborate some of the points left vague in the written constitution.

appointed in Britain, as in America, by the Head of State, the Queen, in fact it is the prime minister who chooses his team of ministers and allots their departmental responsibility. The prime minister then presents the Queen with the list of his cabinet, and in modern times the Queen cannot refuse to accept it. Her function is limited to the purely formal one of receiving each new Minister and handing over to him the badge of his new office.

The prime minister himself is not only a member of parliament, but is the leader of the strongest party in the House of Commons. Each political party elects its leader in its own way. When a new parliament is elected, the prime minister who was in office at the time of the dissolution remains in office if his party has retained a majority. If his party has lost the election, he resigns, and his whole cabinet resigns with him. He advises the Queen to send for his rival, the leader of the majority party in the new parliament, and to invite him to form a Government. The Queen of course accepts this advice, and the new prime minister sets about the task of choosing his ministers and allotting to them their departmental posts. In modern times, this process is very quick; for the practice has grown up that while in opposition, a party sets up what is called a 'shadow cabinet'. The leader of the opposition appoints certain leading members of his party to take special responsibility for certain subjects and to lead the opposition's attack upon the Government in their own subjects. It is understood that these men will normally become ministers when the party next is returned to power. Thus, when the leader of the opposition is invited by the Queen to become prime minister and form a government, he usually has the list of all his senior Ministers ready prepared, and it is only a question of filling in the minor posts. As long as there are only two main parties, each with its recognized leader, the Queen has no choice in the matter; though there have been one or two cases during this century in which this state of things has not existed. In 1894 and again in 1906 the Liberal party was in power, but it was not entirely united under a leader. In 1931, the Labour Government had fallen. It was a moment of great national danger, and the leaders of all three parties agreed that it would be a mistake to have a party Government; it would demonstrate Britain's unity to the world if the new Government was a coalition of parties. Having received this advice from all three leaders, the King invited the outgoing Labour prime minister to form a new Government with the support of the other two parties. He did so, and won an overwhelming victory in the election. Some people have thought that the King should have invited the Conservative leader to form a Government; but most think that with the advice he received, he did the only possible thing. In the two earlier cases, the only problem was to find a leader who would command the support of the party; once he had been found, the matter was settled.

The system of appointing the leader of the majority party in parliament to be prime minister has been copied in many African constitutions. In Sierra Leone for instance, the independence constitution of 1961 provides that the Governor-General shall appoint as prime minister a member of the House of Representatives who appears to him likely to command the support of a majority of the House. There are similar provisions in Nigeria. In 1951, the Governor of the Gold Coast saw that the Convention People's Party had won an overwhelming victory at the elections. The leader of the party was serving a prison sentence for sedition, but the Governor did the only possible thing under British constitutional practice: he let him out and invited him to form a Government. Under the system of cabinet government, the Head of State has no discretion in this matter: the leader of the majority party in parliament must be invited to form a Government, for no one but he will be able to get anything done.

The next characteristic of cabinet government is that the cabinet is collectively responsible to the parliament. In theory at least, if the Government is defeated on one aspect of its policy, the whole Government falls, not merely the one Minister concerned. The theory is picturesquely illustrated by a story of a nineteenth-century prime minister who is alleged to have said at a cabinet meeting, 'Now, what are we going to say? It doesn't matter very much what we say, but we must all say the same thing.' A Government may be very popular as regards its foreign policy, its agriculture, its health, and a dozen other matters; but if it is defeated over its educational policy, the popular Ministers will resign along with the unpopular Minister of Education; the prime minister will advise a dissolution of parliament, and there will be a general election.

That is the theory, and there is still much truth in it. But in modern times the practice is not quite so strict, and the hardening of the party system has changed parliament's attitude towards Government mistakes. The theory of the cabinet's collective responsibility now has to be qualified.

Qualifications of the theory of collective responsibility

The rule that the cabinet should 'all say the same thing' was not established as a convention of the constitution until the early years of the nineteenth century, and it was not until the 1830's that it became the practice for a cabinet to resign if defeated in the House of Commons. Before then, it was always possible for parliament to censure an individual Minister without bringing down the whole Government, and even possible for a Government to be defeated as a whole without resigning.

It is still possible for an individual Minister to resign because he disagrees with the policy of the rest of the cabinet, or because there has been some trouble and he feels that he or his department is to blame. The initiative is not always left to the Minister. The prime minister may decide that it is better to sacrifice a Minister, and he may call on the Minister to resign. There was an example of this in 1935. Italy had been at war with Ethiopia since October, and the League of Nations (the precursor of the United Nations of today) was trying to stop the fighting. Fifty member-states of the League drew up a plan to weaken Italy (whom they regarded as the aggressor) by refusing to buy from Italy or sell to her. But the League could not make up its mind to refuse oil supplies to Italy; that would have hit Italy very hard, and Italy said that she would regard it as an act of war against her. At this moment, the British Foreign Secretary, Sir Samuel Hoare, worked out with the French Government a plan of his own: Italy was to cease fighting, and in return for doing so would receive a large piece of Ethiopian territory, and economic rights over another piece. Sir Samuel Hoare was a member of a Government with an overwhelming majority; but when his 'peace plan' was announced, no parliamentary majority could save him. There was such a great outburst of indignation in Britain that the Government was embarrassed. If it supported Sir Samuel Hoare, the indignation would be turned against the Government as a whole. The Government had to decide quickly whether to support its Foreign Secretary or to drop him. It dropped him; he resigned his post and left the cabinet.

Three years later, Sir Samuel's successor as Foreign Secretary, Mr Anthony Eden, wished the Government to be firm in resisting Italy's foreign policy. The prime minister would not support him, and Mr Eden resigned. There have been other recent cases in which a Minister has resigned to show that he disapproves of his colleagues' policy.

In the middle of the nineteenth century, party discipline was weak, and the House of Commons could easily vote against a Government. We are told[2] that in fact it did so no fewer than ten times between 1832 and 1867. But today, party discipline is strong, and such a thing never happens; at least, it never happens unless the House is in committee on the clauses of a Bill. As we have said, Governments are seldom so much attached to a particular detail that they will go to the trouble of summoning their followers to turn

[2] A. H. Birch, *Representative and Responsible Government*, p. 135.

PRESIDENTIAL AND CABINET GOVERNMENT 117

out in strength. If in a thin House the Government is defeated on section 133 (b) by 87 votes to 83, there will be mocking Opposition cries of 'Resign!' But nobody will really expect the Government to resign over such a small matter. It would be very different if the Government were to be defeated on a vote of confidence; but such a defeat nowadays is unthinkable. No matter how seriously the Government may have blundered, its party will support it, and its majority will see it safely over the vote of censure. A few of its supporters may abstain, as in the case of Suez. One or two may even vote against it; but the Government will be in no danger whatever of defeat.

The criticism is indeed sometimes made that Governments nowadays are too apt to treat every question as a vote of confidence, and to cling to office by means of their obedient majority when it would be more honest of them to resign. This tendency is shown by both parties. There have been several instances, both in the time of the Labour Government of 1945-1951 and of the Conservative Government that followed it, when serious blunders were revealed which raised a storm of criticism; but the Government sat tight, called on its followers to vote for it, won its vote of confidence, and waited for the public to forget about the incident before the next general election. On such occasions, the Government argues, 'If we resign now we shall certainly be defeated in the election. But this parliament has two more years to live before a general election falls due. That gives us plenty of time to cover this blunder with good work in other directions, so that we can choose our own moment for resigning and can go to the country with a good chance of being re-elected.' Any political party will naturally reflect, 'The country is better off in our hands, even if we do make an occasional mistake, than in the hands of the other party, who would ruin it altogether.'

It may seem from this that we have qualified the doctrine of collective responsibility so much that we have destroyed it. But an important part of it remains: the doctrine that Ministers must stand together and speak with one voice. There must sometimes be differences of opinion, but they must be settled in the cabinet room before the Ministers face parliament. The Government is never embarrassed by finding that one Minister has made a speech in Edinburgh which conflicts with a speech made by a colleague in Liverpool; the public never has to ask itself which of these speeches it is to take as Government policy. Then again: as we have seen, individual Ministers do sometimes resign, either because they cannot support the policy which their colleagues have adopted, or because they feel that they are a weakness to the Government, not a strength. But when the prime minister decides that the moment has come for him to resign, all his colleagues go with him. There is no unseemly break-up of the team, each member thinking of his own interests and trying to obtain office in the next Government. Collective responsibility makes that impossible.

If it is impossible for the House of Commons to bring down a Government by a hostile vote, what power has the House to control the Government? In the first place, as we have seen, the Government may not fear the Opposition's voting power, but it does fear its own back-benchers. A prime minister will listen very seriously to his chief Whip when he is told, 'I am afraid there is a good deal of uneasiness over this Bill; X and Y have told me their constituency associations have written to them strongly about it.' In the next place, the Government fears the Opposition's tongue. It must all the time be thinking about its election prospects, and a weighty Opposition attack, well supported in the newspapers and on the radio, will affect the electors' opinions. (We have seen that the swing of only a small proportion of the electorate may make a big difference to the results of an election.) Parliament's control over the Government is less than it used to be, and is exercised indirectly through the constituencies rather than directly through a vote in the House.

Power of the Prime Minister

In cabinet government, the prime minister chooses his colleagues he has as complete a power and freedom in this matter as the President has in the United States. Naturally, he cannot order a man to take a particular post: he can only offer him the post. No doubt it must often happen that a man who particularly wants to be Home Secretary is offered the Ministry of Education, or a prime minister finds himself with three good candidates for Foreign Secretary and nobody who particularly wants Agriculture and Fisheries. There must be difficult negotiations and compromises. But the decision lies with the prime minister and nobody else; and if he has made up his mind that X is to be Minister of Education and not Home Secretary, X must accept his decision. In Britain, this is a matter of convention; in some countries it has been made part of the written constitution. In Sierra Leone, for example, it is laid down that the prime minister advises the Governor-General on the appointment of ministers, and on their dismissal.

All executive power is in the hands of the cabinet. The cabinet draws up its policy and writes the 'speech from the throne' in which the Queen, at the opening of the session, announces the Government's plans. The cabinet approves the budget, and there is a well-established rule that no financial proposals may be made in parliament except by the Government. The Government's programme of legislation is so heavy that there is little chance for any other Bill to be carried unless the Government—that is to say, the cabinet—agree to help it by finding parliamentary time for it. A cabinet with a working majority in the House can assume that it will stay in office for the full five years of the parliament's life, unless it chooses its own suitable moment to resign a few months beforehand. As we have seen, there is no serious fear of its being defeated. Though all the cabinet ministers are members of parliament, it would be easy for them, if they chose, to reduce the House of Commons to insignificance.

If they do not do so, it is because they were members of parliament before they were ministers, and they have been brought up to regard parliamentary debate and criticism of the Government as important. They are in office today, but they may be in opposition tomorrow; so the rights of the Opposition must be preserved. Parliament carries a heavy load of business, so heavy that it has to set up committee after committee to report to the whole House on the details of legislation and of finance. The Government is constantly tempted to take more time for its own business, and it sometimes goes so far as to take time away from private members. But it will never take away the days which are allotted to the Opposition. By agreement 'through the usual channels,' that is, through the Whips, so many days in each session are allotted to the Government, so many to the Opposition, and a few to private members. This agreement between Government and Opposition is never broken. The tradition is strong that the Government, all-powerful though it could be, must submit itself to the criticism of its rivals. It must allow them to choose the points of attack and the lines of the debate: 'Answer this if you can,' says the Opposition; 'the electors will be interested to hear what you can say in your defence.' This two-party rivalry is the setting in which the cabinet system has developed.

Such a system in modern times (with collective responsibility and a strong party organization) gives great power to the prime minister. With his cabinet behind him, and a solid parliamentary majority, a prime minister can do anything he likes. He must be careful not to go further than his own party will stand; but it is surprising how much a party will stand from a leader whom it trusts, rather than break up the Government and put its rivals into office. A British prime minister, as long as his majority is safe, can meet an American president on equal terms. He is restrained by no such checks and balances as restrain the president. He can agree to a treaty, confident that parliament will back him; the president's agreement has to be ratified by two-thirds of the Senate, and when President Woodrow Wilson signed the charter of the League of Nations, the Senate refused to ratify. The prime minister can promise money; if he puts it in the budget, parliament will vote it. The president can not, for Congress is very likely to refuse him the money. The prime minister has just as much power as the president to dismiss a colleague. He controls the business at cabinet meetings; he can have an item placed on the agenda paper or kept off it, and he can encourage or close discussion. If there is disagreement, he can, if he chooses, say to the minority group, 'Now, the cabinet has made its decision. You disagree with it. Very well; will you resign, or will you keep quiet and support the decision loyally?' It is almost an African attitude.[3] The prime minister is the leader of a team; he picked each one, and he can dismiss each one.

Politics is the art of using power. The prime minister in a cabinet system has very great power; the most important quality for him to possess is the skill to know just how great his power is, and the strength to use it. He must above all be a strong leader, strong enough to know his own mind, to take unpopular decisions when necessary, and to convince his party that they are sound.

[3] See page 96.

CHAPTER IX

Some Problems of Parliament

A. *One House, or Two? Historical reasons for two Houses in England. Reasons why two Houses have been set up in America. Examples of two Houses, chosen in different ways: Sweden, Ireland, Turkey, Britain.*
Advantages of two Houses: (i) a second House can act as a revising body; (ii) a second House may bring in useful members who are not strong party men. Examples in Britain and Nigeria.
B. *Too Heavy a Load of Business. Modern Governments are busy, and work their parliaments hard. Devices for speeding up parliamentary procedure: (i) the guillotine, (ii) selecting some clauses for debate and not others, (iii) mechanical voting devices; (iv) committees. Value of debates in the House even though the result of the vote is known beforehand.*
C. *Lack of Expert Knowledge. Parliament is not an assembly of experts, but of ordinary men and women chosen by the electors. Vast and varied business of parliament beyond the scope of any one member. Special interests and pressure groups outside parliament. Do we agree that expert criticism should come mainly from sources outside parliament? The proposal to use specialized committees. A specialized committee would have more control over Government policy than the whole House now has: this has always caused the British to reject the idea. The danger would not arise in a country which works on the principle of the separation of powers.*

THE function of parliament is to express the wishes of the electors and to guide the executive according to those wishes. We have seen that it is not an easy matter to obtain a parliament which accurately expresses the wishes of the electors; nor is it easy to ensure that the executive is willing to be guided. But if these difficulties have been solved, others remain.

ONE HOUSE, OR TWO?

Some countries have two Houses of parliament, others have one. Britain has two. The United States and Canada have two; so has every other country in the New World except Costa Rica, Guatemala, Honduras and Nicaragua. Russia has two Houses, and so have most countries in Europe; but Albania, Bulgaria, Denmark,

Finland, Greece, Rumania and Spain have one. Six countries in Asia, including India and Japan, have two Houses; Israel and Lebanon have one. New Zealand has one House, Australia two. In Africa, most countries have only one House, but there are two Houses in Ethiopia, South Africa, Liberia and Nigeria. Out of this survey of sixty parliamentary states, thirty-eight have two Houses and twenty-two have one.

The system of two Houses grew up very early in Britain: not because anyone sat down to consider whether one House or two would be more democratic, but simply because it seemed more convenient. The king must have his council of great nobles, men whom he knew personally. If the king and his council proposed to tax the people, it was advisable to consult the representatives of the people who would actually have to pay the tax: the townsmen and the small freeholders in the country. But the king and the nobles would not wish to have their council crowded with these strangers, whose faces they did not know and whose opinions on state affairs they did not desire. They had only one thing to say to these commoners: 'How much money are you willing to provide for these very necessary wars that we propose to fight? Go away to your own room and talk it over, while we discuss important business. When you have decided, come back and tell us, and then you can go home while we continue our council.' This arrangement, which began as a mere convenience, developed into an important constitutional principle.

But why have so many other states adopted the same principle? Well, for one thing it satisfies a natural desire. Every ruler likes to obtain the advice of the old and the wise, and a council of elders or wise men is common all over the world. But where modern democratic ideas have come in, the common people are not prepared to take without questioning whatever the old men decide. It is convenient to have an assembly in which the common people can make their views heard. One of the problems which the British never solved in West Africa during the colonial times was how to develop the chief's council of elders so as to give the 'young men' some voice in affairs. It was all very well for the elders to say, 'It is not our custom to admit young men;' but when the young men became educated it was natural that they should wish to be heard, and the elders were the poorer for excluding them.

Apart from this general reason for having two Houses, there are special reasons in certain countries. The Americans found difficulty in agreeing on their constitution. The small States of the new Union wanted the parliament to represent all States equally; the large States wanted it to give representation to States proportional to their population. Each point of view was natural. Rhode Island and

Delaware asked, 'Why should we give up our freedom to a parliament in which New York and Pennsylvania will be able to do whatever they like without troubling about us?' New York and Pennsylvania on the other hand replied, 'Why should a handful of people in these small States have just as big a voice in parliament as our great numbers?' The matter was settled by a compromise: the parliament (Congress) would consist of two Houses, the lower House being elected in proportion to population, the upper House consisting of two representatives from each State, whether large or small. This means that every law passed by Congress must satisfy not only a majority of the people of the whole country, but a majority of the States. There being now fifty States in the Union, the Senate has a hundred members. No doubt, similar thoughts have led to two-chamber parliaments in other federal countries, such as Canada, Australia, Brazil, Switzerland, West Germany, and Malaysia. When the Federation of Nigeria was first established, the Federal legislature had only one House; but a second House was added in 1959, five years later.

Many countries with a unitary (that is, non-federal) form of government have parliaments of two Houses. The upper House is usually chosen in some different way from the lower. In Sweden, for instance, the lower House of 232 members is elected by a popular vote in the usual way every four years. The country is divided for local government into twenty-four counties, plus the city of Stockholm. Each of these bodies elects members to the upper House of 151 members, every eight years. The upper House thus represents the local government bodies; and since it lasts twice as long as the lower House, it is possible that a swing in public opinion may bring the two Houses into disagreement. In Ireland there is a lower House of 147 members and a Senate of sixty. Eleven are nominated by the prime minister, and six by the universities; the rest are chosen by an electoral college of 990 members made up of members of parliament and of local government bodies. The upper House in Turkey has fifteen members nominated by the president, and 150 elected by the people; but they are elected for six years, whereas the lower House is elected for four years. In Britain, the House of Commons is elected, but the members of the House of Lords hold their positions for life. Some of them sit because their fathers have sat in the House, and their sons will sit after them. In the last few years, laws have been passed which enable the Queen to nominate men and women to life peerages, and enable members of the House of Lords to renounce their hereditary peerages. A life peer has the right to sit in the House of Lords for his life-time, but his son does not inherit the right. Similarly, a hereditary peer who gives up his peerage can give it up only for his own life-time; the peerage remains in existence for his son to inherit if he chooses.

It seems that most countries in the world have a feeling that although it is democratic to be governed on the principle 'One man, one vote', a parliament elected on this basis is imperfect. It is imperfect in two ways. First: there are many good men whose help in the legislature would be valuable, but who will not go through the business of seeking party support and fighting a contested election on party lines. A second House gives such people an opportunity to make their special contribution. Second: public opinion may change suddenly, and the public and its representatives in the lower House may become very excited and act hastily and unwisely. A second House slows down hasty and unwise action and gives the public time to reflect.

Both these purposes are plain in some modern constitutions. In Britain, a peerage (that is to say, membership of the House of Lords) is given to men and women who have distinguished themselves not only in party politics, but in industry, administration, science, medicine, education, or public service. Such people are often not strong party politicians, and the party machines are not strong in the House of Lords. They are appointed so that they may contribute their individual experience and wisdom. As a result, the House of Lords contains members who are experts on many subjects, and both the Government and the Opposition find its debates well worth studying. In Ireland, forty-three out of the sixty senators are chosen to represent five different fields: labour, industry and commerce, agriculture and fisheries, public administration and social service, and the field of art, literature, and education. In Nigeria, the republican constitution of 1963 retains the system of adding a few 'special members' to parliament, which existed in the 1960 independence constitution and, of course, in colonial times. In the federal senate there are four such special members, nominated by the president on the advice of the prime minister; and there are special members too in the regional legislatures. But there are only few, compared with the large numbers in Britain and in Ireland.

The second purpose of a second chamber is to act as a revising body, criticizing and amending the work of the lower House. When the upper House begins to act in this way, a problem immediately arises. Since the lower House is directly elected by the people and the upper House usually is not, how much power should the upper House be given? It should not be able to block the wishes of the lower House altogether, for that would be to block the people's wishes. On the other hand, a popular assembly is sometimes moved

SOME PROBLEMS OF PARLIAMENT 125

by emotion, and if unchecked, may do things that it afterwards regrets. So the upper House should be given enough power to enable it to delay action and suggest improvements.

During the nineteenth century, the House of Lords in Britain was predominantly Conservative, and when a Liberal Government was in power, the House of Lords often blocked or seriously modified its measures. We have seen in Chapter Three that by two Acts in 1911 and 1949, the power of the House of Lords has been greatly restricted; it cannot now delay Bills by more than two sessions of parliament, or one year. The House of Lords has accepted its new position. It recognizes that it should not attempt to act in a party spirit to block a programme which the people clearly has determined to carry through. Its function is to suggest improvements in the programme: to introduce Bills (to be sent down to the House of Commons for consideration) which the programme of the Commons cannot find time for: to debate general questions of Government policy: and only seldom to use its limited powers of delay. From time to time there has been talk of 'reforming' the House of Lords. But the reply is always made, 'If you reform it, you will have to give it more power;' and neither party is willing to give more power to the Lords.

The Nigerian Senate has a similar position. In Nigeria, as in Britain and most other countries, a Bill imposing taxation (a 'money bill') must be introduced in the lower House. The House of Representatives sends a money bill to the Senate, and the Senate must pass it without amendment within a month. If the Senate keeps it longer than a month, the House of Representatives will send the Bill to the President over the head of the Senate, and the President will sign it and pass it into law without the Senate's approval. In the case of bills other than money bills, the Senate has some power of amendment and of delay. It may send down its amendments for consideration by the House of Representatives. If there is a serious difference of opinion between the two Houses, the House of Representatives being determined to carry a Bill to which the Senate objects strongly, the constitution provides a special procedure. The House of Representatives will send the Bill to the Senate at least a month before the end of the session. If the Senate rejects the Bill altogether, or makes amendments which the House of Representatives cannot accept, the Bill will stand over until the next session. If the House of Representatives is still of the same mind, it will send the Bill up to the Senate a second time; it must be at least a month before the end of the second session, and at least six months after the Bill was passed by the House in the first session. If the two Houses still cannot agree, the Senate's power of delay is exhausted.

At the end of this second session, the Bill will go from the House of Representatives to the President over the head of the Senate, and it will become law. There is one session of parliament every year; so the Senate has power to delay a Bill for at least six months, but cannot delay it as long as two years.

TOO HEAVY A LOAD OF BUSINESS

We have said that one convenience of a second House is that it has time to debate general questions, and to introduce Bills which have no chance of finding a place on the programme of the lower House. This leads to one of the biggest problems of all modern parliaments: How can they find time to get through their work?

This is a problem which affects all modern states. A hundred years ago, it was the general opinion that the fewer new laws that parliament made, the better. Many of the subjects that concern parliaments today, such as education, health, housing, agriculture, industrial relations, were then thought to be no part of a Government's business; it was not until 1872, for example, that the British Government began to build schools, which until then had been left entirely to private individuals and the Churches. The world seemed larger, life was more leisurely; parliaments could get through their business without hurrying.

But during the last hundred years, the idea has taken hold on all nations that it is the Government's business to be active in remedying evils and deficiencies. The programme of legislation becomes heavier and heavier; parliamentary sessions become longer, the parliamentary working day too becomes longer. The party discipline becomes more rigid, and it becomes a more serious matter for a member to miss an important division; it becomes harder and harder for a member to work to earn his living and attend parliament in his spare time.

Consider the position of the British parliament. It sits continuously for about twelve hours a day on four days a week; on Fridays it sits for only five or six hours, so that members can get home to their constituencies for the week-end—not necessarily to rest there. It sits in this way in three terms corresponding very closely to the three terms of a school year, with a long vacation in the late summer and shorter vacations at Christmas and Easter. Being a member of parliament is nearly a full-time job. A member must not only attend in his place as much as possible, but must keep up a heavy correspondence, keep in touch with his party organization in the constituency, and be available for any of his constituents that wish to consult him. It would hardly be possible to lengthen parliament's working day or session. And yet parliament is too busy to do its work as well as it would like. It is driven to adopt various devices to speed things up.

Some of these devices are designed to shorten the debates on the details of a Bill. One of these is nicknamed the guillotine; the real guillotine is a machine used in France for executing criminals by cutting off their heads. The parliamentary guillotine is a motion, moved by the Government, that a given stage of the discussion shall end at a fixed hour. No matter how little ground has been covered and how much remains, that stage of the discussion is to end and the vote is to be taken, so that the House may pass on to the next item of business. Governments try not to use the guillotine, for it looks brutal, and always provokes the Opposition to protest fiercely that the Government despises parliament and is undemocratic at heart. But all Governments use it, whenever they have a long and highly controversial Bill which the Opposition is determined to cut to pieces.

A less conspicuous device is to select certain clauses or amendments for debate and leave the rest undiscussed, to be passed or rejected by a plain vote. This happens when a Bill is not so bitterly opposed. What happens in effect is that the Opposition gives up its right of debating every detail of a Bill in order to gain more time for debating the details that it thinks really important. The Whips on each side get together and make the selection by a process of bargaining, and then notify the Speaker of the agreement they have reached. We must remember that under modern conditions of party discipline, the Opposition has no real hope of defeating the Government in a vote. The Government can carry every one of its clauses if it wishes; if it should happen that by some bad luck, late at night, the Government is defeated by 43 to 39, the Government will reintroduce the lost clause, and the Whips will see to it that it is carried next time by 223 to 187.

Why then spend time in debating? Because the Opposition, though it cannot defeat the Government in a vote, hopes to be able to do two important things. In the long run, it hopes to show the public how much better a Government it would provide than the group of men now in office. And for the moment, it wants to improve an imperfect Bill: to delete from it what is bad, to make what is good yet better. It does not often happen that one party considers the other party's Bill to be so hopelessly bad in principle that it cannot be improved. It may be so bad that the best to hope for is to render it harmless; but it cannot be remedied harmless without discussion of details.

The Government in its turn must be reasonable. It may be

attached to the principles of its Bill: but no Bill of a hundred or more clauses is faultless in detail. A great deal of work goes on behind the scenes. Members put their criticisms of this or that clause in private. The Minister in charge of the Bill says, 'Yes, I see your point. I will look into the matter and see what we can do.' The result may be that the Government introduces an amendment to its own Bill before the clause has been reached in discussion. Or when a clause is reached, an Opposition member will say, 'We do not want to delay this by a long debate. I would like to put one point briefly to the Minister. . . .'—and he then states the ground of his opposition. The Minister replies, 'I am grateful to the hon. Gentleman, who we know has great experience in these matters. I will undertake to give further consideration to the point he has raised.' The clause may be skipped for the moment, and returned to later when the Government is ready with its amendment; or it may be agreed to temporarily and amended at a later stage of the Bill's progress. It is important to remember that under a two-party system, parliament is not like a battlefield or a football ground, where if I find I cannot win, at least I do my best to stop the other side winning. Every voter who goes to the polls to elect his member does so with the idea of choosing the best man to carry on the government of the country. Every member of parliament has a loyalty and a responsibility greater than that to his party: it is his loyalty and responsibility to the nation—to the Queen or the President, if you like to personify the nation in that way. Both Government and Opposition are responsible for passing wise laws, and both must realize that there must be a reasonable give-and-take. They may disagree on some matters, but they are agreed that—as one prime minister said long ago—'the Queen's Government must go on'. The Opposition has a duty to be reasonable and constructive in its criticisms, and the Government has a duty to listen to such criticism and take it to heart.

We should remember that if clause 12 of a Bill is debated, and then clause 28, clauses 13 to 27 being passed over, this does not necessarily mean that parliament is giving up its duty of considering them.

Another device, which has been adopted in some parliaments, but not yet at Westminster, is a speeding-up of the process of voting on a motion. Voting is always lengthy. If there are three hundred members in their places, it is not practicable for the clerk to count the raised hands for Aye and No; it takes quite a time, and it is very easy to make mistakes. In the United Nations, they call the roll, and each delegate says Yes or No, which the clerk writes down. This again is slow, but it does not matter very much, for votes are

SOME PROBLEMS OF PARLIAMENT

not taken very often. At Westminster, members vote by walking out through two separate doors, being counted as they go: probably the slowest method of all. The device has been tried of giving each member an electric switch on his desk, so that he can light a green lamp for Yes and a red one for No. But these, like raised hands, have to be counted. The real difficulty is that so many members are not in the chamber, and have to rush in from outside to vote. No really satisfactory solution has yet been found to this problem. If one could be found, it would save several hours a week.

All these are ways of speeding up business when parliament is sitting as a whole. But they do not speed it up enough. A more drastic way is to split parliament into committees, and get as much of the work as possible done in committee. Without such a system, the British House of Commons could not possibly hope to cover its ground. The House has four standing committees: one each on Public Accounts, Estimates, Statutory Instruments, and Nationalized Industries. In addition, every Bill affecting Scotland goes to a committee of all the Scottish members. Every Bill at a certain stage of its progress is 'sent upstairs' to one of the many select committees which exist for the purpose of giving a closer and more detailed examination than the House as a whole can possibly give. These committees are selected so as to represent the parties in the same proportions as in the whole House. Discussion in committee is freer than in the whole House, and the committees have more leisure to do their business thoroughly. After being discussed in committee, a Bill is reported to the whole House with the committee's amendments, and proceeds through its remaining stages.

LACK OF EXPERT KNOWLEDGE

The complaint is often made that the work that parliaments have to do is not only vast in amount, but vast in complexity and variety. In one session, a parliament may find itself turning from foreign affairs to education, agriculture, housing, and several other subjects, each of which has formed a life-long study for those who earn their living in it. It is impossible for any member of parliament to become familiar with more than one or two of these large subjects. Consequently, when parliament is debating any one of them, it may be that not more than one-fifth of the members present understand the subject well enough to make useful speeches; a good many, without much understanding, have strong views; but most will be content to follow the party's line and vote as the Whips tell them.

On the face of it, this seems unsatisfactory. It means that the Government receives skilled and useful criticism from only a small group of members, and expects to find most of the criticism it needs outside parliament. In Britain, for example, any Bill on agriculture or education would be discussed with the powerful professional organizations of farmers and teachers; and there are many organizations (called 'pressure groups', because an important part of their work is to bring pressure on the Government if their interests seem in danger) which will be ready to give advice and criticism on their special subject where it is needed: such as the Road Haulage Organization on any matter concerning roads and lorry traffic, the Federation of British Industries and the Trades Union Congress on any matter concerning industry and labour. It is the same in America; the United States policy towards China and South-East Asia, for example, has been greatly influenced by what they call 'the China lobby'[1]—that is, the group of business men, missionaries, army officers and others who regard themselves as specially knowledgeable on Chinese matters and are anxious to guide their Government's policy. (It will be noticed that a lobby need not be united in its views.) No doubt the same is true in other countries. But this means that parliament is only one of the sources—and perhaps not the most important—from which the Government obtains the advice and criticism it needs; and it lessens the importance of parliament. Another important source of comment is the Press; any Government in Britain will pay careful attention to the articles written by specialists in a few of the daily and weekly papers, and will probably find more useful comment in them than in the parliamentary debates.

This is true; but it would only be a serious criticism of a parliamentary system if we believed that parliament should be the main source from which Government proposals receive skilled advice and criticism. If we wanted that sort of a parliament, we should need a different system of election. The voters do not go to the polls to elect wise and expert leaders and critics; nor does the party system provide such candidates. The voters are thinking mainly of electing representatives who will understand their wishes and needs: people like themselves. And most of the voters think much more about their own rents and taxes and the cost of living than they do about wider issues of statesmanship. The value of parliament is not that it is a collection of clever men with specialist

---

[1] The 'lobby' is the passage or ante-room just outside the parliament chamber. The word hence comes to be used for a group of people who are not members of a parliament and so are not allowed inside the chamber, but who wait 'in the lobby' to explain their views to Ministers and members when they come out. The noun 'lobby' gives rise to the verb 'to lobby', meaning to behave in this way.

knowledge; its value is that it is a collection of men who are fairly representative of the people. The whole theory of democracy rests on the faith that the people as a whole has common sense, loyalty, decency, and a sense of justice and fair play; and that these qualities make it able to govern itself. Abraham Lincoln once said, 'You can fool all of the people some of the time, and you can fool some of the people all of the time; but you cannot fool all of the people all of the time.' If you do not have this faith, then do not have parliamentary government.

This does not mean that the people have no need of leaders. They have. The art of government, like other arts, needs skill and practice. If we want to be cured of illness, we go to a qualified doctor; if we want a bridge to be built over a river, we go to a qualified engineer; and likewise, if we want our public affairs to be properly run, we go to people who have made a study of public affairs. In a parliamentary democracy, we believe that we shall find suitable leaders among the members of parliament, and that the people, and the representatives whom it elects, will judge when to support them and when to withdraw support. We look to parliament for the heavy detailed work of government and legislation; we do not look to it to provide six hundred specialist experts.

But if this is so, we are in effect saying that we do not expect parliament to exercise effective control over Government policy. Do we really mean as much as this?

There are many who would say No. They do not wish to accept that parliament cannot effectively control Government policy. They would propose means of strengthening parliament's control: the principal means being an extension of the committee system. They propose a new kind of committee: a specialized committee. Existing committees of parliament, as we have seen, are selected so as to keep the party balance, but not to provide expert knowledge. The specialized committee which is proposed would be a committee of members who have special knowledge of some field of policy: foreign affairs, for example. All matters concerning foreign affairs would be referred to the committee. Its members would become more specialized; having less need to be well informed on education or housing, which belonged to other committees, they could be better informed in their own field. As the committees meet in private, the Government could reveal confidential information which it dare not reveal to the whole House and the newspaper reporters in the Press gallery. It would follow that the specialized committee would take over some of the powers which now belong to the whole House. Such a specialized committee could exercise real control over policy, a control which would be wisely used because based on full information.

A specialized committee of this kind would not be a new thing. Such committees exist in France and the United States. But so far, no British Government has favoured the idea. The chief argument against it is that the House of Commons as a whole should not give up any part of its powers to a committee, however expert. The House can adopt or reject any advice given it by the committees it now has. To give a committee the power, not merely of making recommendations to the House, but of taking action in the name of the House would be so foreign to the British tradition of parliamentary government that it has hitherto always been rejected. It is admitted that a specialized committee, armed with powers entrusted to it by the whole House, would soon come to exercise a stronger control over policy than the House itself has ever exercised. That is the very reason why Governments dislike the idea. They do not want the House to control them; they want it merely to criticise. In fact, the attitude of all British Governments to the House of Commons is rather like the attitude of the House of Commons itself to the House of Lords. 'We agree that the House as it is needs improving if it is to do its work properly. It is not difficult to suggest ways in which it could be improved. But if we improved it, we should have to give it more power; and the House has enough power already. It is better to have an imperfect House with its existing powers than to have a more powerful House, even if a better one.'

That particular fear would not arise in a country, such as the United States, whose system is based on the idea of the separation of powers. The American Congress cannot control the Government: however energetic and well-informed, all it can do is to make the Government's task easier or more difficult. But in any country like Britain or Nigeria, where there is no separation of powers, and the Ministers are chosen from the members of parliament and have to depend on a parliamentary majority, the fear is a real one. Do we want a parliament which is merely a debating chamber to criticize, but not to control policy, or do we want a parliament which exercises real control? So far, Britain has always chosen the first.

CHAPTER X

Federal and Unitary Government

All Governments experience a tension between central and local needs. Modern nation-states are built up out of many separate units, and separate loyalties often persist. In a unitary state like Britain or France, loyalty to the central Government is stronger than any local loyalty. If local loyalties are so strong as to be serious rivals to the central Government, a federal system may be better. Federal Government usually the result of the combination of a number of hitherto independent units, who do not wish to give up all their independence: for example, Switzerland, Malaysia and others.

Obstacles to the formation of a federation: (i) fear; 'That other country will dominate us;' (ii) selfishness: 'Why should we take on the burden of this other backward country?' Examples from South Africa, the United States, the Caribbean.

A federal constitution is always a compromise between need for a strong central Government and rights of separate states. The constitution may limit the powers of the Federal Government, so that as time goes on, the states become relatively stronger; or may limit the powers of the states, so that the Federal Government gradually becomes stronger. The United States, Australia, Nigeria limit federal powers; Canada limits provincial powers.

Advantages of federalism: (i) it brings about a union which would otherwise never be brought about at all; (ii) its constitution can be drafted to meet the needs of the situation.

Disadvantages: (i) federalism is expensive in money and man-power, for each state of the federation must have the same kind of government machinery. (ii) Tension is always likely between state and federal Governments. (iii) Policy and action may vary greatly between one state and another, in matters which belong to the separate states. (iv) Some Government action is slowed down or made difficult because a majority of the separate states have to agree to it.

Thus, a unitary government is best, if the people can be persuaded to accept it; but if not, a federal government is much better than no form of common government at all.

Federal states need not be republics, or have a presidential type of government, or work on the principle of the separation of powers. Canada and Australia are monarchies, and they, with Nigeria, have cabinet government. On the other hand, France is a strongly unitary state, but has presidential government.

IN almost[1] every country in the world there is a certain tension or suspicion between the central Government and the people living some distance away from it. In Britain, this tension was shown very plainly in 1963, when the Government set up a commission of inquiry into local government, and the commission recommended, among other things, that the smallest county in England, the county of Rutland, should be absorbed into its neighbours. The people of Rutland protested so strongly that the Government gave up the idea. Britain is a small country, and local feeling is not as strong as it is in many other countries.

Every country recognizes the strength of this feeling, and divides itself into provinces or districts, giving each of them certain powers to govern itself within certain limits. Even a large city like London is divided into self-governing local districts; the powers of the districts depend on an Act of Parliament which lays down the limits of the district's authority.

In very early times, a people is divided into tribes or clans or family groups, and often there are differences of custom and of dialect. It is only gradually that they come together and form one nation. Twelve hundred years ago, there were ten or a dozen main tribal groups in England and four or five in Wales. It was not until the ninth century that any tribal ruler dared to call himself King of all England; it was not until 1707 that the two independent countries of England and Scotland joined into one United Kingdom. In France too, it took several hundred years for the different provinces to become firmly united into one country. Every country in Europe has gone through this slow process of unification; some have succeeded in it, others have failed. Austria, for example, grew into a very large state ruled by one king, inhabited by peoples speaking many different languages. But when the French Revolution brought about the spread of nationalism, it became harder for Austria to hold together, and in 1919 she split into three independent states, while parts of her territory were taken by her neighbours.

A small country like Britain or France may be able to hold together under one Government, though even here, as we have seen, local or provincial feelings may be strong. A large country whose peoples are very different from one another may fly into pieces like Austria. But there is a system of government by which some countries are able to hold together, though more loosely than Britain or France. This system is called federalism.

---

[1] There are a few very tiny independent countries, such as San Marino and Monaco (which have an area of only 23 square miles and half a square mile respectively), Andorra and Luxembourg, where this problem can hardly exist.

FEDERAL AND UNITARY GOVERNMENT

In a federal state, the central Government hands over some of its power to a number of separate regional (or state, or provincial) Governments. The division of powers is laid down in a written constitution. There is an important difference between this system and the system of a unitary Government, like the British Government, which has a number of subordinate local government bodies like county councils or town councils. The powers of a county council or a town council in Britain depend on an Act of Parliament. If the council exceeds its powers, it can be (and sometimes is) sued in the courts. Parliament, which passed an Act to create county councils and to give them certain powers, could equally well pass an Act to abolish them and take all their powers back into its own hands. Likewise, parliament makes laws for the whole country, and is not bound to consult the county councils before doing so; and the laws made by parliament take precedence over any local laws which a county council may make under the authority which parliament has given it.

Under a federal system, the central (or 'federal') Government has parted with some of its powers, and cannot take them back. There are certain powers which the constitution reserves to the federal Government, and others which it reserves to the regional Governments. Neither side can go beyond the powers which it holds under the constitution. The constitution may of course be amended; but as we have seen, constitutions are usually made so that they cannot be easily amended, and federal constitutions are always made so that the federal Government alone cannot amend them; the regional Governments too must consent. It might easily happen that the British parliament should pass an Act which abolished the county of Rutland, and in fact, that very thing nearly happened. But it is unthinkable that the United States Congress should pass an Act to abolish the State of Alabama, or the Nigerian parliament pass one to abolish the Northern Region and declare it to be Federal territory like Lagos. The American example is unthinkable, because, although the necessary amendment to the constitution would not need the agreement of Alabama itself, it would need the agreement of three-fourths of the States. Every State would think, 'It is Alabama today; will it be our State tomorrow?' and it would be impossible to get three-fourths of the States to agree. The Nigerian example is unthinkable, because the constitution expressly provides that any alteration of this sort must be approved by the Region concerned; thus, the Northern Region could not be abolished without its own consent.

A federal system of government usually comes into being when a number of states who have previously been independent of each other agree to join together. There is no reason in theory why such states should not agree to form a unitary government like that of Britain or France. In practice, the old loyalties usually make them unable to give up all their independence to a unitary central government. Switzerland came into being in this way: one canton after another won its freedom from Austria and joined the federation. It was the same with the United States, which began with thirteen separate British colonies: with Canada, South Africa, and Australia, which began in the same way; with Malaysia, which began with several separate Malay states and one or two small British colonies. Brazil is a very large country, formerly a Portuguese colony, which has grown in much the same way as the United States: many separate settlements on the coast expanded into the interior. India and Nigeria may seem at first sight to be exceptions, for each was ruled as one country by Britain before independence—though Nigeria was given a federal constitution by Britain seven years before independence. But these two countries are not really exceptions. Each consists of a very large number of peoples with different languages and cultures. There had been no unity before the days of British rule; such national unity as exists is the result of the work done by the British administration. It would not have been surprising if, when the British left, India and Nigeria had fallen into several independent states. India did, in fact, break into three: India, Pakistan and Burma. But it might have broken into many more, and by adopting a federal form of government, it held together. The Caribbean islands are an example of a federation that nearly came into being, but not quite. The British Government tried hard to persuade the British islands in the Caribbean to join into a federation, along with the two mainland countries of British Honduras and British Guiana. Many island statesmen too did their best to form a federation, and long conferences were held. But in this case, the local feeling in the separate islands was too strong, and they did not succeed in reaching agreement.

It seems that a federal government is not always easily reached. A federation becomes possible only when the separate states feel that some such form of joint government is better than continuing in their separate existence. The commonest obstacle is fear and selfishness. Fear makes a country say, 'I am small, that other country is big; if we join together, it will dominate me, and will care nothing for my feelings.' Selfishness makes a country say, 'I am rich, that other country is poor; if we join, it will expect me to pay for it.' Both these feelings amount to the same thing; the fear that if I join in a federation, I may give up more than I shall gain.

FEDERAL AND UNITARY GOVERNMENT

Thus, the British tried to get the four South African countries to join into a federation in the eighteen-seventies, but they failed. The Transvaal and the Orange Free State were afraid that a federation would bring them under the rule of the Cape; the Cape was busy building railways, and did not want to burden itself with poor countries like the Transvaal and the Orange Free State in the days before gold had been found on the Rand. There were similar difficulties over the United States federal constitution. The thirteen colonies declared their independence and formed a military alliance to fight for it. But the United States government which won the war was much too weak to govern the country in time of peace. Four years after the end of the war, delegates from twelve states met to try and improve their constitution; the state of Rhode Island refused to send anyone, because it valued its independence too highly. Fifty-five men from the twelve states met on May 25, 1787; thirty-nine of them signed the new constitution on September 17th. It had been hard work. One delegate had refused to attend the convention because he knew it would recommend a stronger central government, and he did not want one. Three who did attend refused to sign the constitution because they disagreed with parts of it. The main point of dispute was how to have a strong enough federal Government without limiting too much the powers of the states. This question arose in settling the way in which Congress should be elected. The small states wanted a Congress in which all states would have equal representation, the large states wanted representation to depend on a state's population. As we know, a compromise was reached by which the Congress was to consist of two Houses, one composed in one way and one in the other. The same difficulty arose over the question of Negro slaves. The slave-owning states would not of course allow their slaves to vote, but they wanted to count them as part of their population, so as to have more members in Congress. The free states replied, 'If you will not count your slaves as citizens for one purpose, you cannot expect to count them for another.' Here too a compromise was reached: a state was allowed to count three-fifths of its slaves for the purpose of reckoning how many members of Congress it was entitled to. Eleven states ratified the new constitution within a year, but Rhode Island and North Carolina refused to ratify it or to take part in the new Government until a number of amendments were introduced.

The establishment of a federal government does not put an end to these difficulties. A federal constitution is always a compromise between the views of those who want a strong federal government and those who insist that the rights of the separate states must be respected. This battle over state rights is still being fought in America today. The Civil War was fought a hundred years ago to decide whether a state could leave the Union or not. The war decided that it could not: the Union must be preserved. The trouble that occurs when the Federal Government tries to make a southern state admit Negroes to white schools comes from this same conflict over state rights. Education is one of the subjects which are controlled by the states, not by the Federal Government; thus, a southern state protests that, 'The way we run our schools is our business; the Federal Government has nothing to do with it.' The Federal Government replies that the Constitution forbids any state 'to abridge the privileges or immunities' of any citizen, and the Supreme Court has interpreted this provision to mean that a Negro's privileges are being abridged if he is kept out of a school or college simply because of his colour. Each side has to keep a careful eye on what the Supreme Court says; but those in the South who wish to keep Negroes down are able to get more support than they otherwise might because they are able to raise the cry, 'The Government is trying to limit the rights of our State!'

The federal constitution is thus always a compromise; and the compromise may be made either so as to give much power to the Federal Government and little to the states, or to give little power to the Federal Government and much to the states. There are examples of both. The United States constitution limits the powers of the Federal Government, but not those of the states. The Tenth Amendment says, 'The powers not delegated to the United States by the Constitution, nor prohibited by it to the States, are reserved to the States respectively, or to the people.' This makes it clear that the Federal Government has no powers except those it can find in the Constitution; but the states can do anything which the Constitution does not expressly prohibit. Thus, if a state, or an individual citizen, thinks that the Federal Government is exceeding its powers, he can challenge the Government, 'Show me the clause of the Constitution which permits you to do this.' On the other hand, if the Federal Government thinks that a state is exceeding its powers, the state can challenge it, 'Show me the clause in the constitution which prohibits me from doing this.'

The Australian constitution, like the American, limits the powers of the Federal Government, but not those of the states; but it allows rather more power to the Federal Government than the United States Government possesses.

The Canadian constitution tilts the balance the other way; it limits the powers of the provinces, and leaves to the Federal Government powers which are not expressly reserved to the provinces. It says,

'It shall be lawful for the Queen, by and with the Advice and Consent of the Senate and House of Commons, to make Laws for the Peace, Order, and good Government of Canada, in relation to all Matters not coming within the Classes of Subjects by this Act assigned exclusively to the Legislatures of the Provinces; and for greater Certainty, but not so as to restrict the Generality of the foregoing Terms of this Section, it is hereby declared that (notwithstanding anything in this Act) the exclusive Legislative Authority of the Parliament of Canada extends to all Matters coming within the Classes of Subjects next hereinafter mentioned. . . .'

The language is not as simple or as terse as that of the United States constitution, but it is just as definite. The Act (the British North America Act of 1867) assigns certain subjects exclusively to the provinces. All other subjects belong to the Federal Government. The Act lists some of them 'for greater Certainty', but is careful to explain that the list is not exhaustive. Any subject which is not listed either as belonging to the provinces or to the Federal Government must be taken to belong to the Federal Government.

The Nigerian constitution follows the United States pattern of defining the powers of the Federal Government but not those of the Regional Governments. It does so in a new way. It lays down two lists of subjects: one list of subjects which are reserved to the Federal Government, and a second list of subjects in which a Regional Government may make laws and the Federal Government too may make laws, which will be applied to a Region if the Regional Government so decides. For example, a Regional Government may not make laws about citizenship or defence or railways; these are matters which concern the whole of Nigeria, and are reserved to the Federal Government. On the subjects of bankruptcy, or electricity, or national parks, a Region may make laws of its own, or it may prefer to wait for the Federal parliament to make a law, and then adopt the Federal law. (The constitution provides that if a Region does make its own law, and the Federal parliament too passes a law on the same subject, the Federal law is to prevail if there is any disagreement.)

But there is no list in the Nigerian constitution of subjects which are reserved to the regions. Any powers which are not reserved to the Federal Government or listed as joint ('concurrent' is the term used) powers must be taken to belong to the Regions, and the Federal Government must keep away.

When the United States, Nigeria and Australia are on one side, and Canada on the other, no one can say in general terms whether it is better to specify the powers of the Federal Government and give all others to the provinces, or to specify the powers of the provinces and give all others to the Federal Government. Each country must consider its own situation and decide for itself. If you want your Federal Government to grow stronger as the years go by, then limit the powers of the provinces so that they cannot expand. If you want to make sure that your Federal Government never grows any stronger than it is now, then limit its powers and leave the provinces to develop.

ADVANTAGES AND DISADVANTAGES OF FEDERALISM

Federalism is a way of government which is invented to suit one situation. You have several local units which are too suspicious of each other to agree to join under one unitary government, but which realize that it is necessary for them to join together in some way if they are to survive and prosper. Each local unit wishes to keep some of its freedom, and to give up to the central authority only as much power as it finds necessary. Federalism makes this possible. It enables the different units to hold together tightly, or loosely: to give up much of their power, or only a little. Its constitution can be drafted so as to ensure that the central or federal Government remains weak, or to ensure that it gradually becomes stronger. It can be so drafted that it is easy to amend, or difficult, and so that it becomes easy, or else impossible, for a unit which is dissatisfied to break away and resume its original independence. This is the great advantage of federalism: in such a situation, a federal form of government can be drawn up so as to meet the wishes of the different units exactly.

But these great advantages are bought at a price. In the first place, federalism is expensive in man-power, and so in money. The United States has one central legislature and executive, and fifty State legislatures and executives. Since all the States are equal in importance —or think themselves so—each must have the same type of government machinery. Texas has nearly ten million people, and an area of over 260,000 square miles; Rhode Island has fewer than one million people and less than one thousand square miles of land. But Rhode Island has its governor, lieutenant-governor, secretary of state, attorney-general, just like Texas; and its own legislature of 46 senators and a hundred representatives. Texas has a legislature of 31 senators and 150 representatives. And there are 48 other

States in the Union, each with its state government on similar lines. We can see the same difficulty in the Federation of Nigeria. Before 1954, Nigeria was governed as one country, with one governor, one director of education, one director of health services, and similarly one head of each Government department. Today, there is not only the President and the Federal Government, but there are four Regional Governments, each with its own administrative service as well as its own legislature. If ever a fifth Region is established, Nigeria will at once have to appoint a fifth governor, elect a fifth Regional assembly, build a fifth set of parliament and administrative buildings, and get together a fifth set of administrators. A federal system of government is a heavy burden on a country which is short of trained men.

It may be said that in a country with a unitary government like Britain, the counties and other local government units have their own chief education officers and educational administrative staff. That is true; but there is only one Ministry of Education. The general educational policy of the country is laid down in London, and the local authorities administer their schools according to that policy, and within the limits of the power allowed them by the central Government. One Ministry of Education in Washington or in Lagos could quite well run education over the whole of the United States or Nigeria. If the United States and Nigeria choose to have, instead of one Minister, fifty Ministers, or four, they do so for political reasons. Administratively speaking, it is less convenient, and more expensive.

A second disadvantage, as we have seen, is that you are always liable to have tension between the Federal Government and the Regional or State Governments. It may not occur all the time; but it is the nature of all Governments to try and stretch their powers a little further. Sooner or later, the Federal Government will do something which the States say is unconstitutional; or else the other way round. The matter of civil rights for Negroes in America is a case in point. It leads to friction and much wasted effort. Trouble of this kind is bound to occur when both the Federal and the State Governments derive their power from the same source, the constitution. It cannot occur when the local government bodies are subordinate to the central Government, and draw their powers from an Act of the central parliament.

There is another characteristic of a federal system of government which may lead to a third disadvantage, though it need not. Since each member state of the federation is independent in certain respects, policy and its execution may vary greatly between one state and another. Educational facilities, for instance, may be much better in one state than in its neighbour: perhaps because one is richer than the other, perhaps because one has a more enlightened policy than the other. Minor variations may occur under a unitary government; it is sometimes said, for example, that certain local education authorities in Britain are willing to spend more on education than others. But when all authorities are administering one centrally-planned policy, only minor variations are possible. If it ever were found that a boy from the county of Norfolk had twice as good a chance of university education as a boy from the neighbouring county of Suffolk, there would be such an outcry that Suffolk would soon be forced to come into line with its neighbours.

A federal Government is at a fourth disadvantage compared with a unitary Government. In certain matters, the constitution may provide that the consent of the Regions,[2] or of a majority of them, is necessary before the federal Government can act. Thus in 1919, when President Wilson of the United States was trying to draw up a peace treaty along with the prime ministers of Britain, France, and Italy, all four men agreed to establish a League of Nations. The three European statesmen were sure that their parliaments would support them. But by the United States constitution, the consent of two-thirds of the Senate—that is to say, the consent of two-thirds of the states—was necessary for making a treaty; and Wilson could not get this consent. Thus, the president of the federally governed country was at a disadvantage in this important matter compared with the prime ministers of the three unitary governments. Not all federal constitutions have this particular proviso.

Thus, although a federal government may be the only government possible for a certain country, the alternative being no common government at all but a group of completely independent states, federalism has disadvantages. If a country can endure a unitary form of government, it should choose that form. Unitary government is cheaper in men and money; it is more efficient; it is likely to suffer less from internal tensions. Dr Nkrumah was certainly right in insisting on a unitary government for Ghana in 1956; the British Government was certainly right in urging a unitary government in Uganda in 1960. Dr Nkrumah won, the British Government lost. The people of Uganda had the right to decide for themselves whether to hold together as a unitary state (as they had been in colonial times) or to break apart into a federation. They chose federation, and no doubt they chose wisely. But their British

---

[2] The units that compose the federation have different names in different countries: in Nigeria they are called regions, in Australia and the United States, states, in Canada, provinces, in Switzerland, cantons, in West Germany, lands.

advisers were right when they warned them, 'Uganda is a small country; for such a country there are great advantages in a unitary form of government. Do not break up into a federation unless you feel that you must.'

There is one warning that we should bear in mind when discussing federalism. The United States is such an old-established and powerful federal state that we tend to think that all federal constitutions embody the theory of the separation of powers and have a presidential government, like the United States. This is not so. Many federal countries have a federal government in which the cabinet, like the British cabinet, is completely responsible to parliament. Canada, Nigeria, Australia are three examples. On the other hand, presidential government is found in some unitary states, as in France (under the de Gaulle constitution), Spain and Ghana.

PART TWO

*Political Institutions of
West African States*

CHAPTER XI

Constitutional History Before 1945

The four Commonwealth countries of West Africa all began from British trading settlements on the coast.
The standard type of colonial government, consisting of governor, executive council, and legislative council; relationships with Britain.
Development of the executive council; the addition of unofficial members. How did the executive council differ from a cabinet?
Development of the legislative council: first purely official, then nominated unofficial members added; the system of the official majority. Development until 1945 in the Gambia, Gold Coast, Sierra Leone, Nigeria.
The Gold Coast Aborigines Society, and the National Congress of British West Africa: the beginnings of pan-Africanism. The 1925 constitution of the Gold Coast.
The 1922 constitution of Nigeria; the Richards proposals of 1945.
The link between political, economic and constitutional progress; general principles of the constitutions established soon after the 1914 war.

THE four Commonwealth countries of Gambia, Sierra Leone, Ghana and Nigeria came into existence in much the same way, and under British rule they went through a similar process of gradual constitutional development.

All of them began as British settlements on the coast. The British trading settlements in the Gambia and in Ghana were founded in the seventeenth century. Freetown was founded in 1787 on land bought from the local chiefs, to serve as a home for slaves who had been set free on the high seas by the British navy. The settlement became a colony in 1808, and a protectorate was proclaimed over the interior in 1896. On the Gold Coast (now called Ghana) the British bought out the Danish and Dutch trading settlements in the nineteenth century; in 1874 the country as far inland as the Pra river was proclaimed a colony, and in 1901 Ashanti and the North were added. Nigeria grew from the British colony of Lagos and the British protectorate over the Niger delta. Lagos was occupied in 1861, the Oil Rivers Protectorate was proclaimed in 1885; the colony and protectorate of Southern Nigeria came into being in 1906. Northern Nigeria was conquered and became a separate protectorate in 1903, and the two territories were joined under one

Nigerian government in 1914. The small country of the Gambia was often joined with Sierra Leone; it was separated from Sierra Leone in 1843, joined with it again in 1885, and separated once more three years later; it has remained separate ever since.

In the early days of British colonial rule, all these territories were provided with governments of the usual British colonial pattern. There was a governor, who was responsible to the Queen, through the Secretary of State for the Colonies. He was assisted by British officials, who were selected by the Secretary of State on behalf of the Colonial Government. An official was appointed by the Colonial Government, and paid from Colonial revenues. He received his letter of appointment from the Governor as soon as he arrived in the colony for the first time. He was thus a servant of the colony, not of the Government in Britain. No colony was ever asked to pay any tax to Britain, nor did Britain ever claim any other direct financial benefit; for example, African cocoa, cotton, timber and other produce was bought by British merchants at the prevailing world prices. On the other hand, these world prices were fixed in Europe and America without regard to the needs of the African produces; and Britain never gave a colony any financial help, unless it was so poor that it could not even pay for the essentials like a governor, a police force to keep law and order, customs officers to collect revenue, and a few secretariat clerks. If a colony was as poor as this, the British Treasury would give some help to set it on its feet. As we have said, Britain received no direct financial benefit from her colonies; the benefit she received was indirect. The trade in African produce was profitable; moreover, the expatriate officials were all British, and when a colony was rich enough to build railways and buy materials of any kind for official use, the rails, the engines that ran on them, the paper and the typewriters in the secretariat, the picks, spades and shovels used by the public works department were all made in Britain.

The usual pattern of colonial government was to assist the governor with an executive council and a legislative council: the executive council to advise him on policy, and the legislative council to help him in making laws. This pattern was followed in West Africa.

DEVELOPMENT OF THE EXECUTIVE COUNCIL

The executive council always consisted of a small number of senior officials, presided over by the governor. The governor was not bound to accept the advice of his executive council, but if he rejected it, he had to tell the Secretary of State in London why he had done so; and if any member of the council felt strongly on the matter, he would put his views in writing and ask the governor to forward them to the Secretary of State.

The Governor's executive council in the Gambia in 1888 consisted of the lieutenant-governor (if any), the treasurer, the chief magistrate, and the collector of customs. In 1902 it consisted of the lieutenant-governor (if any), and the colonial secretary, with other members to be appointed by the governor with the Secretary of State's approval. The governor of Sierra Leone was given a similar executive council in 1863. In 1924 his executive council consisted of the officer commanding the troops, the colonial secretary, the attorney-general, the treasurer, and the director of medical services. Two African unofficial members were added in 1943.

From 1874 (when the Gold Coast Colony was set up) until 1903, the executive council in the Gold Coast consisted of four senior officials: the colonial secretary, the treasurer, the attorney-general, and the inspector-general of the troops. In 1903 the soldier was replaced by the director of public works; by then, Ashanti and the North had been pacified, and it was now time to begin opening up the country with roads. But the executive council had nothing to do with Ashanti and the North; its function was limited to the Colony. In 1925, Governor Guggisberg was given power to add other members: in 1934 the council's jurisdiction was extended to Ashanti and the North, and the two chief commissioners became members. In 1937 the office of treasurer was replaced by the new office of financial secretary; and a new member was added to the council, the secretary for native affairs. In 1942, the first two African members were appointed, Mr K. A. Korsah (now Sir Arku Korsah) and Nana Sir Ofori Atta; they were not officials, but were nominated unofficial members of the legislative council. A third African member was added in 1943, and one or two official members were dropped so as to reduce the size of the council to eight—five European official and three African unofficial members. But this council, though beginning to look like the beginnings of a cabinet, was not at all like a cabinet in reality, for two reasons: first, the governor was not bound to accept its advice, and second, it was not in any way responsible to the legislature.

Nigeria did not become one country until 1914. In that year, the two protectorates of Northern and Southern Nigeria were united with the colony of Lagos under one governor. There was an executive council of the usual type, and a legislative council, whose jurisdiction was confined to the Colony. The executive council in 1914 consisted, in addition to the governor, of ten senior officials. This purely official council lasted until 1941, the numbers occasionally rising to twelve and once falling as low as eight. The first unofficial members took office in October 1942: they were Mr[1] Adeyemo Alakija, Mr G. H. Avezathe, and Mr S. Bankole Rhodes. From then onwards, there were always unofficial members on the executive council. In 1951, on the eve of the new constitution, the council consisted of eight ex-officio members and six unofficial members, five African and one European.

If we sum up this story of the development of the executive councils before 1945, we see a uniform pattern. The councils begin with a few senior officials, all of them British. As the country develops, the governor drops his military adviser from the council, and adds instead someone from the social services or someone who is in close touch with African opinion. At the very end of the period, there comes about the great change, when for the first time African unofficial members are added to a council which has hitherto consisted entirely of European officials.

DEVELOPMENT OF THE LEGISLATIVE COUNCIL

The legislative councils developed in much the same way. They began by including, as well as the officials, one or two nominated unofficial members, either British or African. Then they began to add a few African elected members. But up till 1945, all the legislatures were carefully arranged so that the official members were in a majority. Thus, if all the official members voted solidly together, they could defeat any motion proposed by the unofficial members. And the official members always did vote solidly together. Laws were proposed by the Government, and it was their duty to vote in support of every Government measure. They were not allowed to vote as they thought fit. This arrangement was made to prevent the unofficial members from doing damage by carrying unwise proposals through the House. On the other hand, the strictness of this Government control was modified by a constitutional convention which grew up. If the Government found that the unofficial members were nearly unanimous in opposing a measure, the Government would nearly always drop it. Thus, the unofficial members were in a position somewhat like that of the Opposition in the British parliament today: they could not hope to defeat the Government in a vote, but they could often defeat the Government by argument, or even by an opposition based on emotion rather than reason. Thus, the Gold Coast Government tried more than once to introduce direct taxation. The African unofficial members of the legislative council always opposed it; they argued that the legislative council as then constituted was not competent to impose taxation.

[1] Afterwards Sir Adeyemo Alakija.

That could only be done, they said, by an elected assembly. The Government did not in the least agree with their argument. But it felt that it would be useless to press the matter against such solid opposition; and it dropped its proposals.

The Gambia legislative council in 1888 and 1902 consisted of the members of the executive council, with other official and unofficial members to be nominated by the governor. The number of nominated members was not specified, but in 1888 it was laid down that at least one of them must come from the protectorate. The Sierra Leone legislature in 1863 was mainly composed of officials, but the governor was instructed to add two unofficial members. He nominated one African, and invited the most important business men in the colony to choose the other. There were two candidates, one European and one African; the African was elected. This was not what the Colonial Office had intended, and there were no more elections for a long time; future unofficial members were nominated by the governor. In 1923 the number of nominated unofficial members was increased to five, and in 1924 the legislative council was reconstituted. It then consisted of eleven official members, seven nominated unofficial members (three of whom were paramount chiefs from the protectorate) and three members elected by constituencies in Freetown and the neighbourhood. There were thus eleven official and ten unofficial members; six of the ten unofficials were Africans. This formula of x plus 1—a given number of unofficial members, and the officials outnumbering them by one—was commonly used in order to secure an official majority for all Government proposals. It may seem insufficient for the purpose. Certainly, any responsible Government which relied on a majority of only one would feel very insecure. But the colonial Governments were not responsible to the legislature. Moreover, it was unlikely that all the unofficial members would ever unite against the Government. The unofficial members did not form a united body. Some of them were European business men representing merchants or miners; on many subjects they would be likely to support the Government. Among the Africans, some were paramount chiefs and others were educated men (doctors, lawyers and the like) representing the towns; and there were often differences of opinion between these two groups. So the x plus 1 formula gave the Government more security than it might seem; Governments did not often find themselves faced with a solid unofficial opposition. As we have said, if they ever did so, they nearly always gave way.

The Legislative Council in the Gold Coast (Ghana)

The Gold Coast legislative council in 1897 consisted of four official and three unofficial members; in 1901 a fourth unofficial member was added, but the official majority vote was preserved, because the governor had an original as well as a casting vote.

In 1916 the four unofficial members were increased to nine, and although no instructions were given on how the nine unofficial members were to be chosen, the governor, Sir Hugh Clifford, introduced a convention of nominating three Europeans, three paramount chiefs, and three educated Africans. There were thus six African members in the council. At the same time, the official element was increased from four to eleven; all these senior officials were Europeans.

These years from 1897 to 1916 were a time of great political activity. In 1897 the Gold Coast Government caused a great stir by its Lands Bill, which was defeated because a group of Africans led by Mr John Sarbah[2] sent a deputation to London and persuaded the Secretary of State, Joseph Chamberlain, to order the Gold Coast Government to withdraw the Bill.

This group of Africans founded the Gold Coast Aborigines Rights Protection Society, which included chiefs as well as lawyers and teachers and other educated men. The Aborigines Society (as it was affectionately called for short) was founded in 1898, and had a large membership among the chiefs; in fact, it claimed to be the official spokesman for the whole body of Gold Coast chiefs, and for a good many years was treated as such by the Government. Thus, alongside the legislative council with its official majority, there existed this completely unofficial African body, including educated men as well as chiefs, which the Government consulted on policy.

The Aborigines Society was not satisfied with the new legislative council in 1916. In the next year, one of its leading members, Mr J. E. Casely Hayford, founded the National Congress of British West Africa. His idea was to unite the four British territories into a sort of federation, so that they could deal with the British Government as one body instead of as four separate groups. The Congress had representatives and members in all four territories, but drew most of its strength from the Gold Coast.

In 1920 the Congress drew up a petition to the British Government containing their proposals. These were: (i) a West African legislative council, with one half of its members nominated and one half elected; (ii) a West African House of Assembly to consist of all the members of the legislative council plus six elected financial representatives; this House was to control revenue and expenditure; (iii) an African majority on every municipal council; (iv) the appoint-

[2] 1864-1910; the first Gold Coast African to be called to the bar; an unofficial member of the legislative council from 1901 till his death.

ment of African judges and magistrates—all judges and magistrates at that time were Europeans; (v) the establishment of a university for British West Africa.

These proposals were sent to London, and a deputation of the Congress went to London to see the Secretary of State (Lord Milner) and press the proposals upon him. But a group of Gold Coast members of the Aborigines Society cabled to London that the Gold Coast members of the Congress deputation had no authority to speak for the Gold Coast chiefs and people. The Secretary of State rejected the petition, and the Congress deputation achieved nothing. This was the first important split between the educated Africans and the chiefs, and it weakened not only the National Congress but also the Aborigines Society.

This early move towards pan-Africanism having failed, the initiative now passed to the Aborigines Society, and it continued to press for a revision of the 1916 constitution. In 1923 the new governor, Sir Gordon Guggisberg[3] consulted the Aborigines Society on his ideas for a new constitution, and two years later the new constitution was brought into effect.

The constitution of 1925 was an advance on its predecessor, but by no means all features of it pleased the Aborigines Society. The legislative council was increased from twenty members to twenty-nine, fifteen officials and fourteen unofficial members—again the Government's favourite x plus 1 formula. Of the fourteen unofficial members, five were Europeans: two elected by the Chamber of Mines and the Chambers of Commerce to represent the mining and commercial interests, and three others nominated by the governor. Three of the remaining nine were municipal members, elected to represent the towns of Accra, Cape Coast, and Sekondi. There was no provision in the constitution that the three municipal members should be Africans, but no doubt the British Government expected that they would be, and in fact they always were.

The remaining six unofficial members were Africans, elected to represent the provincial councils of chiefs: one from the Western Province, two from the Central, and three from the Eastern.

These provincial councils were a novelty, created by the 1925 constitution. Each council consisted of all the paramount chiefs in the province. The council elected its own president, and usually sent its president as its representative to the legislative council in Accra, with additional representatives from the Central and Eastern provincial councils. The provincial councils had other work besides electing representatives to the legislative council. They naturally discussed matters of traditional interest; but they also discussed all

[3] Governor, 1919-27.

Bills that were to be introduced in the forthcoming session of the legislative council. The provincial commissioner (the senior administrative officer of the province) attended the opening of the session of the provincial council; he explained the Government's purposes in introducing the new Bills, and then withdrew, leaving the council to discuss them. In 1932 the three provincial councils met together at Saltpond in a joint conference, and after that they met similarly every year. In 1944 the Government gave formal recognition to this joint provincial council.

In setting up this system of provincial councils, the Government's idea had been to associate the chiefs and their councillors more closely with the work of the central Government The governor pointed out that councils of paramount chiefs were no new thing in Gold Coast history; what was new was that the Government had set up these regular councils and recognised them as advisory bodies on behalf of their people. The chiefs in council, he said, would not give an opinion on any Bill until they had consulted their people in the traditional way; thus, the Government was justified, he thought, in regarding them as truly representative of the people. A Gold Coast nation would be built up by uniting the chiefs, and through them, their people.

That was the Government's idea; but the system of provincial councils was never popular, and it was bitterly attacked by the Aborigines Society. It had one great weakness. By Gold Coast tradition, a chief was the spokesman of his people. If a provincial council had discussed a Bill and come to a decision, its representative on the legislative council ought to do no more than express its decision. If he was answered by a Government speaker, who gave reasons for disagreeing with him, he ought to reply simply, 'I will go back to my people, tell them what you have said, and come back and tell you what they think about it.' As Nana Sir Ofori Atta, representing the Eastern Province, once said in the legislative council, 'After all said and done, we are merely here as messengers, and we carry messages from the people to you, and vice versa.' But could the people always trust their representatives to hold fast to this strict African tradition? The people doubted it. There were cases in which a provincial representative in the legislative council used his discretion and did not follow closely enough the decisions which his provincial council had taken. Such cases were resented. The people disliked the system of using the provincial councils to elect representatives to the legislative council, because it seemed to bring chiefs under strong temptation to exceed their powers, to think for themselves and express their own views, instead of acting merely 'as messengers'.

The Aborigines Society had a special reason for disliking the whole system. The Society had originally claimed to represent all the people of the Gold Coast, chiefs and their councils as well as educated townsmen. But by establishing provincial councils, the Government had recognised the chiefs and their councils as a section of the people apart from the educated townsmen; and had gone further, and given six members to the provincial councils but only three to the towns. It was not until 1929 that the two groups of African members came together and agreed to co-operate.

This Gold Coast constitution of 1925 had other defects. As we have seen, there were no Africans on the governor's executive council. This meant that, however much African members of the legislature might try to take a broad and statesmanlike view of the Government's proposals, none of them had any executive responsibility, and they were constantly tempted to regard themselves simply as an opposition party. It was the Government's business to introduce Bills, their business to criticize them. Under the 1925 constitution, this tendency always existed, in spite of all the discussions and consultations that went on outside the legislature, in the provincial councils and elsewhere.

Next: there was little provision for African elected members, and although the Government had power to set up new town councils, it did not exercise it. The Government introduced a Bill to give the town councils an elected majority. The Bill was supported by the African members in the legislature, and was carried; but it aroused strong public opposition, and was never put into effect. The public disliked the idea of paying local rates, and the chiefs and their councils in the towns disliked the idea of having a mayor and an elected body of councillors as their rivals. Thus, the only opening for educated Africans in the legislature was the three municipal seats. Educated men too had little scope in the traditional state councils. Thus, local government remained weak, and the cleavage between the chiefs and their elders on one side, and educated men on the other, became wider and wider. The Government's hope that the 1925 constitution, and especially the provincial councils, would be effective in building up a nation, was never realized.

Lastly: the constitution did not apply to Ashanti or the North; there were no members of any sort from Ashanti and the North, either nominated or elected. In 1934 the jurisdiction of the executive council was extended to Ashanti and the North, but the legislature still made laws for the Colony only, though it discussed the estimates of revenue and expenditure for the whole country.

The 1925 constitution, then, though a great advance on that of 1916, did not satisfy African opinion, and did not succeed in its aim of building up an African nation. In 1934 the Government introduced two Bills which roused intense opposition, the Sedition Bill and the Waterworks Bill. A national delegation was sent to London to protest. It requested not only that the two Bills should be withdrawn, but that Africans should be appointed to the executive council, there should be an unofficial majority in the legislature, and that provincial representatives in the legislature should not be chiefs. The delegation had no immediate success, not even in securing the withdrawal of the two Bills, which were duly enacted. But all three of their requests for constitutional advance were put into force, as we shall see, in 1946, twelve years later.

The Legislative Council in Nigeria

Nigeria, as we have seen, did not become one country until 1914. At that time, there was a legislative council for the colony, a very small area around Lagos. For the rest of Nigeria, there was a 'Nigerian Council', which had no legislative powers, but was merely an advisory body which the governor could consult. Both councils were abolished in 1922, and a new legislative council was set up for the whole of Nigeria.

The 1922 legislature consisted of 26 officials and 15 nominated unofficial members; these numbers were afterwards increased to 'not more than 30' officials and 'not more than 17' nominated unofficials. In addition to these nominated unofficial members there were four elected members, three for Lagos and one for Calabar. The nominated unofficial members in 1945 included ten Africans and seven Europeans. The governor had both an original and a casting vote. There were no unofficial members from the North. The governor and his executive council made laws for the North, just as the governor of the Gold Coast and his executive council did for Ashanti and the North in that country.⁴ But, again as in the Gold Coast, the legislative council considered the estimates of revenue and expenditure for the whole country, so to this extent all Government activities in Nigeria came before it.

In 1945, the governor of Nigeria, Sir Arthur Richards (now Lord Milverton) told the Government in London that he thought the time had come for a big step forward. He said that he had three aims in his constitutional proposals: (i) to promote the unity of Nigeria; (ii) to provide adequately, within that unity, for the diverse elements making up the people; (iii) to give Africans a greater share in the discussion of their own affairs. Nigeria, he said, falls naturally into three regions (North, West, and East). But although these

⁴ From 1934 onwards; before 1934 the governor of the Gold Coast made laws for Ashanti and the North by himself.

CONSTITUTIONAL HISTORY BEFORE 1945 157

regions were separately administered, each with its chief commissioner, this administrative division,

'besides being incomplete in itself through the lack of an adequate regional organization at each chief commissioner's headquarters, has no counterpart in the constitutional sphere. Apart from chiefs' conferences, no bodies exist at which public affairs can be discussed on a less narrow plane than the purely local, or one less wide than the Nigerian. Nor is there any constitutional link between the legislative council and the native authorities.'

Sir Arthur Richards here points out several weaknesses of the existing system. First of all, there was an administrative weakness. The chief commissioner of a region was head of the regional administration: all the provincial and district administrators (the Residents and district officers) were under him. But he was not equally in command of the technical officers—the education, agricultural, forestry, public works, medical and similar officers. These men were controlled by their head offices in Lagos.

Next, there was no consultative machinery by which a chief commissioner (or, for that matter, a Resident) could discuss matters with representatives of the people in his region, or province. There were of course the chiefs; every administrative officer, whether district officer or Resident, was in the habit of holding gatherings of the chiefs in his area, and a chief commissioner, though more rarely, could do the same. But in Nigeria, as in the Gold Coast, the chiefs and their state councils contained no representatives of the young educated men. The only places in which educated Nigerians had regular opportunities of expressing their political views were the 'purely local' town councils and the legislative council itself.

Lastly, there was no means by which the native authorities, who were responsible for so much of the routine work of local government (schools and dispensaries and hospitals and roads and so forth) could be brought into contact with the Nigerian legislative council. It would help the native authorities to take a broader view of their work if they could work in touch with the legislative council; and it would help the legislative council if it were in close touch with the everyday realities of local administration.

To remedy these weaknesses, Sir Arthur proposed to widen the scope and the membership of the legislative council, and to set up three regional councils. The legislative council should have an unofficial majority, and an African majority, and the whole range of Nigerian affairs should be open to it. The regional councils should discuss regional affairs and should be linked with the legislative council: some of the members of the legislative council should be appointed from the members of the regional councils.

There is a similarity here to Sir Gordon Guggisberg's idea of the place of provincial councils in the Gold Coast. But the Nigerian system worked more successfully than the Gold Coast system. For one thing, in many parts of Nigeria the chiefs had more power than they had in the Gold Coast Colony; they were not so liable to find themselves in trouble with their people if they expressed views of their own, and so they did not feel themselves to be attending the legislative council 'merely as messengers'. For another thing, whereas the provincial councils in the Gold Coast consisted entirely of chiefs, the regional councils in Nigeria included other members as well, so that educated men could attend the legislative council to represent the regional councils.

This despatch of Sir Arthur Richards led to the establishment of the 1946 constitution, in which his ideas were carried out.

Political, economic and constitutional history go together. There could not be a legislative council for Nigeria until Nigeria had come into being as one country: till its boundaries had been settled, and peace and order had been established. Nor could a legislative council have done any useful work until Nigeria had made some economic progress: until it could pay for an administration to carry out the laws, for roads and schools and other forms of development to supply educated people to do the work and to make it possible for them to move easily round the country. This economic progress depends on exploring and opening up the country's natural resources, timber, minerals, and agricultural crops.

As we look back on the period of constitutional development which ended in 1945, we can see how closely the constitutional development depends on political and economic conditions. The boundaries of Sierra Leone were fixed in 1895, and the Protectorate came under effective British rule after the war in 1898. British rule was established in Ashanti and the Northern Territories of the Gold Coast on 1st January 1902, after the end of the Yaa Asantewa war. Northern Nigeria became a British protectorate in 1900, but it took Lugard another three years to stamp out slave-trading and establish peace.

At first, all three countries were poor. The Government's first duty was to open them up and discover the possibilities of trade. Geological surveys had to be established to look for minerals. Sierra Leone did not discover its iron till 1926, and its diamonds till 1931. In the Gold Coast, it was not until the war of 1914-19 that cocoa exports became so profitable that the Government had a large surplus revenue. Diamonds and bauxite were not discovered until after the war, manganese in 1915. In Nigeria, tin was known to exist on the plateau, but the mines did not develop much until the railway was built as far as Jos in 1914; the large exports of groundnuts did not become possible until the railway reached Kano. The trade in palm oil had been running since the eighteen-eighties, and until 1920 or later this was the country's chief source of revenue. No great constitutional development is possible until some economic progress has been made.

The first big constitutional step forward was taken in all three countries just after the 1914-19 war: 1922 in Nigeria, 1924 Sierra Leone, 1925 Gold Coast. The principles followed were the same in all three countries. The legislative council was enlarged to include a good number of nominated unofficial members, and a few elected members; the elected members were all Africans, and so were some of the nominated members. In Sierra Leone there were three elected and three other Africans out of a council of twenty-one members: in the Gold Coast, three elected and six other Africans out of twenty-nine: in Nigeria, four elected and ten other Africans out of forty-seven. The proportions are strikingly similar: in each case the African members form slightly less than one-third of the total membership.

The period from 1920 to 1945 was one of very rapid economic growth. New minerals were discovered, new exports began, the national wealth increased, education was greatly expanded. The Governments tried to develop native authorities and to give them much more responsibility for local administration. There was a great increase in the number of educated men and women; it is not surprising that not only these educated Africans themselves but also enlightened governors like Sir Arthur Richards in Nigeria and Sir Alan Burns in the Gold Coast began to feel that the time was coming for a further constitutional advance which should give these educated Africans a much bigger share in the government of their country. The Gambia lagged behind the other three countries. Its constitution did not change between 1902 and 1946; but after the second world war it shared in the general move towards self-government.

CHAPTER XII

Partial Self-Government

Reasons for the rapid constitutional progress after 1945.
General similarity of the process in all countries: (i) an unofficial majority in legislative council; (ii) an elected majority; (iii) an unofficial majority on executive council. The governor's reserved powers.
The Gold Coast: the Burns constitution of 1946. The Watson commission and the Coussey commission; the new constitution of 1951. The Gold Coast executive to 1951; Dr Nkrumah decides to accept the constitution.
Nigeria: the Richards constitution of 1946. The regional councils. Nigeria not yet a federation: limited powers of the regions. The 1951 constitution: regional executives and legislatures; the central Government. How does this constitution fall short of full self-government?
Sierra Leone: the constitutions of 1951 and 1953; the system of 'official members'. The 1954 elections. Government in the Sierra Leone protectorate: native authorities, district councils, the Protectorate Assembly.
Gambia: changes made in 1946 and 1951: elected members and a minimum number of unofficial members. Unofficial majority in 1954; the Gambia system of Ministries.

THE second world war ended in 1945, and in all the British West African territories, constitutional development speeded up greatly after the war was over. Ghana became fully independent in 1957, Nigeria in 1960, Sierra Leone in 1961. The Gambia reached full internal self-government in 1963, but is not yet (1964) fully independent.

There were various reasons for this rapid advance. One reason was that (as we have seen) the economic development which had taken place in the last twenty-five years had brought the British authorities to feel that it was high time for a fresh advance. Another was that in 1945 the British Government passed a Colonial Development and Welfare Act which enabled it to give large sums of money for education and other social services, and for economic development such as communications and hydro-electric schemes. Economic development was thus speeded up; and constitutional development naturally followed. A third reason was that many thousands of

PARTIAL SELF-GOVERNMENT 161

West Africans had served overseas in the war and had come to know the outside world; and they were determined that their country should take its proper place in the world. Fortunately, leaders like Dr Nkrumah, Dr Azikiwe and Dr Margai were available to take this popular demand, organize it, and give it expression in a way which the British could not have ignored even if they had wished to.

All four countries passed through the same process. First, the legislative council was given an unofficial majority; the old colonial system of an official majority which could carry through any measure the Government wanted was finally abandoned. The next step was to transform this majority of unofficial members, some of whom were elected and others nominated, into a majority of elected members. At this stage, the elected members were in a majority over all the official members and the nominated unofficial members together. This would have given the legislative council an unlimited power of discussing, criticizing, and blocking any Government proposal; but it would not have given it any power of making policy. But at the same time, another step was taken which gave the legislature a great deal of control over policy, though not yet complete control. The governor's executive council already contained African members (Gold Coast 1942, Sierra Leone 1943, Nigeria 1942). It was now given a majority of unofficial members, drawn from the members of the legislature; they were appointed Ministers, and became individually responsible to the legislature, under a leader who was in fact prime minister, though he was not at first given that title. But the executive council was not at once transformed into a cabinet. It was not collectively responsible to the legislature. And more than that, it still contained two or three officials, who were directly responsible to the governor for certain subjects which the British Government still feared to entrust to African hands—notably external affairs and defence. Moreover, the governor was given reserved powers: powers, that is, to overrule the legislature in an emergency. It was hoped of course that there would never be an emergency; but the reserved powers were there just in case. We end this chapter when this stage of partial self-government is reached.

The dates can be summarized in a table:

	Gambia	Sierra Leone	Gold Coast	Nigeria
Unofficial majority in legislature	1954	1951	1946	1946
Elected majority	1954	1951	1951	1951
Unofficial majority on executive	1954	1951	1951	1951

In the last chapter, we began by describing the development of the executive council, and then we came to the development of the legislature. In this chapter we take the legislature first, because, as the table shows, two of the legislatures developed in this period before there was any change in the executive.

THE GOLD COAST LEGISLATURE, 1946-51

A new governor, Sir Alan Burns, came to the Gold Coast in 1942. It was a difficult time, for it was in the middle of the war; but Sir Alan, like his contemporary Sir Arthur Richards in Nigeria, thought that the war should not stop him from making proposals for constitutional development. We have seen that he appointed two African unofficial members to the executive council in 1943. He tackled the question of local government: in 1944 his Government passed two important laws, the Native Courts (Colony) Ordinance and the Native Authority (Colony) Ordinance. The first of these made some very necessary reforms in the working of local tribunals; it was based on the report of a committee of inquiry mainly composed of Africans. The Native Authority Ordinance brought all the chiefs and their councils into much closer relationship with the central Government. The idea behind this legislation was that the chiefs and their councils should be developed into useful organs of modern local government. The joint provincial council accepted the Bill; the African municipal members opposed it, on the usual grounds that if it made the chiefs stronger, it would be contrary to Gold Coast constitutional traditions, and if it made them mere tools of the colonial Government, it would make that Government much stronger than it had ever been. The municipal members were elected, and they saw the future development of local government as an extension of the electoral system. The governor disagreed. He told the council,

'I am most anxious to see the Native Administrations take their full share in the government of this country because I believe that indirect rule by Government through the Native Authorities is the best training-ground for the self-government which we are aiming at.'

In October 1944, the governor announced his plan for the new constitution, though it was not put into effect until March 1946, the war having delayed the work of the Colonial Office in London.

The new legislature contained six official members, six nominated unofficial members, and eighteen elected members; thus, the elected members were in a majority over the official and the nominated members together. The governor presided, but had no vote.

The eighteen elected members were made up thus: nine by the joint provincial council of the Colony, four by the electors in the municipalities (Accra two, Cape Coast and Sekondi-Takoradi one each), and five from Ashanti (four from the Ashanti Confederacy Council and one from the Kumasi Town Council). Of the first six unofficial members nominated, three were Africans. There was an African majority on the standing finance committee. The governor had considerable powers reserved to him. Not only could he disallow a Bill, but if he thought it necessary 'in the interests of public order, public faith, or good government', he could carry a Bill into law even though the legislature refused to pass it. (Naturally, if he took this extreme step, he had to make a full report to the Secretary of State, who might disavow his action.) The Government in London thought it wise to reserve these powers to the governor in case an inexperienced African legislature made a real mess of affairs. Its fear was unnecessary: in the remaining eleven years until independence, the governor's reserved powers were never needed.

This 1946 constitution was a great step forward in many ways. It replaced the old official majority not only by a majority of Africans, but by a majority of elected members. It brought Ashanti members into the council for the first time. Africans controlled the finance committee of the council. But it had one great weakness. All policy was begun by the governor and his permanent officials and the executive council; and the executive council and the officials were responsible to the governor alone. The legislative council did not control policy, it did not make policy; all it could do was to criticize policy.

This weakness was quickly shown in the difficult times which followed: high prices and shortage of goods, swollen shoot and compulsory cutting-out of cocoa, difficulties over ex-service-men's pensions and re-settlement, shortage of housing. The African members of the legislature had no power to introduce measures to deal with these troubles; all they could do was to criticize measures proposed by the Government. In 1947, Dr Danquah and others started the United Gold Coast Convention, a party which aimed at further constitutional advance through gradual and legitimate means. Late in that same year, Dr Nkrumah arrived in the Gold Coast to become the Convention's secretary. In 1948 there came the riots and the inquiry by the Watson Commission.

The Watson Commission rightly saw that one of the underlying causes of the troubles was that Africans had far too little political responsibility, and it recommended great constitutional advances.

The Gold Coast Government, under its new governor Sir Gerald Creasy (1948-49), who had been unlucky in arriving in his new post just in time for the riots, set up an all-African commission, the Coussey Commission, to discuss the Watson proposals for constitutional advance.

We need not set out the Coussey recommendations in detail, for they were almost entirely adopted and put into force in the 1951 constitution. It will suffice if we point out the few respects in which the 1951 constitution differed from what the Coussey Commission proposed. The Government in London announced that it accepted the Coussey report on the same day that the report was published. But there was one respect in which the Government in London felt that the Coussey proposals were unrealistic. The Coussey report proposed that the Gold Coast should have a cabinet mainly composed of elected members, and collectively responsible to the legislature. The Government in London did not see how this could work when there was no party system in the legislature; and so, although it modified the governor's executive council a good deal, it did not completely transform it into a cabinet.

As far as the legislature was concerned, the 1951 constitution was very close to the Coussey proposals. It was to consist of one house of 75 elected members and nine nominated members; the Coussey Commission, by a majority of 20 to 19, would have preferred two houses, but its report said that if the Government decided to have only one House, it should be thus designed. Of the 75 elected members, 37 were to be elected by the state councils in the south, and by the regional councils in Ashanti and the North; five were to be elected by the municipalities; and 33 were to be elected by electoral colleges in the rural areas of the Colony and Ashanti. All this was according to Coussey, except that the Coussey commission recommended that only one-third of the House, not one-half, should be elected by state and regional councils. Of the elected members, half represented the Colony, and one-quarter each Ashanti and the North. The nine nominated members comprised three senior officials *ex-officio,* one commercial and one mining representative, and four others. Only the ex-officio and the commercial and mining members had votes: the other four had none. The Coussey commission had recommended the three ex-officio and the commercial and mining members, but the four other nominated members were added by the Government, though not recommended by Coussey.

The Gold Coast Executive to 1951

The Burns constitution of 1946, which made such a decisive break with past tradition in the matter of the legislature, made no

PARTIAL SELF-GOVERNMENT

such decisive break when dealing with the executive. The governor's executive council in the 1946 constitution remained in just the same position as far as its constitutional function was concerned: that is to say, it was a group of individuals, each giving the governor his personal opinion, which the governor was not bound to follow. The council was not collectively responsible even to the governor, much less to the legislature. It was not even explicitly provided that the unofficial members of the executive council must be members of the legislature, though in practice they were so.

The executive council of 1946 was of course presided over by the governor. It comprised the colonial secretary, the financial secretary, and the attorney-general (the three senior officials who continued to sit in the 1951 legislature), the three chief commissioners of the Colony, Ashanti and the North, one other official (the director of medical services) appointed *ex-officio*: and four nominated members: one official (the secretary for rural development) and three African unofficial members. Apart from the governor, it thus contained eight European officials and three African unofficial members.

The Coussey commission proposed to revolutionize this old-fashioned executive. It proposed a council of twelve members, presided over by the governor. Not more than three should be Government officials; at least six members of the council (one of whom should be the leader of the legislature) should be called Ministers, and should have ministerial responsibilities. The executive council should be collectively responsible to the legislature; if defeated there, it should be bound to resign. This would turn the executive council almost into a cabinet on the British pattern: not quite, for the governor would still be in the chair, whereas in the British cabinet it is the Prime Minister who is chairman.

In drawing up the 1951 constitution, the Government in London felt unable to go as far as this. It accepted the idea that the executive should include a group of Ministers chosen from the members of the legislature, but it left to the governor the task of choosing them. It made the executive council still responsible to the governor, not collectively responsible to the legislature; the legislature should be able to force the resignation of individual Ministers, but not of the council as a whole. And thirdly, it did not see how the legislature could elect its own leader; instead of this, it laid down that the African members whom the governor chose for his Ministers should elect one of themselves to be leader of the legislature.

The Government in London was unnecessarily cautious. In practice, the governor would have to choose the leader of the majority party in the legislature to be one of his Ministers, and of course the other African Ministers would elect that man to be leader of the legislature. The governor would have to choose him, and the Ministers would have to elect him, for the simple reason that the legislature would listen to nobody else. So why not let the legislature elect its leader in the first place?

At the elections of 1951, the Convention People's Party, led by Dr Nkrumah, won thirty-four out of the thirty-eight seats which were directly elected. The governor, Sir Charles Arden-Clarke, invited Dr Nkrumah to form a Government. There were eight African Ministers, and three British ex-officio Ministers. Dr Nkrumah gave six Ministries to members of his own party, and one each to members from Ashanti and the North. Dr Nkrumah was called Leader of Government Business; next year, 1952, he was given the title of Prime Minister, and the executive council was renamed the cabinet.

This 1951 constitution was far short of complete self-government. The governor still had reserved powers; he could still (in theory) make a law by himself if the legislature refused to pass his Bill. The executive council, or cabinet, was responsible to him, not collectively to the legislature; and there were still three European Ministers whom the legislature could not dismiss. Dr Nkrumah had been demanding Self-Government Now, and he might well have decided that this constitution was so far short of complete self-government that he and his party would not accept it. But he saw that if he took office under the constitution, his power would be greater in fact than it seemed on paper; and he judged that the governor was sincere in regarding the 1951 constitution as only the first step towards full self-government. There was quite enough useful work to be done in developing education and agriculture and other social services, reforming local government, and pushing forward the economic development of the country, to keep the Government busy without getting into more constitutional quarrels; and after a few years of this, the British, he thought, would be ready for further steps towards independence.

NIGERIA, 1946-1951

We have seen that in 1945 the governor of Nigeria, Sir Arthur Richards, proposed a new constitution which should give Nigeria, like the Gold Coast, an elected majority in its legislature. In 1946, very shortly after the Burns constitution in the Gold Coast, Sir Arthur Richards' proposals resulted in a new constitution for Nigeria.

PARTIAL SELF-GOVERNMENT

One of its new features was the establishment of three regional councils in the North, West, and East, though Nigeria was not yet formally divided into the three Regions, each with its lieutenant-governor. That came five years later, in 1951. In the 1946 constitution, the Northern regional council was divided into two Houses, but the councils of the West and the East consisted of only one House. The Northern House of Chiefs contained all the first-class chiefs in the North, and 'not less than ten' second-class chiefs, elected by the second-class chiefs of the region. The House of Assembly contained nineteen officials, with between twenty and twenty-four unofficial members nominated to represent the people generally, with six more to represent special interests or special communities. All these unofficial members were nominated; there were no elected members.

The regional councils in the West and the East followed the same general pattern. They both contained fourteen officials and rather more nominated unofficial members: in the West, three head chiefs, from seven to eleven representatives of native administrations, and five members to represent 'special interests or communities'. In much of the eastern region there were no powerful chiefs, for people governed themselves in small clans. So the Eastern House of Assembly contained from ten to thirteen representatives of native administrations, with five special members, as in the West.

The regional councils had only limited powers. The Government laid before a regional council its estimates of revenue and expenditure for the region, and the council could consider the estimates and make recommendations to the Government about them. All Bills which were to be introduced in the Nigerian legislative council at Lagos were shown first to the regional councils for their advice, and the Governor might if he chose consult the regional councils on any other matter. Members of a regional council might introduce a resolution, and the council might discuss and carry it; but resolutions on finance were out of order. In accordance with the British tradition that taxation must be discussed first by the Commons, it was laid down that in the North, where there were two Houses, any recommendations concerning the estimates must be proposed and considered first in the lower House, the House of Assembly.

In addition to these powers, the regional councils had one other function: they appointed representatives to sit on the legislative council in Lagos.

The powers of the regional councils were limited. The councils could not act, nor could they stop the Government from acting; they could neither vote money nor refuse it. They were limited just as Sir

Arthur Richards had proposed: they gave Africans more opportunity to discuss their own affairs, they provided a link between the native administrations and the legislative council, and they brought together members from all over a region so that 'public affairs could be discussed on a less narrow plane than the purely local but one less wide than the Nigerian'. The Nigerian constitution of 1946, like the Gold Coast constitution of the same year, gave Africans a great opportunity of discussion, but no responsibility for action.

The legislative council of 1946 contained thirteen ex-officio members, three nominated officials, twenty-four nominated unofficial members, and four elected members representing the Colony and Calabar. Of the twenty-four nominated unofficial members, twenty were nominated (on the advice of the regional councils) to represent the councils; one represented the Colony, and there were three special members.[1] The council had legislative powers for the whole of Nigeria; no longer was it confined to the South. No proposal for expenditure could be made except by the Government; this of course is the standard practice in Britain itself. The governor presided at the council, with a casting vote but no original vote. He was given powers (as in the Gold Coast) to introduce and even to carry a Bill or a motion if he thought it necessary for 'public order, public faith, and good government', even though the legislative council refused to agree. But if ever he used these powers—and he never needed to—he must report to the Secretary of State in London, and must forward to the Secretary of State any written protest which a member of the council gave him.

Thus Nigeria, like the Gold Coast, now had an elected majority in its legislature. Twenty names were given to the governor by the regional councils, and it would have been unthinkable for him to refuse to nominate any of them: four more were directly elected. Against these twenty-four members, there were sixteen officials and four others nominated by the governor at his discretion. But no assembly will long be content with having the right to talk, but not to act. The Nigerian legislature in 1946 had no more control over the executive than the legislature in the Gold Coast. The next step must be to bring the executive nearer to being a cabinet, with a responsibility to the legislature.

The Constitution of 1951

The next step in Nigeria, as in the Gold Coast, was taken in 1951; but Nigeria too reached only partial self-government. The central

[1] I use this short term to stand for 'members nominated to represent special interests or communities not otherwise represented'.

legislative council and the regional councils were increased in size, but the most important change was that a beginning was made in making the executive responsible to the legislature.

The division into three regions was made formal, and each region was given a lieutenant-governor. The Northern regional council again consisted of two Houses. The House of Chiefs contained all the first-class chiefs, with thirty-seven other chiefs; it had three ex-officio members and an adviser on Muslim law. The lieutenant-governor of the North presided. The House of Assembly had four officials, ninety elected members, and some special members; it had an unofficial president. The regional council in the West, which had consisted of one House in 1946, was now divided into two. Its House of Chiefs, presided over by the lieutenant-governor, contained three officials, and not more than fifty chiefs; its House of Assembly, with an unofficial president, had four officials, with eighty elected members and some special members. In the East, there was still only one House, presided over by the lieutenant-governor; it had five officials and eighty elected members, with some special members.

In each region there was to be a regional executive. There were to be not more than five official Ministers in a region, with from six to nine unofficial Ministers. As in the Gold Coast, the lieutenant-governor chose his Ministers, but he submitted the names to the regional assembly, and the assembly might approve or reject them. In the North and the West, where there were two Houses, this duty of approving or rejecting the Ministers was carried out not by the two Houses separately, but by a joint council of not more than eighty members, composed of unofficial members of both Houses. This joint council also performed the duty of nominating regional representatives to the central legislature. If a Minister when in office lost the confidence of the regional assembly, he might be dismissed by a two-thirds majority. He might also be dismissed by the lieutenant-governor if he seemed to be going against the policy which had been laid down by the executive of which he was a member. In Kaduna, Ibadan and Enugu, as in Lagos and Accra, the legislature had no power of dismissing an official Minister.

The Government in Lagos was planned on the same lines as in the regions. The Nigerian legislative council consisted of 136 elected, six official, and not more than six special members; half the 136 regional representatives came from the North, and one-quarter each from the West and East. The governor had the same reserved powers as his three lieutenant-governors had in the regions: powers of making laws necessary to public faith, public order, or good government. In the North and West it was possible that the two Houses might disagree; if this happened and the disagreement could not be resolved, the lieutenant-governor had power to summon a joint session of not more than twenty members of each house, and this joint session of not more than forty men had power to pass the disputed Bill by a simple majority.

The executive in Lagos was similar to that in the regions. The governor presided over his council, and he had six official Ministers and twelve unofficial, four from each region. He chose them himself, but submitted the names to the legislature for approval or rejection.

This Nigerian constitution of 1951, like the Gold Coast constitution of the same year, can be regarded only as the first step towards self-government. The executive still contains official Ministers, who cannot be dismissed by the legislature. Individual unofficial Ministers can be dismissed by the legislature, but the council as a whole cannot, and the governor still has large reserved powers. Nothing has been done to settle the relationship between the central and the regional governments; Nigeria is not yet a federation, but a unitary state, held together by the strong framework of the official administration. The governor and his three regional lieutenants, the heads of department in Lagos and their regional deputies, all understand one another and have a uniform policy which they will try and persuade the new unofficial Ministers to adopt. But this is an unstable situation. It will not be long before a Minister refuses to follow the policy which is advocated by the expatriate official; it will not be long before one region wishes to follow one policy, and its neighbour wishes to follow a different policy. What is to happen then? These questions will have to be answered before long.

On the other hand, we must always remember, as the British officials in Nigeria and in London assuredly remembered, that there are such things as constitutional conventions; and with their help, paper constitutions usually work better than we might expect. If an official Minister were to follow a policy quite contrary to the wishes of the legislature, he and the governor would hear about it long before matters came to open friction in the House, and we may be sure that the policy would be modified. Much depends on personal relationships; and many official and unofficial Ministers were pleasantly surprised to find how easily they came to trust each other and work together as colleagues. Unofficial African Ministers and members of the regional and central legislatures had in fact more influence and power than the constitution seemed to give them. But everyone, in London as well as in Lagos, could see that the 1951 constitution could not last for long.

SIERRA LEONE FROM 1951 TO 1956

The 1924 constitution of Sierra Leone lasted until 1951. In that year, when both the Gold Coast and Nigeria had taken the important step of giving the legislature some—even if only a little—control over the executive, the Government in London began to modernize the Sierra Leone constitution also. The 1951 constitution was modified in 1953; we may take the two versions together.

The legislative council was increased from twenty-one members to thirty, without counting the governor, who might himself preside or be represented by a vice-president. There were seven ex-officio members, seven African members elected to represent seven electoral districts in the Colony, and fourteen members elected from the protectorate. (Twelve of these fourteen were nominated by district councils—as in the Gold Coast and Nigeria—and two were nominated by the Protectorate Assembly.) Two other unofficial members were nominated to represent commerce. Thus there was an unofficial majority of twenty-three to seven, but only seven members were directly elected.

The executive council consisted of five ex-officio members and 'not less than four' elected members of the legislative council, whether directly elected from the colony or indirectly from the protectorate; actually, the governor chose six. The constitution did not require the governor to give executive responsibility for administration to members of his executive council, but said that he might do so if the legislative council desired it. In 1952 the legislative council did desire it; and the governor, Sir George Beresford Stooke, set up the system of 'official members'. He did not make each individual member of his executive council responsible for one department, but grouped all the departments into five groups, and gave one group to each member. The sixth member had no direct responsibility, but was free to advise on Government business as a whole; he was what we should now call a Minister Without Portfolio. Since all these 'official members' were unofficial members of the legislative council, they were able to speak there on the subjects they were specially interested in.[2] But there was no question of their being directly responsible for the administration of these branches. Any one branch requires a Minister to itself. And nothing was said about giving the legislative council power to dismiss a member. Still, it is something when the legislature forms the habit of looking to one of its own unofficial members for information on a particular branch

[2] The groups of subjects were: (1) Health, Agriculture, Forests; (2) Local Government, Education and Welfare; (3) Works and Transport; (4) Trade, Commerce, Posts and Telegraphs; (5) Lands, Mines, Labour.

of the administration. Again, much will depend on personal relationships: not only on the relationship between the African Minister and his permanent officials but on that between official and unofficial members of the executive. Members of the legislative council had always been able to ask formal questions in the House. But there is a great difference between that, and an informal question on these lines: 'There is a point in your policy which I have always found it hard to understand; and so, I know, have many of my fellow-members. Would you mind explaining why. . . .' The official explains. 'Yes, thank you. I see your point; but I still think that you are paying insufficient attention to such-and-such, which *we* all think very important. I am sure the House would give you much more cordial support if you paid more attention to that point, even at the price of lowering your technical standards a little.' Officials would find it difficult to resist that sort of pressure; and in such ways as these, African Ministers would have more real power than the constitution would appear on paper to grant them.

In April 1953, the title of 'official member' was dropped, and was replaced by 'Minister'. In July 1954, Dr Margai, leader of the Sierra Leone People's Party, who was Minister of Health, Agriculture and Forests, was styled 'Chief Minister', while continuing to hold his portfolio. Dr Margai's party had won a sweeping victory in the 1951 elections over its rival, the National Council of Sierra Leone led by Dr. Bankole Bright. The S.L.P.P. won two out of the seven Colony seats, but all fourteen of the seats in the Protectorate. The governor naturally gave all the ministry posts to Dr Margai's party, following the British democratic tradition. In 1956 the legislative council was renamed the House of Representatives.

Government in the Protectorate

From 1896 onwards, the protectorate was governed in the usual colonial way by district commissioners responsible to the governor; there were five districts, each containing a number of chiefdoms. Two ordinances, the Protectorate Ordinance of 1901 and the Protectorate Native Law Ordinance of 1905, introduced the ideas of indirect rule; the district commissioners began to work indirectly through the chiefs and their councils, and the Government tried to develop these traditional units into native authorities capable of undertaking the tasks of modern local government. In the nineteen-thirties, this policy had succeeded so far that the native authorities had become the main units of local government: they were levying their own taxes and drawing up their budgets of revenue and expenditure, subject to the Government's approval.

In 1946 (by which time the original five districts had been divided

PARTIAL SELF-GOVERNMENT 173

into twelve) a district council was set up in each district to advise the native authorities and co-ordinate their work. Four years later these district councils were given a new status: they were made bodies corporate, able to hold property and to sue and be sued. A district council consisted of all the paramount chiefs in the district, with one or more chiefs elected to represent each chiefdom, and three other members elected by the councillors themselves. There were over 200 native authorities, so co-ordination was very necessary. From 1950 onwards the district councils began to share the responsibility of local government with the native authorities. They became higher grade local government bodies, with the lower grade bodies, the native authorities, subordinate to them.

From 1946 to 1957 there was a Protectorate Assembly, which served much the same purpose as the Nigerian regional councils in 1946 or the provincial councils in the Gold Coast from 1925 onwards. It considered Bills which were to be introduced in the legislative council, and discussed the Government estimates. It had no legislative powers, and did not nominate representatives to the legislature, as the Nigerian regional councils did. But it was a useful means of bringing the Government and the protectorate representatives in touch with one another and helping them to understand one another's views. The assembly consisted of the chief commissioner, nine official members, two representatives from each of the twelve district councils, and six unofficial nominated members, four of whom were usually Africans. There were thus usually twelve Europeans and twenty-eight Africans: ten officials and thirty unofficials. When the 1958 constitution came into force, and the protectorate began electing members to the House of Representatives in Freetown, the assembly was no longer needed, and was abolished.

THE GAMBIA FROM 1946 TO 1954

The year 1946, the first year of peace, was a great year for new constitutions, and even the Gambia, which had had no constitutional changes since 1902, began to move with the times. Not that the Gambia moved very fast. There was no guarantee of an unofficial majority on the legislature, which was to consist of the usual three ex-officio members, an unspecified number of nominated members, both official and unofficial, and one elected member to represent Bathurst and Kombo St Mary. The one elected member is the great change. Once the elective element appears, further change becomes certain. The Government in London evidently realized this, for next year (1947) it gave the governor of the Gambia the same reserved powers as it had given elsewhere in West Africa—powers which might never be needed, and certainly could not be needed unless there were an unofficial majority. Evidently the Government in London was looking ahead to an unofficial majority in the Gambia legislature.

In 1951 the next cautious step was taken. For the first time in the history of the Gambia, a minimum number of unofficial members was laid down. There were to be at least four nominated unofficial members; and instead of only one elected member there were to be three—two for Bathurst and one for Kombo St Mary.

The decisive step was taken in 1954. The legislative council was enlarged and given an unofficial majority. The governor was to preside, but there was to be a Speaker (who would preside for most of the time), five official members (four ex-officio and one nominated) and two nominated unofficial members. There were to be fourteen elected members. Three of them were to represent Bathurst, and one Kombo St Mary. Four were to be elected by the divisional councils in the protectorate, three elected by head chiefs in the protectorate; and these eleven members were to choose three others out of a list of nine to be submitted by the Bathurst town council and the Kombo St Mary rural authority. Thus, there was to be an unofficial majority (16 to 5) and an elected majority (14 to 7); but it is to be noted that only four of the fourteen elected members were directly elected by the people; the remaining ten were indirectly elected.

The executive too was transformed. It consisted of four ex-officio members, the one nominated official member of the legislature, and at least six 'appointed members'. The 'appointed members' must be chosen from the unofficial members of the legislature, whether nominated or elected. Since the legislature contained only two nominated unofficial members, this meant that at least four of the 'appointed members' must be from the elected members.

In the matter of Ministries, the 1954 constitution was very cautious. It was laid down that at least two—but not more than three—of the 'appointed members' were to become Ministers. But a Minister's power in the Gambia was limited in a way which we do not find elsewhere. A Minister was provided with an advisory committee, which was to consist of 'the appropriate public officer' and others. The 'appropriate public officer' means the departmental head; the director of agriculture, for instance, in the case of the Minister of Agriculture. The Minister was not bound to follow the official's advice. But if he did not follow it, the official was authorized to ask his Minister to refer the matter to the governor; and the Minister was bound to do so. This is a situation very like the situation of a colonial governor in relation to his executive council. He was not bound to follow his council's advice, but any councillor who felt strongly could ask the governor to forward his views to the Secretary of State. The Government in London was clearly afraid that an inexperienced African Minister might ignore professional advice and make a serious mistake.

Still, this 1954 constitution had taken the step from which there can be no going back. There were African Ministers and a legislature with an elected majority. Nothing was said about making even individual Ministers responsible to the legislature; that was yet to come. But the essential principle had been conceded: the legislature was to represent the people, and it would henceforth look for a lead not simply to the Government officials, but to African Ministers who were chosen from among its own members.

Thus the Gambia in 1954 reached the stage of partial self-government which the other three countries had reached in 1951. In all four legislatures there was not merely an unofficial majority, but an elected majority, though not all the elected members were directly elected: some of them were nominated or elected by local councils of one sort or another. There was an unofficial majority on the executive also. Some of the Ministers in the Gambia, the majority of the Ministers in the other three countries, were chosen from the unofficial members of the legislature. The worst feature of the old colonial constitutions was that all policy was laid down by the governor and his European officials; the African members of the legislature had no share in making policy; their job was to criticize policy with no responsibility for putting their criticisms into effect. This was now a thing of the past: Africans were now making and executing their own policy.

CHAPTER XIII

Towards Independence

The partial self-government reached in 1954 (Gambia) and 1951 (the other three countries) compared with the system before 1946. Five limitations on full independence still to be removed:
  (i) ex-officio Ministers on the executive council;
  (ii) governor's reserved powers;
  (iii) external affairs, defence, internal security not yet in African hands;
  (iv) some members of legislature not directly elected;
  (v) executive council not yet a cabinet.
Ghana, 1951-57: Dr Nkrumah's position under the 1951 constitution. Changes made in 1952 and 1953. The 1954 constitution; only two limitations on independence still remaining. The National Liberation Movement: should Ghana be a federal or a unitary state? Differences of policy between C.P.P. and N.L.M.
The Lennox-Boyd compromise. The 1957 independence constitution.
Nigeria, 1951-60: the federal constitution of 1954. Composition of regional executives and legislatures.
The federal and concurrent legislative lists. The constitution of the federal government.
1957, removal of ex-officio Ministers.
1958 and 1959, modifications in regional legislatures; 1959, establishment of federal Senate. Human rights in the constitution.
The independence constitution of 1960.
Sierra Leone, 1956-61: the 1958 constitution. Modifications of 1960: cabinet, public service and judicial service commissions. Limitations on full self-government remaining in 1960. The independence constitution of 1961. Colony and protectorate.
Gambia, 1960-63: constitution of 1960; increase in powers of Ministers. Constitution of 1962, and modifications of 1963.
Political Parties in West Africa: Ghana, Nigeria, Sierra Leone; they are based on tribal feeling and on loyalty to a leader; they have attained their object of securing national independence. What will happen now?

ALL four countries had now reached partial self-government. All of them had legislatures in which the great majority of the members were elected[1] and executive councils in which most of the members

---

[1] Gambia, 14 to 7; Sierra Leone 21 to 9; Gold Coast 75 to 9; Nigeria 136 to 12.

were Africans chosen from the members of the legislature. The executive councils had begun to develop towards something like a cabinet: the members had taken on the duties of departmental Ministers, and had begun to exercise an influence over departmental policy, even if they had not yet taken complete control over it. In Ghana and Nigeria the constitution provided that an African Minister could be dismissed by the legislature; this was not explicitly provided in Sierra Leone and the Gambia, but in practice a Minister's position would be impossible if the legislature decided that he was not the man for the job and carried a vote of censure against him by a reasonable majority.

If we compare this with the colonial system as it existed before 1946, we can see what a great advance had been made. Before 1946, there was an official majority in all the legislatures, and all policy was laid down by the governor and his departmental officials. The business of the African members in the legislature was to criticise the policy produced in the Secretariat, and it was only in the last two or three years before 1946 that Africans had been admitted into the governor's executive council to be given as it were a preview of Government proposals before they reached the legislature. There were of course all sorts of consultations in regional or provincial councils and other less formal gatherings. But the fundamental position of a colonial Government remained: 'This is what we propose to do, but if you have any comments we should be interested to hear them.' There is a very great advance from this position to the new position which the governors held in the middle of the nineteen-fifties: 'It is for you to say what you propose and to secure the support of the legislature.'

Five limitations on self-government

What limitations were there which had to be removed before this partial self-government could develop into complete independence? There were five of them.

The first was that the executive council still contained ex-officio Ministers: European permanent officials who were not members of any African political party, who sat in the executive (and in the legislature too) because of the official positions they held, and could not be dismissed by a hostile vote in the legislature. These men might be pleasant colleagues, and in fact more than one African chief minister was surprised to find how well he could work with them. But that did not alter the fact that the African leader was not in full control as long as these men were holding power. They must be got rid of.

The second was the governor's reserved powers. They might

never be used, but a country was not independent while they still existed. These reserved powers were the same in all four countries. They were defined by the phrase 'public faith, public order, and good government'. The governor was still responsible for seeing that the Government kept public faith: that is, kept its promises, including the promises of previous Governments. For example, if a Government had borrowed money at four per cent, it would be contrary to public faith if a new Finance Minister proposed to reduce the interest to two per cent. A measure contrary to public order would be one which was so clearly aimed at one section of the community that it was certain to provoke riot or rebellion. The Western Region of Nigeria, for example, would clearly be risking serious disorder if there were a housing shortage in Ibadan and the Government proposed to expel all Ibo and other non-Yoruba people from the city so as to make their houses available for Yoruba citizens. Similarly, if the Ghana Government had introduced a law to abolish chieftainship and confiscate all stool property without compensation, it would have risked large-scale disorder from those who regarded the chiefs as essential. The fact that we have to imagine such absurdities shows how very unlikely it was that the reserved powers would ever be needed.

'Good government' is a much vaguer phrase: so vague, in fact, that it would seem to give the governor an unlimited power of intervening 'in the interests of good government'. 'Good government' might be taken to mean whatever the governor thought right. But of course it was not intended to be taken in such an extreme sense. It would be possible for a Government, without breaking faith or provoking violent opposition and disorder, to mismanage affairs to such an extent that it would be difficult to get things right again. For example: in its enthusiasm for education, a Government might draw up an enormously expensive plan of free secondary education, and propose to find the money by unwise economies in other directions. It might propose to cut down maintenance work on the roads and railways and to curtail other social services. The governor might find himself compelled to tell the Ministry, 'Education is a fine thing, and I am entirely with you in your attempts to expand it. If you proposed new taxes to pay for your schemes, I should have nothing to say. But I cannot let you throw away all the good work that has been done in the last five years in building up the maternity service; and if you once let the roads and railways deteriorate beyond a certain point, it will cost millions of pounds to restore them. I warned you of this three months ago when you first told me of your scheme, but you ignored my warning. Now I must act to save the country from the suffering which your inexperience will cause it.' Again, this may seem an absurd case. In fact, nothing like this ever happened. But that is the sort of possibility which the Government in London had in mind when it drafted the governor's reserved powers to act 'in the interests of good government'.

What then were these reserved powers? In the first place, the governor could refuse his assent to a Bill. This is normal; the Queen can do it in England, though she has not in fact done it since 1707, and the president of the United States frequently does it today. But the governor had much more power than this. If there were a Bill before the legislature which it seemed the legislature was likely to reject, the governor could send a message to the House certifying that the Bill was necessary under one or other of these three heads;[2] and in this case, even if the Bill were rejected by the legislature, he would be empowered to declare that it had become law. If there were no such Bill before the legislature, and no unofficial member were willing to introduce one, the Governor could send a message to the Speaker or president, telling him that such a Bill was necessary, and requiring him to have it introduced by a fixed date. If the legislature still contained official members, the governor of course would order one of them to introduce the Bill; if not, he could still have the Bill introduced in this way through the Speaker. Once the Bill was introduced, the governor could declare in due course that it had become law, even if all the members objected to it.

On the other hand there was a check on these large powers. No governor would ever dare to use them without the support of at any rate a good proportion of his executive council. If he did use them, even with his executive council solid behind him, he had to send a full report of the circumstances to the Secretary of State in London, along with any written protest or counter-statement which a Minister or a member of the legislature might require him to send. The Secretary of State would then have to decide whether to support the governor or the legislature; and if the governor had managed to get so thoroughly at cross purposes with his Ministers as this, it would be very doubtful whether he had the qualities of tact and wisdom that were necessary in his position. It is quite likely that the Secretary of State would have felt compelled to support the legislature against the governor. Anyway, it never happened, for governors and Ministers had too much sense to let it happen. All the same, the very existence of the governor's reserved powers was

---

[2] In all this discussion of the governor's reserved powers I shall assume that they are limited to these three heads of public order, public faith and good government; and when in future I refer for short to 'the usual reserved powers', this is what I shall mean.

a limitation on independence which every African Minister would naturally wish to have removed.

The third limitation was somewhat similar. Certain functions of government were not entrusted to African hands; the governor kept the responsibility for them himself. These reserved functions were usually three: external affairs, defence, and internal security. These African countries were not yet allowed to have their own ambassadors in foreign countries; their foreign affairs and their relations with other Commonwealth countries were still handled by Britain. A scheme was introduced by which Africans were attached to British embassies in foreign countries for training in the arts of diplomacy; but meanwhile, external affairs were in British hands. Britain, through the governor, kept the responsibility for defending the country against outside enemies: the British army, navy and air force undertook this task, with help from the country's own forces. Lastly, the police were directly under the governor through a British commissioner of police. It is understandable that a governor should tell his new African Ministry, 'You get on with your job of running the country. I will see that peace and quiet is maintained while you are doing it, so as to give you a chance to settle down to the job.' These are reasonable limitations for that period; but they had to be thrown off if the country was to become independent.

The fourth limitation was that the legislature still contained members who were not responsible to the people. There were some ex-officio and nominated members; and many of the elected members were not directly elected by the people, but were elected to represent houses of chiefs, or local councils of some kind. This is a much less serious limitation on independence. There is nothing wrong with indirect election: the presidents of Ghana and the United States are elected indirectly, and the United States senate was elected indirectly until 1913. A country might be perfectly independent while some—even a majority—of its legislature was indirectly elected. But there were special reasons in West Africa why African Governments should wish to fill their legislatures with members directly elected by the people. It was the British Government that required indirect election: the Coussey commission in Ghana recommended that one-third of the legislature should be elected by state and territorial councils, but the Government increased this to one-half. Then, the chiefs and their elders tended to be conservative in their outlook, and to stand aloof from party politics. Party leaders naturally wanted to extend their party organization into the towns and villages all over the country, but many chiefs and elders did not welcome the young party agents sent out from Freetown, Accra or Lagos, who seemed to them to compete against their traditional position as heads of their people. There had always been some rivalry between chiefs and educated townsmen; the development of national political parties sharpened the rivalry and spread it all over the country. To a party leader like Dr Nkrumah, the solid block of members of the legislative council elected to represent the chiefs and their elders must have seemed like a brake on his machine, permanently screwed down so as to prevent him from travelling as fast as he and his party wished. For these and similar reasons, it came to be looked on as a necessary condition of independence that all the members of the legislature should be elected by the people.

This would mean too that the ex-officio members and the special members would have to leave. Clearly there could be no foreign members sitting ex-officio in the legislature of an independent country. There seems no reason in theory why a legislature should not include four or five special members; the British House of Commons, for example included until 1948 a few members representing the universities, and the Irish senate is mainly composed of members representing special interests. However, no political party likes to see members in the House who are non-party men; so the special members too had to go. Political leaders took it for granted that when they achieved independence, all the members of the legislature—at any rate, of the lower House—would be party men, elected by the people on a party basis.[3]

The fifth limitation was that the cabinet was not yet fully formed. Not only did it contain ex-officio members, but it was not fully responsible to the legislature. African party leaders wanted a cabinet in which all the members would be chosen by the prime minister and which would hold office only as long as it retained the support of an all-elected legislature: a cabinet which (like the British cabinet) would be collectively responsible as long as the prime minister chose, but from which he could compel an individual Minister to resign if that seemed in his judgment the best course for the party and for the country. Such a cabinet seemed still far off in 1954.

We must now trace the process by which these limitations were overcome, ending this chapter at the attainment of independence, and leaving to the next chapter the story of constitutional developments after Independence Day. Ghana became independent in March 1957, Nigeria in 1960, Sierra Leone in 1961; the Gambia is

---

[3] Though as a matter of fact there are still four special members in the Nigerian Senate, and twelve paramount chiefs, nominated by district councils, in the Sierra Leone legislature.

not yet (1964) fully independent. We will take the countries in this order.

GHANA 1951-1957

Dr Nkrumah and his Convention People's Party won thirty-four out of the thirty-eight contested seats in the 1951 election, and the governor could not possibly have invited anyone but Dr Nkrumah to form a Government. But the thirty-four C.P.P. members in the House were faced not only by the tiny group of four opposition elected members, but by three European ex-officio, six European nominated, and thirty-seven territorial members; so they were a minority Government, depending for support on at least a section of the African territorial members. This would be an unsatisfactory position for any party leader. In the executive, six Ministries were held by the C.P.P., and two more by African unofficial members. Dr Nkrumah had wished to have all eight held by his own men, but for reasons of state he thought it advisable to appoint one Minister from Ashanti and one from the North. Three Ministries—defence and external affairs, finance, and justice—were held by European ex-officio Ministers. In March 1952, Dr Nkrumah, hitherto called Leader of Government Business, was given the title of Prime Minister; but the change gave him no more power. At the same time, the executive council was renamed the Cabinet. The new arrangement was that the governor should choose a prime minister, and should submit his name to the legislature; if the legislature elected him, the prime minister would henceforth be responsible to it, not to the governor. When elected, the prime minister would nominate his Ministers; the governor would submit their names to the legislature, and they too would be elected by the legislature and would thus become individually responsible to it. The ordinary constitutional conventions would of course make it impossible for the governor to nominate anyone for the office of Prime Minister except the leader of the majority party in the House.

These changes made hardly any difference to the realities of the power situation, and Dr Nkrumah soon began pressing for further advance. In the latter part of 1952 and throughout 1953 there was much discussion all over the country. Dr Nkrumah and the C.P.P. wisely saw that the country was not yet ready for complete independence—in particular, they must have a few more years to train their future army officers and ambassadors and departmental heads. So for the time being it was a question of an interim constitution to give the essentials of internal self-government, while leaving Britain still the responsibility for such matters as defence and external relations.

In June 1953, the Government published its proposals, and in April 1954, the British Government brought the new constitution into force. The legislative council of 84 members was replaced by one of 104. All ex-officio and nominated members were removed, and the block of territorial members also vanished; all the 104 were popularly elected. Moreover, the electoral colleges which had elected the rural members under the 1951 constitution were abolished, and all members were directly elected. The 104 members consisted of 7 municipal members, 39 rural members from the Colony, 13 from Trans-Volta, 19 from Ashanti, and 26 from the North. In the June elections, the C.P.P. won 79 out of the 104 seats. The official Opposition was the new Northern People's Party, with 14 seats; 11 members belonged to small parties, or to no party at all. An interesting constitutional point arose here. The Northern People's Party was a regional party, aiming to preserve the interests of the North from being ignored by the more powerful South. The Prime Minister protested that, being a regional party, it ought not to be regarded as the official Opposition. The Opposition surely, he said, must be a national party. The leader of the N.P.P. took up the challenge. His party, he said, might be based on the North, but it was perfectly ready to form an alternative Government if ever Dr Nkrumah and the C.P.P. resigned office. Dr Nkrumah's point was sound; but the Speaker followed British tradition, and declared that since the North could form an alternative Government, it was entitled to be regarded as the official Opposition. Had the N.P.P. been weaker—had it held, for example, only eight seats instead of fourteen, it would have been too weak to form a Government, even if it were the strongest opposition party in the House.

The 1954 cabinet was to consist of at least eight persons, chosen by the Prime Minister from the members of the assembly. The cabinet was to be collectively responsible to the legislature. There were no ex-officio Ministers; the cabinet was an entirely African, entirely C.P.P. group. The governor was to retain the usual reserved powers.

To see the effect of this constitution, it will be convenient to cast our minds back to the 1951 limitations, and see how they had now been set aside. They were: (1) ex-officio Ministers; (2) governor's reserved powers; (3) reserved functions—defence, external affairs, security; (4) ex-officio and nominated members in the legislature; (5) cabinet not fully and collectively responsible. Of these five limitations, numbers 1, 4 and 5 had now been removed, but 2 and 3 remained. The 1954 constitution satisfied Dr Nkrumah for the time being; he had no objection to these two limitations for another two or three years till he considered the country ready for full independence.

Dr Nkrumah hoped that he might not have to wait even as long as this. But in September 1954, only three months after the election in which the C.P.P. had won such a triumphant majority, there arose a new opposition party calling itself the National Liberation Movement; and in October the new party was strengthened by receiving the support of a powerful ally, the Asantehene. This meant that the influence of all the Ashanti chiefs was thrown against the C.P.P. and in favour of the N.L.M. The Northern People's Party made common cause with the N.L.M., and both parties adopted a policy of advocating a federal government for an independent Ghana. This policy brought in some support from Togoland, and a good many cocoa farmers who were not specially interested in federalism joined the new party because they were dissatisfied with the Government's policy of paying them (through the Cocoa Marketing Board) only a moderate price for their cocoa and using the Marketing Board's large profits for national development projects. The threat had to be taken seriously; for although the C.P.P. had won such a comfortable majority of the seats in the legislature (79 out of 104), it had not received a proportionate majority of the total vote; 392,000 against 315,000 opposition votes. As in Britain, the electoral system tended to give a strong majority in the House to the party winning a slight majority of the votes. If seats in the House had been allotted in proportion to the votes cast, the C.P.P. majority, instead of 79 out of 104, would have been 58, compared with the Opposition's 46. Dr Nkrumah dared not ignore the possibility that the floating vote might reverse his position in the House; and indeed the Opposition declared that at the next election it would.

We need not go into the story of the difficult, and sometimes bitter negotiations which began in October 1954 when the Asantehene and fifty Ashanti chiefs signed a petition to the Queen asking for a commission to be set up to consider the possibility of a federal constitution for an independent Ghana.

Dr Nkrumah was utterly opposed to the idea of a federal constitution. He pointed out that Ghana was a small country, no bigger than Great Britain. The differences between the South, Ashanti, and the North were not big enough to make federalism necessary. Once regional units had been set up, he feared that it would never be possible to establish a unitary government; the country would be permanently divided. And Ghana, though richer than many other African countries, was not rich enough either in money or in trained men to staff and maintain a central government and four regional governments. Dr Nkrumah in fact took the view that the objections to federalism are so strong that a unitary government is best, provided the citizens can make up their minds to accept it.

The National Liberation Movement advocated federalism because it saw that wealth and education were concentrated in the south, and so too was the power of the C.P.P. Under a unitary constitution, they feared that this concentration of wealth and education and power would increase, and Ashanti and the North would be completely dominated by the Convention People's Party. They were deeply afraid of what they called a 'creeping dictatorship', and all their policy was designed to make such a thing impossible. They wanted a fully federal system, with regional assemblies with large powers of raising taxes and passing laws. They wanted a two-chamber federal parliament, the upper House to include chiefs, and perhaps also some distinguished men nominated by the Government, perhaps also even some elected members. (The Opposition was not quite united in its views on the composition of the upper House, but it was united in demanding that there should be an upper House, and that it should be largely composed of chiefs.) They wanted a Council of State which should advise the governor-general on appointments to the public service and similar matters. The Council was to be a non-party group; it was to consist of the Prime Minister, the leader of the opposition, the attorney-general, and the heads of the four regions. Its main duty was to keep the governor-general above party politics and to see that the judges and the civil service too were non-party. They wanted the powers of the regional assemblies to be laid down in the constitution, and they wanted the constitution to be made difficult to amend. All these demands were made because the Opposition was afraid of the C.P.P's immensely strong position in the legislature. For a two-thirds majority, the C.P.P. needed seventy seats; but it already had seventy-nine. With such a majority, the C.P.P. Government could do what it liked. The only hope for the Opposition was to get the powers of the regions, of the upper House, and the Council of State written into the constitution, with a Supreme Court to defend them in the American style.

In July 1956, fresh general elections were held, and to the disappointment of the Opposition, the C.P.P. majority was only slightly reduced: from seventy-nine seats to seventy-two. The party still had its two-thirds majority. The independence constitution which was finally settled after the personal mediation of the Secretary of State (Mr Alan Lennox-Boyd) was a compromise, the C.P.P. giving up a little and the Opposition giving up a good deal more.

There was no Council of State, and no second House. There were to be regional assemblies; but nothing was laid down about their powers. A constitutional commission was to consider what sort of regional assemblies were needed, who should sit in them, and what they should do; it was to report to the Ghana parliament within nine months of independence, and 'as soon thereafter as may be', the Government was to introduce a Bill to put its proposals into effect. Until this happened, there were to be interim regional assemblies, consisting of all the members of parliament elected from the region. Ghana was thus to be a unitary state, and Dr Nkrumah was not to be compelled to set up powerful regional assemblies; for if he disliked the recommendations of the constitutional commission, he could always say that his Bill was not yet ready and other more important matters must come first. The regional assemblies were thus to depend, not on the constitution, as the Opposition had wished, but on an Act of the Ghana parliament, as Dr Nkrumah and his party wished.

On the other hand, some concessions were made to the Opposition. Amendments to the constitution were to be made by a two-thirds majority of all members of parliament, instead of by a two-thirds majority of the members present and voting.[4] Some amendments would need also the approval of two-thirds of the regional assemblies, and amendments affecting the status of chiefs would need the approval of the regional Houses of Chiefs. Bills altering the boundaries of a region must be approved by the regional assembly.

Another concession dealt with appointments to the public service. Though there was to be no Council of State, there was to be a public service commission, which should advise the governor-general on all matters concerning appointments to the public service: appointments, promotions, transfers, dismissals and discipline. Dr Nkrumah went further, and announced that he would make a practice of consulting the leader of the opposition when making appointments to the public service commission; and he hoped that this constitutional convention would be followed by his successors.

Judges were to be appointed by the governor-general on the advice of a judicial service commission; this was a body of distinguished lawyers, who would recommend the most suitable candidate from their professional point of view. This arrangement, like that of the public service commission, was made to ensure that the judges, like the civil service, were above politics. The chief justice however was to be appointed on the prime minister's advice. Any judge could be dismissed if two-thirds of the legislature requested

[4] See page 28.

it. These arrangements were similar to those in England; but in England a two-thirds majority of both Houses of parliament is needed, and this would be impossible to obtain in practice unless a judge had shown himself manifestly unfit for his post through infirmity or defect of character. It could never be obtained for political reasons. But in Ghana, with a one-chamber parliament in which one party had a safe two-thirds majority of the seats, this provision of the constitution did not give the judges as much security as they had in Britain.

The parliament of Ghana was unchanged from the 1954 parliament.[5] The assembly again consisted of the Speaker and 104 elected members. All men and women of twenty-one years were entitled to vote if they had lived for six months in their constituency or 'electoral district'. There were of course certain disqualifications, such as a criminal record, unsound mind, corruption, non-payment of rates or taxes. Such disqualifications as these are usual in all countries; and we shall not mention them again; when we speak of all men as entitled to vote, we shall mean all men except those disqualified in some such usual way. Voting was to be by secret ballot. Members of parliament must be Ghanaian citizens of twenty-five years old, able to speak and read English. Here too, there were certain disqualifications. The assembly was to sit every year; its life was to be not more than five years, and within two months of its being dissolved, fresh elections must be held.

The executive power was held by a cabinet of not less than eight members of parliament. The governor-general appointed them, but he did so on the advice of the prime minister, and it was the prime minister who allotted each to his Ministry. The prime minister could advise the governor-general to dismiss a Minister, and his advise would of course always be taken. The prime minister, by the usual convention, must be leader of the majority party in the assembly. If the assembly passed a vote of no confidence in the Government, it was for the prime minister to decide whether to resign or to ask for a dissolution. If he resigned and a new prime minister were appointed, the whole cabinet automatically went out of office. A minister lost his post if he lost his seat in the assembly, unless the assembly were dissolved, in which case he stayed in his office until a new prime minister was appointed. The effect of this was that a new prime minister had a clear field: all the Ministries were vacant, so he could arrange his new cabinet as he pleased.

[5] Strictly speaking, the term parliament means the combination of the governor-general and the assembly—or, today, the president and the assembly. But the word is often used loosely to refer to the assembly alone, though we shall try to avoid using it thus in this book.

There were no ex-officio members in the cabinet; all the Ministers were members of the C.P.P. chosen by the prime minister. The governor-general was in exactly the same position as the Queen in England: he received each Minister and formally appointed him, but he had no power to choose for himself, or to reject anyone whom the prime minister had chosen. All the subjects (defence, external affairs, and security) which had hitherto been reserved to the governor were now handed over to African Ministers, and the governor's reserved powers were taken away. The governor-general of independent Ghana had ceremonial functions, but no real power. He formally opened parliament, and read a speech announcing the programme of legislation for the session; but the speech was written by the cabinet, and the governor-general had no voice in what was to be put in or what was to be left out. He retained the theoretical power of refusing his assent to a Bill; but since the power has not been used in England for over 250 years, it was highly unlikely that any governor-general would try and revive it. Ghana was completely independent.

NIGERIA 1951-1960

Under the constitution of 1951, Nigeria was formally divided into three regions, each with a lieutenant-governor. But it was still a unitary state, governed from Lagos. The regional Governments had their legislatures and their executives, but the constitution made no attempt to define the relationship between the central and the regional Governments, and nothing was said about what might happen if a regional Government wished to adopt a different policy from the one laid down in Lagos. Such an arrangement was clearly unsatisfactory, and in 1954 the decisive step was taken of giving Nigeria a federal constitution.

The general structure of the Government was unchanged. As in 1951, there was a central (now a federal) legislature and executive, and there were three regional legislatures and executives. There was a general tendency to reduce the number of ex-officio members and to increase the number of elected members. These unimportant changes in the membership of the councils can be summarized in a table:

	1951	1954
Northern House of Chiefs	All 1st-class chiefs, 37 others, adviser on Muslim law	No change, but Ministers who are members of the lower House are added

	1951	1954
Northern House of Assembly	4 officials, 90 elected, special members	4 officials, 131 elected, not more than 5 special
Western House of Chiefs	3 officials, 50 chiefs	50 chiefs, with special members
Western House of Assembly	4 officials, 80 elected, special members	80 elected, with special members
Eastern Legislature	5 officials, 80 elected, special members	84 elected, no officials
Central Legislative Council	6 officials, 136 elected, and specials	3 officials, 184 elected, up to 6 specials
Northern Executive	5 officials, 6 to 9 unofficial	3 officials, 13 unofficial
Western Executive	5 officials, 6 to 9 unofficial	at least 9 unofficial
Eastern Executive	5 officials, 6 to 9 unofficial	at least 9 unofficial
Central Executive	6 officials, 12 unofficial	3 officials, 10 unofficial

The 184 elected members of the central legislative council in 1954 comprised ninety-two from the North, forty-two each from the West and East, six from the Southern Cameroons, and two from Lagos. The ten central Ministers comprised three each from the three Regions, and one from the Southern Cameroons.[6]

It is noticeable that the officials disappear altogether from the legislatures of the Eastern and Western regions, and even from the executives, though they remain in the North and in the federal Government. The thirteen unofficial Ministers in the North were a prime minister and twelve others appointed on his recommendation. The executive in the West must not include more than three chiefs. The official influence was weakened too in the federal executive, for it was provided that voting was to be by majority, and the

[6] The Southern Cameroons was at that time administered as part of Nigeria; it was a separate region of the federation, with its own legislature. In 1961 the Southern Cameroons decided by a plebiscite to join its neighbour, the Cameroon Republic.

governor-general was to have only a casting vote. This is a clear step away from the old colonial idea of a group of individual advisers towards the idea of a cabinet.

The most important change made in 1954 was the replacement of unitary by federal government. As in all federal systems, the question at once arose, what were to be the powers of the federal and the regional Governments? The 1954 constitution answered this question by drawing up two lists. The first was the federal list: a list of subjects on which only the federal Government had power to make laws. It included

> aviation, banks, census, citizenship, copyright, currency, customs, defence, deportation, external relations, certain higher educational institutions, immigration and emigration, mining, police, railways, inter-regional commerce, trunk roads, inter-regional water, weights and measures, radio and television,

and other matters. The second was the concurrent list: a list of subjects on which regional Governments might make laws, but the federal Government too might make laws, though federal laws on these subjects would not apply to a region unless the regional Government approved. This list included

> antiquities, bankruptcy, commercial combines, electricity, other higher education, labour (conditions of labour, industrial relations, trade unions, welfare), national parks, tourist traffic, surveys, water power, public safety,

and others. For example, if the federal Government decided to change the currency from £ s. d. to some form of decimal currency, and to abandon British measures and change to the metric system, no region could continue in the old way; for currency and weights and measures are matters reserved to the federal Government. On the other hand, if a region wishes to make a law about trade unions, it is empowered to do so, and its trade union law may differ from that in other regions. But the region may think it better to have a law which is the same as that in other regions; if so, it may wait for the federal Government to make a law on the subject, and adopt the federal law in its own legislation.

It would of course be easy to make a list of subjects not included in either the federal or the concurrent list. Primary and secondary education is the first item that comes to mind. This, and any other subjects not already listed, are exclusively the affair of the regional Governments. Thus the federal constitution of Nigeria is like that of the United States and Australia in restricting the powers of the federal Government but leaving the regional Governments free to do anything which the constitution does not expressly forbid them to do. The constitution provides that if there were a conflict between regional and federal law, the federal law must prevail. Similarly, the executive authority of a regional Government must not impede that of the Federation.

The Nigerian judiciary was reorganized to correspond with the federal structure; the federal Supreme Court would hear appeals from the regional High Courts. The Nigerian finances were arranged so as to provide the regions with a revenue. The income tax receipts were divided among the regions in proportion to their assessments, the receipts from motor spirit and tobacco duties in proportion to their consumption. The federal Government kept none of this money. But it kept roughly half of the customs revenue, the other half being divided among the regions.

There were the usual provisos that the governor general and the regional governors should have reserved powers, and that only the Government could initiate proposals for expenditure.

Nigeria was thus established as a federation, with one federal House of Representatives, and two-chamber regional legislatures in North and West, with a single-chamber legislature in the East. There was a weakening in the official influence, but no clear advance towards independence. In the next few years however, several steps were taken towards the full independence which came in 1960.

In 1957, the ex-officio Ministers were removed from the federal executive, the Council of Ministers. This body was now to consist of the governor-general and not less than eleven Ministers, all chosen from the federal House of Representatives. The governor-general was no longer required to preside; the prime minister might preside. The ex-officio members were removed too from the federal House of Representatives. Similar changes took place in the regions. Two of the three ex-officio Ministers left the Northern executive, and it was laid down that the governor need not preside; the Northern premier,[7] it was laid down, must be a member of the House of Assembly (the lower House) and able to command a majority there. This proviso was applied also to the two-chamber legislature of the West.

[7] *Premier* is a French word used in England as an alternative to *prime minister*. There is no difference whatever in meaning, and both are used. In Nigeria however, a usage has grown up which confines the term *prime minister* to the federal Government. The chief minister of a region is called the premier.

In 1958, the strength of the Northern House of Chiefs was increased by ten, from thirty-seven to forty-seven chiefs (other than the first-class chiefs, who were all members). At the same time, the governor ceased to be a member. The Northern House of Assembly was increased from 131 members to 174. The Western House of Assembly lost its special members, and added the members of the executive who were members of the Western House of Chiefs. Similarly, members of the executive in the North who were members of the Northern House of Assembly were made members also of the Northern House of Chiefs. The effect of this is that in the North and the West, members of the executive could sit in either House.

Next year, 1959, there were many more changes. The legislature in the Eastern Region, which had hitherto consisted of only one House, now added a second House, a House of Chiefs. It was to contain all first-class chiefs and fifty-five other chiefs; and as in the other two regions, it was provided that members of the executive could sit in either House.

The federal legislature too was enlarged by the addition of a second House, to be called the Senate. The Senate was to consist of forty-eight members appointed from the four regions (North, West, East, and the Southern Cameroons) in equal numbers, four Lagos representatives, two of whom were to be chiefs, and four other members to be nominated by the governor-general—a total of fifty-six members. In addition, it was provided that members of the federal executive might sit in either House. The federal House of Representatives also was enlarged from 184 to 320 elected members, and the special members were removed. The usual proviso was made that money bills were to originate only in the lower House, the House of Representatives.

In the West, the House of Assembly was increased this year from 80 to 124 elected members.

An important addition was made to the federal constitution: a paragraph on fundamental human rights. It was laid down that no Nigerian was to be made or kept a slave, or subjected to torture or any inhuman punishment. Nigerians were not to be deprived of their personal liberty except by due process of law, and if arrested, they were entitled to a prompt and fair trial. They were entitled to freedom of thought and expression, and so forth. This paragraph was reproduced and expanded in the 1960 independence constitution, so we need not enlarge on it now.

The total effect of these changes from 1954 to 1959 was to put the Federation of Nigeria in about the same position as Ghana was in from 1954 to 1957. Let us glance again at the five limitations on national independence. Nigeria had removed the first of them, ex-officio Ministers. The second and third (reserved powers and reserved functions) still remained. The fourth (ex-officio and nominated members in the legislature) had gone. As for the fifth (limitation on cabinet responsibility), that was not yet formally removed; but since the Prime Minister and the regional premiers must command a majority in the legislatures, they could always get their own way by threatening to resign. In practice therefore, full cabinet responsibility was a fact, though it was not laid down on paper. All that remained for full independence was the removal of the reserved powers and the reserved functions of the governor-general and the regional governors.

Nigerian Independence, 1960

In 1960, the British parliament passed the Nigerian Independence Act and authorized the Queen in Council to draw up a new constitution for an independent Nigeria. This 1960 constitution is the basis on which Nigeria is now governed; the 1963 republican constitution made only a few changes. We shall set out the 1960 constitution in some detail, and note the subsequent changes when they occur.

The federal structure of Nigeria was maintained. Let us first dispose of the regional constitutions and then come to the sections of the constitution which concern the country as a whole.

The Northern House of Chiefs was to consist of all first-class chiefs, 95 instead of 37 other chiefs, and the adviser on Muslim law. The Northern House of Assembly was to have 170 instead of 174 elected members, with not more than five nominated by the governor on the premier's advice. The Western House of Chiefs was to have 115 (instead of 50) chiefs, with not more than four nominated by the governor on the premier's advice. The Western House of Assembly, with 124 members, was unchanged from the 1959 figure. The Eastern House of Chiefs was unchanged, with first class chiefs and 55 others; the Eastern House of Assembly was increased from 84 to 146 elected members. In each region there was to be an executive consisting of a premier (who must be a member of the lower House commanding a majority in that House) and a number of other Ministers chosen by him; the executive was to be collectively responsible to the legislature.

Thus all three regions were provided with fully responsible self-government, subject to the limitations on regional powers. There were no more official members, and the few nominated members were to be chosen by the premier, not by the governor. The governor's reserved powers had vanished.

The first section of the federal constitution lays down the powers of the federation, and the manner of amending the constitution. Nigeria is to consist of three regions[8] and a federal territory. The federal constitution is to prevail over any other law, and over any regional constitution. The constitution may be amended by the federal parliament, provided there is a two-thirds majority in each House. On some points it is not enough to have a two-thirds majority in each House of the federal parliament; there must also be a resolution in support of the proposed amendment in at least two of the regional legislatures. Some of the points on which this regional support is necessary are: fundamental human rights, the composition of the federal parliament, the powers of the federal parliament, the judiciary. If the proposed amendment is to establish a new region or to alter regional boundaries, still further safeguards are required. First, the federal parliament must approve the proposal by the usual two-thirds majority in each House. Then the proposal must be submitted to all the regions, and must receive sufficient support from regional legislatures; in particular, the region that will lose some of its land must agree. Finally, the proposal must be submitted to a referendum among the people who will be transferred to a new region, and they must approve it by a three-fifths majority. This elaborate procedure need not be applied if the proposed change in regional boundaries is a small one, involving not more than 1,000 square miles or 100,000 people. But in such minor cases, both the regions concerned must approve the change by resolutions in each House of their legislatures.

Section Two deals with citizenship, and Section Four with the governor-general. These two sections are not important for our purpose.

Section Three lays down in much detail the fundamental rights of every citizen of Nigeria. He is entitled (a) to his life. No one is to take the life of a Nigerian except (i) in self-defence against him if he is attacking, (ii) in trying to arrest him or to prevent him from escaping after he has been arrested, (iii) if he is one of a riotous crowd, or (iv) in order to stop him from committing a crime which he seems just about to commit. All these exceptions are covered by a sentence which says that a Nigerian's constitutional right to his life is not infringed 'if he dies as the result of the use, to such extent and in such circumstances as are permitted by law, of such force as is reasonably justifiable'. Anyone who kills a Nigerian citizen will have to satisfy the courts that he killed the man in circumstances which justified him in using violence or force, and that he did not use more force than was necessary—for example,

[8] Since 1962 there have been four regions instead of three.

that it would not have been enough to break the man's arm instead of killing him.

A Nigerian is entitled (b) to be free from any torture, or any inhuman or degrading punishment, and (c) from slavery or forced labour. It will be for the courts to say whether a punishment which has been inflicted is degrading or inhuman; and in the matter of forced labour, it is provided that the kind of communal labour which has always been customary (for example, when a village headman calls out his people to repair the road which has been washed away) is not to be regarded as unconstitutional.

He is entitled to (d) his personal liberty, unless he is deprived of it 'in accordance with a procedure permitted by law'. If he is arrested, he is entitled (e) to be promptly told, 'in language that he understands', why he is arrested, and (f) to be promptly tried. If he is unlawfully arrested, he is entitled (g) to compensation. We may comment here that an arrested man is not merely to be charged 'in *a* language', but 'in language that he understands'. It does not mean merely that an Ibo man who knows no English must be charged in Ibo, not in English. It means more than this. It means that whatever language is being used, the charge must be explained plainly so that he understands it, not gabbled at him in complicated legal jargon which bewilders him. As for 'unlawful arrest', this means an arrest made otherwise than in the way prescribed by law. There are some circumstances in which a policeman can arrest you without a warrant, and others in which he needs a warrant from a magistrate. If he arrests you without a warrant in circumstances in which he needed one, or if he arrests you and keeps you for some time in a cell without telling you any reason for the arrest, your arrest is unlawful, and you will be entitled to compensation. But do not hope for compensation merely because, after being arrested, charged, and tried, you have been found not guilty. Your arrest may have been perfectly lawful and justifiable, and the prosecution may have been unlucky in not being able to prove the case against you.

If a Nigerian has been lawfully arrested and charged, he is entitled to (h) several rights in connection with his trial. He must be given time and opportunity to prepare his defence; he must be allowed to have a lawyer to represent him; he must be allowed to examine the prosecution witnesses, and to compel witnesses who can give evidence for his defence to come and do so; he must be allowed to have the services of an interpreter if he needs one, and without having to pay for him. Until he is convicted, he is entitled to be presumed innocent. If convicted, he must not be punished for what he has done unless it was a punishable offence at the time he did it; and he must not receive a heavier punishment than the law provided at that time. If he is being tried for a criminal offence, he is not to be compelled to give evidence at his trial if he does not wish to. And if he has been found not guilty, he must not be tried again for that same offence unless a higher court orders his case to be retried.

Here too some comments are needed. All these provisions are needed to protect the citizen against his Government. If the Government made up his mind to kill one of its political opponents, or to imprison him for life, it could easily get its way if it were able to arrest him on some minor charge—or on a major charge—and then prevent him from making a proper defence at his trial. It could frighten all the lawyers from undertaking his defence; it could prevent his defence witnesses from coming forward, either by frightening them or even by imprisoning them until his trial was over; it could say that it was impossible to allow a vile fellow like the prisoner to insult loyal and faithful citizens who were giving evidence for the prosecution by asking them impertinent questions —thus presuming him guilty, though he has not yet been found so. All these things have happened, long ago in England, more recently in Germany and Russia and elsewhere. Again, the Government might discover that even if the prisoner is convicted, the law only allows a maximum sentence of three years: much too short a sentence for its purposes. It could hastily rush through parliament a law increasing the punishment for this offence to life imprisonment, and ask the judge to impose this heavier sentence. All these things are now declared unconstitutional; no Nigerian may be treated in this way.

A Nigerian is entitled to (i) respect for his private and family life. This would forbid the police, for example, to instal a hidden microphone in a man's house to take a recording of his private conversation; or to arrest a man's wife and threaten him that unless he confessed (or did something else which the Government wanted him to do) his wife would be imprisoned or ill-treated. He is entitled to (j) freedom of thought, conscience and religion. A man's thoughts and opinions are his own, and he is not to be punished for his thoughts, even if they are the sort of thoughts that ought not to be uttered aloud. He may choose any religion he likes, and he is not to be compelled to do anything which his religion tells him is wrong. He is entitled to (k) freedom of expression. He may think as he likes, tell other people what he thinks, and may receive and impart information and ideas without interference. Thus, it would be unconstitutional for the Government to tap a man's telephone or open his letters in the post, or refuse to deliver letters and papers that are addressed to him or those that he sends. He is entitled (l) to freedom of assembly and association. He may go to any public meeting, and may join any group or party that he wishes. He is entitled (m) to move about Nigeria freely; he may not be expelled from his country, and if he has left Nigeria for a time, he may not be refused permission to re-enter it when he comes back.

This group of rights, from (i) to (m), may of course be limited by the law. Clearly, a man cannot claim a constitutional right to join a gang of robbers, or to bolt his door against a policeman who is coming with a warrant to arrest him, or to make arrangements through the post for murdering the prime minister. Accordingly, the constitution provides that any of these constitutional rights from (i) to (m) may be limited from time to time in certain cases by 'any law that is reasonably justifiable in a democratic society'. Notice the wording. If I am told that one of my constitutional rights is to be restricted under a law, it is open for me to argue that the law quoted by the Government is a tyrannical and unjust law, not 'reasonably justifiable in a democratic society'. And the courts will have to decide.

Lastly, a Nigerian citizen is entitled to (n) compensation if his property is compulsorily acquired for the public use; and the constitution declares (o) that there must be no discrimination in Nigeria against any man because of his tribe, place of origin, religion, or political opinion. It is doubtful if under the existing constitution any Nigerian Government could declare the country a one-party state, for in a one-party state the citizen is not free to join any group or party that he wishes (l), his freedom of expression (k) is a good deal restricted, and a citizen whose views are unwelcome to those in authority may very probably find himself discriminated against (o) because of his political opinions. If the Government desired a one-party state, it would need to amend this section of the constitution before taking political action.

This section of the constitution on fundamental human rights was reproduced unchanged in the republican constitution of 1963; the same formula is used about laws which are 'reasonably justifiable in a democratic society'.

Section Five of the constitution is concerned with parliament. The federal Senate is a body of twelve representatives from each region, with four from the federal territory of Lagos, and four others nominated by the governor-general on the advice of the prime minister. Regional senators must be Nigerian citizens at least forty years old; senators nominated by the governor-general need not be Nigerian citizens. The federal House of Representatives had 305 members,[9] who must all be Nigerian citizens at least twenty-one years old. Men and women could represent constituencies in the West and East, but women were not eligible to sit for Northern constituencies. Federal Ministers might take part in the proceedings of either House, but could only vote in the House of which they were members. Nigeria is divided into constituencies by an electoral commission, appointed by the governor-general on the Prime Minister's advice. The division is to be revised every eight or ten years to take account of movements of population. The electoral commission is also responsible for registering voters and supervising the conduct of the elections.

In settling the relationship between the two Houses, the constitution takes into account British experience gained in the Parliament Act[10] and subsequently. Money bills must originate in the lower House, and only on the initiative of the Government. (It is a well-established principle that no private member may propose the spending of public money. If this were allowed, the way would be open for all kinds of 'pork-barrel' expenditure on roads, dams, bridges, hospitals and so forth. Mr A would propose that a new hospital should be built in his constituency, and Messrs B, C and D would all support him, on the understanding that he would support their proposals when their turn came. This sort of bargaining would soon spread all through parliament, and the Government would lose all control of public expenditure.) When the House of Representatives sends a Money Bill up to the Senate, the Senate must pass it without amendment within a month; if it fails to do so, the House of Representatives may send the Bill straight to the governor-general for his approval, over the Senate's head. Thus the Senate has no power whatever of amending a Money Bill, and is able to delay it only by a month.

On other Bills, the Senate has somewhat more power. On many Bills of course, there will be no serious disagreement between the two Houses, and the House of Representatives will be ready to consider the Senate's amendments at leisure. But what if there is serious disagreement, for example if the House of Representatives is determined to pass a Bill and the Senate dislikes it? In this case, the House of Representatives will take care to send the Bill up to the Senate at least a month before the end of the session. The Senate may then reject the Bill altogether, or may make amendments. If the House of Representatives is determined on the Bill as it stands, and is not prepared to listen to any proposal for amendment, it may send the Bill to the Senate a second time in the following

[9] Increased to 312 under the 1963 constitution; see page 220.
[10] See page 30.

session. The Bill must reach the Senate not less than six months after the House of Representatives first passed it, and at least a month before the end of the session. If the Senate still refuses to pass it, the House of Representatives may send it direct to the governor-general for his approval. The effect of all this is that the Senate may delay a Bill (other than a money bill) by one session, but no longer.

There is to be one session of parliament every year. The governor-general has constitutional powers of dissolving parliament; this is one of the few matters in which (like the Queen in England) he has some discretion left to him. He may of course—and usually will—dissolve parliament if the prime minister so advises him. But if the prime minister advises a dissolution, the governor-general may refuse if he thinks that the Government can still carry on, and that a dissolution would not be in the national interest. In other words, he will say to his prime minister, 'I can see that you are depressed at the way things are going. But cheer up; you still have a safe majority, and if we had a general election now, I think you would come back to power with a parliament very much like this one. So a dissolution and an election would not give you an escape from your troubles. I advise you to go on fighting; and if you can announce a few tax reductions in your Budget next month, you will find that all this storm will die down.'

There are other cases in which a dissolution may depend on the governor-general's discretion. The prime minister may lose the confidence of the House of Representatives, which passes a vote of no-confidence in his Government. This should mean the fall of the Government; the prime minister will either resign, or advise the dissolution of parliament. If he does neither within three days, the governor-general may dissolve parliament on his own responsibility. Similarly, if the prime minister has resigned, but the governor-general can find no one in the present parliament to succeed him— no one, that is, who has any chance of commanding a majority in the House—the governor-general may dissolve parliament. He may dissolve, but he is not compelled to; in the 1963 republican constitution, these three situations are all mentioned, and the president is allowed less discretion. He may still, as in 1960, refuse to grant a dissolution when the prime minister advises it; but he has no discretion if the prime minister has been defeated in a vote of confidence and will not accept the House's decision, or if the prime minister has resigned and no successor is in sight. In these two cases, the president *must* dissolve the parliament.

The federal parliament makes laws for the federal territory; for the rest of Nigeria its legislative powers are laid down in the exclusive and concurrent lists, as in the 1954 constitution. Federal law is to prevail over regional law if the two conflict. In times of national danger, the federal parliament may exceed the powers given it by the two lists. Such a national danger may be a war, or a 'state of emergency' which is declared by a two-thirds majority of each House on the ground that 'democratic institutions in Nigeria are threatened by subversion'. Such a resolution has effect only for twelve months at a time. The subversion of democratic institutions presumably means an attempt to set up a dictatorship, or to weaken the authority of parliament, or to interfere with freedom of elections or with the fundamental rights listed in the constitution.

The governor-general is head of the executive (Section Six). He appoints the prime minister, who must be a member of the House of Representatives 'who appears to him likely to command the support of a majority of the members of the House'. (If the governor-general chooses the wrong man, he will soon find out his mistake; for the House will not support the man of his choice.) Other Ministers are appointed by the governor-general on the prime minister's advice, and their responsibilities are similarly allotted to them. The post of prime minister is automatically vacant if the prime minister loses his seat at an election, or if parliament is dissolved; and if the prime minister goes out of office, all the other Ministers go out with him. The governor-general may dismiss a prime minister if he no longer commands a majority in the House of Representatives, and he may dismiss any Minister if the prime minister so advises. As we have mentioned on page 113, a Minister in Britain who is unlucky enough to lose his seat while his party is in power is given some latitude: he may continue in office for a time while he attempts to find another seat. This indefinite arrangement is made definite in the Nigerian constitution: a Minister may hold office without a seat in parliament for four months, but no longer.

The Council of Ministers, which consists of the prime minister and his other Ministers, is declared to be collectively responsible to parliament. The governor-general is bound always to act on the advice of the prime minister, except in the matter of dissolving parliament, when, as we have seen, he has some discretion left to him. There are two other cases mentioned in which, as it is impossible for him to obtain the advice of the prime minister, he may act on his own authority. The first is when he has to select a new prime minister: the second is when the prime minister is unable to give him any advice, either because he is absent or because he is too ill, and in consequence the governor-general has to appoint a temporary substitute. On paper, the governor-general's discretion is unlimited in these cases; in practice, he would be bound by convention to consult his senior Ministers at least. The constitution carefully provides that the question whether the governor-general has received any advice from the prime minister, or has acted upon it, 'shall not be enquired into in any court of law'. The prime minister is to keep the governor-general fully informed on public affairs.

Nigeria is thus equipped with cabinet government on the British plan. As in Britain, the prime minister has very great power as long as he keeps the loyalty of his colleagues and the support of the House. He is much more than 'the first among equals'; he is the head of the Government, and any Minister who cannot work loyally under him will have to go. We have described on pages 118-20 the strength of the prime minister's position in Britain; the prime minister of Nigeria is just as strong.

The remaining sections of the constitution need not occupy us long. Section Seven makes provision for the police, Section Eight for the judiciary. The chief justice is to be appointed by the governor-general on the Prime Minister's advice, other judges on the advice of the judicial service commission, which is similar to the judicial service commission in Ghana. Judges may be dismissed only for inability to do their work, or for misbehaviour, and for no other reason. There is no provision, as in Ghana, for an address by both Houses of the legislature. If a judge is thought to be unfit for his post, the Prime Minister will advise the governor-general to appoint a tribunal of lawyers and judges to gather the evidence. If the tribunal thinks that the evidence is sufficient to have the judge dismissed, it will recommend that all the evidence be sent to England, to the judicial committee of the privy council. It will then be for the Judicial Committee to recommend dismissal or not. We notice here the anxious care which the constitution takes to protect the judiciary from political interference. In the 1963 republican constitution, it naturally was felt inappropriate to refer such matters to England in this way, and the president was empowered to dismiss a judge if requested to do so by a resolution passed in each House of the federal parliament by a two-thirds majority. The Supreme Court, as in the United States, is the interpreter of the constitution, and remains so in 1963.

Section Nine lays down the way in which revenue is to be divided between the federal and the regional Governments; its details do not concern us here. Section Ten deals with the public service, and sets up a public service commission (like the one in Ghana) to advise the governor-general on the appointment, promotion, transfer, dismissal and discipline of public officers. The matter of the relationship between the public service (the civil service) and the Government is one which concerns all Governments, and is better dealt with in a separate chapter.

This 1960 constitution made Nigeria fully independent. All the five limitations on its independence were removed. It is true that the Queen was still Queen of Nigeria (as she is Queen of Canada, Australia and New Zealand, as well as of the United Kingdom); but she acted in Nigeria, through the governor-general, solely on the advice of her Nigerian Ministers. Her Ministers in Nigeria might give advice quite contrary to the wishes of her Ministers in Britain; but the Government in Britain had no power or influence whatever over Nigeria. In Nigeria, the Queen was bound to act as her Nigerian Ministers advised her, and in no other way. Three years later, the Nigerian Government chose to amend its constitution and declare the country a republic, replacing the governor-general by a president. But it did not thereby make Nigeria any more independent; Nigeria was completely independent already.[11]

SIERRA LEONE FROM 1956 TO 1961

The 1960 independence constitution for Nigeria has been closely followed in other countries. In Sierra Leone, the governor put forward proposals in 1957 for a further step towards independence, and these were the basis of the constitution of 1958.

The House of Representatives was improved. The ex-officio members were removed, and the elected members increased from 21 to 51: 14 from the Colony and 37 from the protectorate. The two nominated members remained. The House was presided over by a Speaker; he was not a member, and if elected as a member of the House he must vacate the Chair. He was elected by a two-thirds majority of the House.

The executive council consisted of the governor, who presided, and at least seven other Ministers, all of whom must be members

---

[11] It may be thought that it was a slight limitation on Nigerian independence that the advice of the Judicial Committee in London should be sought when it was a question of dismissing a judge. But it was not. The governor-general had to satisfy himself that the judge really was unfit. He had the advice of the legal tribunal, and it was an additional convenience to have this advice confirmed—or maybe rejected—by an expert body outside Nigeria altogether. If the rule of law is to be maintained, dismissing a judge is always a delicate and anxious matter, especially for his professional colleagues (the members of the legal tribunal) who have to make the recommendation. They would be relieved to have the backing of their professional colleagues in Britain: the more so as all Nigerian lawyers were members of the English Bar.

of the House of Representatives. The premier must be the leader of the majority party in the House; when a new premier was appointed, all ministerial posts automatically became vacant so that he might have a free hand in appointing his colleagues. The council was collectively responsible to the House of Representatives.

Under this constitution, the governor had some spheres of government reserved to him: defence, external affairs, internal security and police, and the public service. The 1958 constitution thus brought Sierra Leone to a position similar to that of Ghana in 1954.

Two years later, in 1960, the executive council was renamed the cabinet. Moreover, the governor was allowed to relax his control over the reserved spheres of government. It was laid down that

'The governor, acting in his discretion, may by directions in writing depute any Minister to exercise or to perform, on the governor's behalf but subject to his control, any power or duty relating to any subject referred to. . . .'

It is difficult to see the precise force of the phrase 'but subject to his control'. If the governor for example gives written authority to a Minister to control the police on his behalf, he at once creates the possibility that the Minister may do what he disapproves of. For if the Minister has to consult the governor before he takes any action, he has no authority; if he acts without consulting the governor, he may act—in the governor's view—unwisely. But he has acted under the governor's written authority, so the governor cannot disavow what he has done. Presumably the governor can withdraw his authority, but the damage has been done. It is an unsatisfactory state of affairs; it seems better either to withhold authority or to give it unreservedly.

In November of the same year, 1960, a public service commission and a judicial service commission were set up, on the same lines as those in Ghana and Nigeria.

Sierra Leone was now very nearly independent. There were no ex-officio members left in the legislature or in the executive, and only two nominated unofficial members in the House. There was a cabinet fully responsible to the legislature. The last remaining limitations were the governor's reserved powers and reserved spheres of government (which he could depute to a Minister if he chose), and the two remaining nominated members of the House of Representatives.

Sierra Leone independence, 1961
In 1961, these last limitations were removed, and Sierra Leone

became fully independent. Except that Sierra Leone is a unitary state, its independence constitution of 1961 is very similar to the Nigerian independence constitution of the year before. Being a unitary state, Sierra Leone needs no section of the constitution to define federal powers; and for some reason its constitution does not give a separate section to the police, as Nigeria's does. Otherwise, the eight sections of the Sierra Leone constitution follow the ten Nigerian sections exactly.

The first section deals with citizenship, defining who may and may not be a citizen of Sierra Leone. Then comes a long section on fundamental rights and freedoms: the same rights as those laid down for Nigeria, and expressed in much the same language. 'Every citizen is entitled to the fundamental rights and freedoms of the individual, whatever his race, tribe, place of origin, political opinions, colour, creed, or sex; but subject to respect for the rights and freedoms of others and for the public interest.' There is one interesting minor difference. It is provided in Sierra Leone that in time of public emergency a person may have to be arrested and held without trial, contrary to normal constitutional usage; but he is entitled to have his case reviewed every six months by a legal tribunal.

Section Three lays down the position and function of the governor-general and Section Four discusses the parliament. The House of Representatives is to consist of a Speaker and not less than sixty elected members,[12] who must be at least twenty-five years old and literate in English. Elections are to be by secret ballot. The Speaker is elected from among the members, or from among people qualified for election as members. (This seems a change from the 1958 constitution, which expressly said that the Speaker could not be a member; but it comes to the same thing, for in both constitutions it is laid down that if a man accepts the Speakership, he must give up his seat in the House, if he has one. In Britain, the Speaker of the House of Commons is also member for a constituency.) There is to be an electoral commission, as in Nigeria, to supervise the division of the country into constituencies of equal population, the registration of voters, and the conduct of elections. If there is a dispute over the validity of an election, it is to be decided by the Supreme Court. Expenditure may be proposed only by the Government. There is to be a session of parliament every year.

Parliament has power to amend the constitution. There is only one House, so there is no question of a resolution in two Houses, as in Nigeria. Some amendments can be made by a simple majority.

[12] Sierra Leone has given itself a House of 62 elected members, to whom it has added 12 paramount chiefs chosen by district councils.

But amendment on certain matters is made more difficult: a motion to amend the constitution on such matters must be passed by two different sessions of parliament, with a general election held between them, and by a two-thirds majority in each session. Examples of matters on which this difficult procedure is required are the whole section on fundamental human rights, the existence of parliament, the system of annual sessions, the existence of the paramount chiefs, the judiciary, and the public service commission. Thus, no amendment of the constitution would be needed if Sierra Leone wished to double the size of its House of Representatives, for the constitution lays down a minimum size, but not a maximum. If it wished to halve the size of the House, it would need to amend the constitution, but could do so by a simple majority. If it wished to make parliament meet only once in five years, instead of once a year, it would need to amend the constitution by the elaborate procedure laid down: a two-thirds majority, a general election, and another two-thirds majority in the new House.

The executive resembles the British and the Nigerian executives. The governor-general appoints as prime minister a member of the House who appears to him likely to command the support of a majority. The prime minister advises the governor-general on the appointment of Ministers, who must be members of the House. The governor-general may remove the prime minister from office if he has lost the support of the House, but in no other circumstances; he will remove a Minister on the prime minister's advice. A Minister will lose his office if he loses his seat in the House; he is not given any chance of staying in office for a time while trying to get re-elected, as in Britain (a short unspecified time) and Nigeria (four months, no more). The cabinet is collectively responsible to parliament. As in Nigeria, the prime minister is expressly made responsible for keeping the governor-general fully informed on public affairs. One minor point not mentioned in the Nigerian constitution is that the governor-general's powers of mercy to criminals and convicted persons are to be exercised on the advice of the prime minister, who is assisted by an advisory committee on this matter.

The constitutional provisions on the judiciary are the same as those in the Nigerian constitution of 1960. There is to be a judicial commission to advise the governor-general on the appointment of judges, other than the chief justice, who is appointed on the advice of the prime minister. The constitution provides that judges must retire at the age of sixty-five at the latest; but they are not to be dismissed unless a legal tribunal has investigated the case, and has forwarded the evidence to the Judicial Committee in London, and unless the Judicial Committee in London recommends the dismissal. This is exactly the system laid down in Nigeria in 1960, but abolished there in 1963.

The remaining two sections of the constitution deal with finance and with the public service. There is to be the usual public service commission. There must be proper estimates of revenue and expenditure to be laid before parliament; all revenue must be paid into a consolidated fund; expenditure must be made according to law.

One of the problems in the constitutional development of Sierra Leone has been the difference between the colony and the protectorate. The colony was for a long time much further advanced in education and wealth than the protectorate, and consequently further advanced also politically. In 1924, the qualification for a vote in Freetown was to be a British subject or a British protected person from the Sierra Leone protectorate, to be literate in English or Arabic, twenty-one years old, and resident in Freetown for at least twelve months; and to occupy a house worth £10 a year or to earn £100 a year. In the rural electoral district of the colony, the qualifications were the same, except that it was necessary to occupy a house of only £6 a year or to earn £60. There was no voting in the protectorate. To be qualified to sit as an elected member, you had to be at least twenty-five, to be a registered elector, and to possess £250 worth of property in Freetown, or £100 worth in the rural district. Public servants were not allowed to sit.

In July 1954, the governor appointed a special commission to examine the electoral systems all over the country, and to report on the question whether to extend the franchise[13] in the colony and to extend the colony's electoral system to the protectorate. The commission included members of both parties, the National Council of Sierra Leone and the Sierra Leone People's Party. The National Council was led by Dr Bankole Bright and the People's Party by Dr Margai. The S.L.P.P. had been in power since 1951, holding two seats in the colony and all the seats in the protectorate. As a result of the commission's recommendations, the franchise was greatly extended in 1957. All British subjects and protected persons from the protectorate were given the vote in the colony, provided they were twenty-one years old, had lived in the colony for six months and earned £60 a year or occupied a house worth £3 a year. In the protectorate, the vote was given to all male taxpayers of twenty-one, and to certain classes of women. But in 1960, universal adult suffrage was introduced in Freetown municipal elections—that is, all men and women could vote, provided they were twenty-

[13] The franchise is the right to vote.

one years old; and this was extended to the whole country by the independence constitution of 1961.

THE GAMBIA, 1960 TO 1963

The 1954 constitution left the Gambia still a long way from independence, and it was not until 1960 that the next step was taken. In that year the House of Representatives was enlarged, and the executive was given slightly more freedom from official control. The House of Representatives was made much more representative of the people. The four ex-officio members remained, but the one nominated official member was removed. In 1954 there were two nominated unofficial members, in 1960 there were to be not more than three. The fourteen elected members were increased to twenty-seven: five from Bathurst, two from Kombo St Mary, twelve elected from the protectorate, and eight elected by the protectorate head chiefs. The governor kept his reserved powers.

The changes in the executive council were only slight. There were still the same four ex-officio members, but the one nominated official member was removed. Whereas in 1954 there were to be not less than six 'appointed members', now there were to be not more than six. On the other hand, in 1954 not more than three of the appointed members were to be Ministers, but now not less than three of them were to be Ministers. And the restriction which the 1954 constitution placed upon the power of a Minister was now removed: the permanent official could no longer require the Minister to forward his advice to the governor. The permanent official henceforth in the Gambia, as everywhere else, must say to his Minister, 'Very well, sir; I have explained to you why I myself would recommend you to act differently. But you are responsible for policy, and I will do my best to make this policy of yours work successfully.'

In this same year 1960, a public service commission was set up in the Gambia, similar to those that existed elsewhere.

In 1961 a constitutional conference was held to discuss the next step forward, and in 1962 a new constitution was granted the Gambia, which made great changes.

The House of Representatives was enlarged from twenty-seven elected members to thirty-six: seven from the colony, twenty-five from the protectorate, and four elected by protectorate head chiefs. The four ex-officio members were reduced to one, the attorney-general, and instead of 'not more than three' nominated unofficial members there were to be 'not more than two'. These two, moreover, were to be nominated by the governor at his discretion, but after consultation with the premier. Here again, we see an opening left for the working of constitutional convention. It would be possible on paper for the governor to consult the premier, who recommends A and B as suitable candidates, but for the governor to ignore this and to appoint X and Y. But it would not be possible in practice. If the constitution is to work smoothly, there must be co-operation between governor and premier. All that the governor could do in practice, if the premier recommended A and B, would be to remonstrate: 'Do you really think they are the best men? I will appoint them if you are sure you want them, but I should have thought X and Y would be better.'

The usual provision was made that public expenditure could be proposed only by the Government. The governor was given the usual reserved powers.

The executive was to consist of the governor, the premier, and at least eight other Ministers. The premier must be one of the elected members of the House of Representatives, who can command a majority in the House; and all the Ministers too must be members of the House. All ex-officio members have vanished. This executive council (not yet called a cabinet) is collectively responsible to the House of Representatives. The governor is bound to act in consultation with the executive council normally. But he is still left some discretion: cabinet government is not yet complete. He may act on his own discretion in unimportant trifles: or if 'Her Majesty's service would sustain material prejudice'—that is to say, if he sees clearly that some important thing needs to be done, but cannot persuade his Ministers to realize how important it is—or if the matter is too urgent to wait while his Ministers, who see that something should be done, are not yet sure what. The governor retains the responsibility for defence, external affairs, internal security and police, and appointments and dismissals in the public service. A public service commission of the usual kind was set up to help him in this last matter.

The usual provision was made to ensure that judges should not be dismissed for political reasons. As in the 1960 Nigerian constitution, if a judge's conduct is called in question, a legal tribunal must be set up to review it; if the tribunal considers that the judge should be dismissed, it will recommend the governor to refer the evidence to the Judicial Committee of the Privy Council in London, and the judge will be dismissed only if the Judicial Committee so recommends.

This 1962 constitution was further modified in 1963. The executive council was replaced by a cabinet, to consist of the prime minister and not less than six other Ministers, all of them to be appointed from the members of the House of Representatives according to the traditional cabinet method: that is to say the prime minister must be able to command a majority in the House, and he himself will select the members of his cabinet for formal appointment by the governor.

The constitution lays down the circumstances in which the governor may dismiss the prime minister from office: all of them in accordance with British constitutional traditions. If the prime minister loses his majority as a result of a general election, the governor may dismiss him. If he suffers a vote of no confidence in the House which has hitherto supported him the position is not so simple. The normal British practice would be that the prime minister should either resign, or else ask the Queen to dissolve parliament, which she will nearly always do.[14] Under the Gambia constitution, the prime minister is given three days to make up his mind: if at the end of that time he has not resigned or advised a dissolution, the governor may dismiss him. And in the rare case we have mentioned, in which the governor refuses to dissolve parliament at the prime minister's request, the governor may dismiss him—though no doubt any self-respecting prime minister would resign the moment he heard that his request for dissolution had been refused, and would not wait to be dismissed.

The subjects of defence, external affairs, internal security and police were reserved to the governor. It was provided that if a Bill or a motion were introduced in the House of Representatives which seemed to the governor to touch on these subjects, he might notify the House, and the House must drop it: and on the other hand, if he thought a Bill or motion in the House was necessary, he was empowered to draft one, send it to the House, require it to be introduced, and declare it to be carried.

The constitution provided that the Minister of Finance must lay the annual estimates of revenue and expenditure before the House; and it provided that there must be a consolidated revenue fund and a fund for contingencies: in other words, it laid down the broad lines of financial administration which the Gambia must follow.

The other important change introduced by the 1963 constitution was that a long section was inserted on fundamental human rights. We need not summarize it in detail, for it follows fairly closely the similar sections in the constitutions of Nigeria and Sierra Leone.

---

[14] As we have said on page 199 in this chapter, it is possible to imagine circumstances in which the Queen would not be bound to grant the prime minister the dissolution he asks for. But they are very rare; in 99 cases out of 100, the Queen would accept the prime minister's advice and dissolve parliament.

All these rights and freedoms of the individual are to be enjoyed without any other limitation than that necessary for 'public safety, order, morality, and health', and for the protection of the similar rights and freedoms of others. Thus, if a Gambian citizen finds his house searched or his letters opened, his freedom to join a club or trade union restricted, or any other of his freedoms, he may call on the Government to show that this is being done to him only because 'reasonably required' for the public good. And the courts will decide.

This Gambian constitution of 1963 renders the Gambia completely self-governing in internal affairs (with the somewhat important exception of police) but leaves its external affairs still in the hands of the governor. It corresponds to the Nigerian constitution of 1959 and the Sierra Leone constitution of 1960.

POLITICAL PARTIES IN WEST AFRICA

It would be wrong to leave the subject of the West African struggle for independence without a word on the subject of the political parties who helped to bring it about. In the chapter on Party Systems, we pointed out that political parties in England are still less than 300 years old, and that both in Britain and in America, party allegiance changes from time to time. It sometimes happens that a party is formed to carry out a certain policy and fulfil certain aims, and that after a time it succeeds. When that happens, either the party must hold together and find a new aim, or it will break up, and its members will regroup themselves into fresh parties. All the political parties in West Africa arose as parties fighting for freedom from British colonial rule. They have attained that freedom, and it remains to be seen what will happen to them.

We have already mentioned the Aborigines Society in Ghana; this was not exactly a political party, but it fulfilled at least one of the functions of a political party, that of arousing and guiding political interest. Political parties in Ghana really began, shortly before the 1939 war, when Dr Danquah started his Gold Coast Youth Movement and afterwards his Gold Coast Convention. The Gold Coast Convention was the main party of opposition to the British, though there were one or two other small groups as well. There was a whole set of parties holding different views on the question of Togoland: for example, should the Ewe people in the Gold Coast and Togoland unite to form an independent Ewe state, or should Togoland be reconstituted as a unit, or should British Togoland join the Gold Coast? But these parties were all local;

they concerned the Ewe people and Togoland only, and not the Gold Coast as a whole.

The Convention People's Party began as a break-away movement from the Gold Coast Convention. Dr Nkrumah was secretary of the older party, and decided to form his own organization because he was dissatisfied with the slow and cautious methods of the Convention leaders. The great majority of the party members left Dr Danquah and joined Dr Nkrumah's new Convention People's Party. The basis of the new party was loyalty to Dr Nkrumah and a belief in his 'positive action' and other energetic methods of fighting for self-government.

As we have seen, the C.P.P. had rivals. Not only was there the small remainder of the Gold Coast Convention, but there was the Northern People's Party, and later on, the National Liberation Movement. And there were some other tiny groups as well. It was the N.L.M., in alliance with the Northern People's Party, which fought for a federal constitution, but was defeated. After independence, all these opposition parties joined together into the United Party under Dr Busia. But after a few years of independence, the Government made Ghana into a one-party state, and the United Party officially ceased to exist.

In Nigeria there were three main parties: the Action Group in the West, the National Council of Nigeria and the Cameroons in the East, and the Northern People's Congress in the North. Each of the three tried to become a national party; thus, there were Action Group minorities in East and North, N.C.N.C. minorities in West and North, and N.P.C. minorities in the two southern regions. It is plain that one element in the parties is tribal: the Action Group was Yoruba, the N.C.N.C. was Ibo, the N.P.C. was Hausa-Fulani. Another element is loyalty to a chosen leader: Mr Awolowo, Dr Azikiwe, the Sardauna. But a party needs more than a leader and a feeling of unity; it needs a policy. It is difficult to say how far the three parties in the Nigerian nation stand for three distinct policies. Old tribal quarrels, such as those between Ibadan and Ijebu-Ode, still have an influence in Nigerian politics.

In Sierra Leone, there are two main parties: the National Council of Sierra Leone and the Sierra Leone People's Party. The National Council draws its main strength from Freetown and what used to be the Colony, the People's Party from the Protectorate. Thus, in Sierra Leone, as in Nigeria, one element (and a strong one) in the party system is tribal or local loyalty.

Party politics, as we shall see in chapter fifteen, have entered local government in West Africa as well as the central Governments. In local government, they have come into matters with which they should have nothing to do; they have been largely matters of personal rivalries, and have often impeded the efficient conduct of local affairs. To check these hindrances, the Central Governments, as we shall see, have taken strong powers to control local authorities.

Political parties in West Africa are still young. They have just attained their great objective: independence for their country. It is too early to say whether they will succeed in finding fresh objectives which are important enough to justify them in continuing to exist in their present form.

Events in Ghana and Nigeria since 1963 show how uncertain is the position of political parties. In Ghana, the victorious C.P.P. refused to allow anyone to criticize the actions of President Nkrumah or his Government. It used its overwhelming majority in parliament to pass laws giving the Government power to arrest and imprison people without bringing any charge against them, and giving the president power to dismiss any judge without giving a reason. Such laws were plainly contrary to the rule of law; the people of Ghana were under arbitrary government. In 1966 the army rose up against this arbitrary government and suspended the constitution. The C.P.P. was dissolved, and no political parties were allowed under the military government. The C.P.P. had gone too far. Its members were entitled to express their support of president Nkrumah and his Government; but no party is entitled to refuse a hearing to its opponents.

In Nigeria too, the political parties were unwilling to discuss their differences peaceably. In the 1964 elections, there were many complaints that minority parties were forcibly prevented from holding their meetings. There was violence and bloodshed, and the result of the elections did not represent the real state of public feeling. The President himself said that tribalism was replacing patriotism. Each of the three parties was thinking mainly of how to get control of the federal government, for reasons of personal power and of 'pork' (see page 112). It all ended in revolution and civil war.

Let us not think that these troubles were caused by bad constitutions. Even a perfect constitution will not by itself ensure peace and good government. The oppressive laws in Ghana were passed in a perfectly constitutional manner; the Nigerian troubles happened because too many politicians put their party and their Region first and their country last.

CHAPTER XIV

Ghana and Nigeria Since Independence

Constitutional changes made by Ghana and Nigeria since 1957 and 1960 have not made them any more independent; they were already completely so.
Ghana: republican constitution of 1960. Emphasis laid on 'the people'. Increased power of executive, diminished power of legislature. Powers of the president: Presidential Elections Act and Presidential Affairs Act.
Nigeria: Constitution Amendment Acts of 1961 and 1962.
The Mid-Western Region Act; the Electoral Act; the Constitutional Referendum Act.
The republican constitution of 1963: position of president. President and parliament: relationship modified. Removal of judges from office.

THERE have been further constitutional changes in Ghana and Nigeria since they became independent. These two countries have used their independence to modify their constitutions; but it is important to realize that the changes they have made since 1957 and since 1960 have not made them any more independent. They were completely independent already. Canada, Australia and New Zealand could all declare themselves republics and elect presidents if they chose, and if they chose, they could leave the Commonwealth, as Burma and South Africa have done. But they choose to retain as the formal head of their state a governor-general appointed by the Queen to be her representative. They are completely independent, and they see no need for any change. India, Pakistan, Ghana and Nigeria, all of whom have chosen to adopt a republican form of government but to remain in the Commonwealth, no doubt have good reasons for preferring republicanism; but they are no *more* independent than the Commonwealth countries which prefer to retain the monarchy.

GHANA

The overwhelming majority which the Convention People's Party held in the parliament made amendment of the constitution easy. The hopes which the National Liberation Movement had of turning Ghana into a federal state were disappointed. The regional councils never became important. In 1958 an Act was passed which enabled constitutional amendments to be made by a simple majority of the parliament, instead of by a two-thirds majority as laid down in the 1957 constitution.

In 1960, Ghana adopted a new republican constitution, with Dr Nkrumah as its first president. Ghana is declared to be a sovereign unitary republic. The vote is given to all men and women of twenty-one years old and 'not disqualified by law on grounds of absence, infirmity of mind or criminality'. The constitution declares that,

'The powers of the state derive from the people, by whom certain of those powers are now conferred on the institutions established by this constitution, and who shall have the right to exercise the remainder of those powers, and to choose their representatives in the parliament now established. . . .'

The constitution is remarkable for its constant reference to 'the people'. Most of the articles of the constitution specify that they may be amended only by 'the people'—which means by a referendum, a special vote in which every elector is invited to answer Yes or No to the question, 'Shall this article be amended in the way that is proposed?' Parliament's power of constitutional amendment is strictly limited:

'The only power to alter the constitution . . . which is or may as aforesaid be conferred on parliament is a power to alter it by an Act expressed to be an Act amending the constitution and containing only provisions effecting the alteration thereof.'

And little is left for parliament to amend, when all power of amendment on the following is 'reserved to the people':

(a) abandoning republicanism or introducing federalism; (b) the presidential functions; (c) the presidential oath; (d) the cabinet; (e) composition and functions of parliament; (f) sessions and dissolution of parliament; (g) taxation and the public debt; (h) the judiciary; the establishment of courts and the appointment and dismissal of judges; (i) the armed forces; (j) the special powers granted to the first president.

The Supreme Court is given the power of scrutinizing legislation, to decide 'whether an enactment was made in excess of the powers conferred on parliament by or under the constitution'. But it is given no such power of scrutinizing the actions of the executive.

The new constitution leaves much of the machinery of government unchanged. The National Assembly consists, as it did in 1957, of 104 members, but there is one small change; it is to have 104 members at least, so is not limited to that figure, as it was in 1957. It is to have freedom of speech and of debate. The President may attend its meetings. Parliament must meet every year; the president may send it messages and deliver addresses, and each session must open with a presidential address on policy and close with a presidential address on the state of the nation. (Here we see a reflection of United States practice.) The president may dissolve parliament at any time, and must do after five years.

Compared with British and United States practice, the tendency of the Ghana constitution is to exalt the executive at the expense of the legislature. The annual estimates are to be laid before parliament, and 'submitted to the vote of the National Assembly, but no amendment of the estimates shall be moved.' The president may assent to a Bill, or assent only to part of it, or refuse his assent. The parliament has no such power as the United States Congress has to override the presidential veto. Even parliament's legislative functions are somewhat circumscribed: 'So much of the legislative power of the state as is not reserved by the constitution to the people is conferred on parliament. . . .'; but it is provided that the people may confer some of its own legislative power on parliament by a referendum. As parliaments go, the Ghana parliament under this constitution is not a very powerful body. It has no power of enforcing its wishes on the executive, not even by the power of the purse; for it cannot amend the estimates, it can only accept them or reject them as they stand. During the lifetime of Dr Nkrumah, Ghana's first president (who has been declared president for life), parliament's powers are still further restricted, for the constitution provides that President Nkrumah (but not his successors) may give directions by a legislative instrument, which may alter any enactment of parliament other than the constitution itself.

The executive consists of the president and his cabinet. Cabinet Ministers are appointed from among the members of parliament by the president, and it is the president who assigns them their departmental posts, and may revoke their appointment. There is no prime minister; the president in Ghana stands in the same relation to his Ministers as the Prime Minister does in Britain. The cabinet must consist of at least eight Ministers; the president of course presides. A Minister's post falls vacant if he is dismissed by the president, or loses his seat in the House ('otherwise than by reason of a dissolution'), or resigns, or if the presidency is vacant and a new president is ready to assume office.

Ghana has paid its first president, President Nkrumah, the compliment of electing him president for life. But normally, the president and the national assembly will be elected together for a five-year term; when the assembly is dissolved, the presidency falls vacant. When the general election is being held, parliamentary candidates must declare which candidate they will support for the presidency if they are returned to parliament. Thus, every general election is both an election of a new assembly and also the election of a new president. Every member of the new assembly is pledged, openly and publicly, to support Mr X or Mr Y for president. Thus, the new president is automatically assured of the support of a majority in the assembly. He is spared the embarrassment that the president of the United States often experiences when elections halfway through his term of office change the political complexion of congress, so that having begun his term with congress behind him, he now finds congress against him. The president of Ghana has no more fear of losing the support of the assembly than the British prime minister has of losing that of the Commons. It is a danger theoretically conceivable, but in practice not worth bothering about.

The president has great powers. The constitution expressly states,

'Except as may be otherwise provided by law, in the exercise of his functions the president shall act in his own discretion and shall not be obliged to follow advice tendered by any other person.'

Not even, it would seem, by the unanimous voice of his cabinet. But no doubt a constitutional convention would make it impossible in practice for the president to ignore all advice. He is commander-in-chief, and may dismiss any member of the armed forces; but he is not allowed to raise any armed force except under the authority of an Act of Parliament. On assuming office, the president is required by the constitution to make a 'solemn declaration' of eight clauses: (1) The powers of his Government spring from the will of the people, and should be exercised in accordance therewith; (2) Freedom and justice should be honoured and maintained; (3) The union of Africa is to be striven for and preserved; (4) Ghana's independence is not to be surrendered except to further the cause of African unity; (5) There is to be no discrimination in Ghana on account of sex, race, tribe, religion or political belief; (6) Chieftaincy in Ghana is to be guaranteed and preserved; (7) Every Ghanaian citizen should receive his fair share of his country's produce; (8)

Except when necessary to preserve public order, morality or health, no Ghanaian is to be deprived of his freedom of religion and speech, or of his right to move and assemble without hindrance, or of his right of access to the courts of law.

These constitutional provisions as to the presidential powers were elaborated by two Acts also passed in 1960, the Presidential Elections Act and the Presidential Affairs Act. A candidate for the presidency must be a Ghanaian of at least thirty-five years old, and must be nominated by a group of at least ten members of parliament. At the general election (the presidency having automatically fallen vacant by the dissolution of parliament), each candidate for a parliamentary seat must tell the Chief Justice that (a) he supports Mr A for the presidency, (b) that Mr A has accepted his support, and (c) that he believes Mr A will be supported by half the candidates. In this way, 'freak' candidates for the presidency (candidates supported by only tiny groups of members) will be squeezed out, and the presidential election will be a straight trial of strength between two candidates, each the head of a parliamentary party. It is provided that no action at law can be brought against the president.

In the great powers which the constitution gives him, the president of Ghana has a position like that of the United States president; in the close link between the presidency and the assembly, and in his relations with his cabinet, the president's position more resembles that of the British prime minister. Since no citizen can bring an action against him, and the Supreme Court apparently has no power of declaring any of his actions unconstitutional, the value of the president's 'solemn declaration' rests less on its legal enforceability than on his own conscience and his interpretation of the declaration.

The constitution does not provide for regional councils of the kind hoped for by the Opposition; but it does establish a House of Chiefs in each region of Ghana, to consist of such chiefs, and to have such functions relating to customary law and other matters, as may be provided by law. The constitution expressly recognizes customary law, along with the constitutions, Acts of Parliament and of the constituent assembly, previous statute law (dating from colonial times) and the common law, as making up the laws of Ghana.

Unlike the constitutions of the Gambia, Sierra Leone and Nigeria, the constitution of Ghana has no section on fundamental human rights. There is however, a reference to such rights in the president's solemn declaration, which mentions freedom of speech and religion, of movement and assembly, and of access to the courts of law.

NIGERIA

Nigeria became a republic in the autumn of 1963, but there had already been some constitutional changes before then.

There were two Constitution Amendment Acts: the first, in 1961, made the necessary arrangements as a result of the United Nations plebiscite, whereby the Northern Cameroons voted to join Nigeria and the Southern Cameroons voted to join the Cameroon Republic. The second Act, in 1962, made only one small change. Under the constitution, there was (as in other countries) an official called the Director of Public Prosecutions, who was responsible for deciding whether the Government should, or should not, prosecute a citizen. His office is important when facts are revealed in the course of a civil action which suggest that a crime has been committed. Under the constitution, the Director was independent of any control; he acted at his sole discretion. In 1962 this was changed, and he was made subordinate to the attorney-general, who was a member of the Government.

Three important Acts were passed in 1962. The Mid-Western Region Act took away the Benin and Delta provinces from the Western Region and set them up as a new Mid-Western Region. The preamble to the Act states that the proposal has been approved by a two-thirds majority in each of the two Houses of the federal legislature, and by a majority in the legislatures of the Northern, Western and Eastern Regions, both Houses consenting.

The two other important constitutional Acts of 1962 were the Electoral Act, which laid down the procedure to be followed in elections, and the Constitutional Referendum Act. This Act provides that the Government may invite the Nigerian people to approve or disapprove of a proposed law in a referendum. It lays down the general principles on which the referendum is to be conducted, empowering the Government to draw up detailed regulations. The vote is to be taken by secret ballot. If it is a party matter, and political parties wish to post observers to watch the voting, they may do so; but not more than two from each party are to be posted at each voting station and counting station. The only question to be put to the voters is, 'Do you agree that the—Act shall have effect?' This shows that the arguments for and against the proposal will have been thrashed out in parliamentary debate, so that the voters will have had every opportunity of making up their minds about it. The voters are not to be confused by several questions: there is to be only the one question, which can be answered by a straight Yes or No. And they are not to be intimidated by crowds of party representatives besetting the polling station; there are to be only two from each party.

The referendum is used in Australia; and, as we have seen, it is used also in Ghana when constitutional amendments are proposed. Australia and Ghana and Nigeria are the only Commonwealth countries which have adopted this method of ascertaining the people's wishes.

The republican constitution, 1963

Nigeria became a republic on September 19, 1963. The republican constitution keeps very closely to the 1960 independence constitution. Nigeria is declared to be a federal republic, consisting of four regions and the federal territory of Lagos. The sections of the constitution on amendment, on citizenship, and on fundamental rights are identical with those of 1960.

The governor-general of course is replaced by a president, who must be a Nigerian citizen of at least forty years old. The president is elected by secret ballot at a joint meeting of the two Houses of the federal parliament. If there is only one candidate, he is declared elected if a simple majority of the members vote for him. If there is a contested election, the procedure is more complicated. A two-thirds majority is required, and balloting will continue until the two-thirds majority is gained. If there are three candidates or more, and none is elected, the candidate with the fewest votes is eliminated, and balloting then proceeds until one candidate obtains his two-thirds majority and is elected.

The president is elected for a term of five years, and is eligible for re-election. He may be removed from office if a certain strict procedure is successfully carried through. First, one-quarter of the members of either of the Houses in the federal legislature may ask to have his conduct investigated. Then a joint session of the two Houses must be summoned, and a motion in support of the investigation must be carried by a two-thirds majority. Thirdly, a joint committee of investigation must meet, and after hearing the president in his defence must recommend that he should be removed. Lastly, their recommendation is laid before another joint session of the two Houses, and a motion to remove the president must be carried by a two-thirds majority. If the president's opponents fail on any one of these points, the president escapes. In other words, the president can be removed if his conduct has been so bad that two-thirds of the members of the federal legislature think he must go, and remain of that opinion for some weeks, if not months, while the process of investigation goes on. But no momentary irritation or fluctuation of party fortunes will touch him; he is above that.

And this is as it should be: it would be a very serious matter to remove the president from office.

The federal parliament is only slightly modified. The Senate is increased by the addition of the senators from the new Mid-Western region. The House of Representatives is increased from 305 members to 312. The president is given slightly less discretion in dissolving parliament than the governor-general had under the 1960 constitution. As we have seen on page 199, there were three cases in which the governor-general was given discretion to dissolve parliament or not, as he thought fit. The president is still allowed to refuse a dissolution if the Prime Minister requests it; but in the other two cases mentioned, he has no discretion: he *must* dissolve parliament.

The relationship between the federal and the regional Governments is unchanged: the exclusive and concurrent legislative lists remain as before.

The only other change is in the manner of removing judges from office. The legal tribunal appointed to investigate a judge's conduct under the 1960 constitution exists no longer, and there is no longer a reference to the judicial committee of the privy council in England. Nigerian judges may now be removed from office if a motion for dismissal is carried by a two-thirds majority in each House of the federal legislature.

THE REVOLUTIONS OF 1966

Both in Ghana and in Nigeria the independence constitutions were overthrown by revolutions early in 1966. In Ghana, the army rose up and overthrew the Nkrumah Government. The constitution was suspended and the country was placed under military government, but it was announced that a new constitution would be drawn up as soon as possible.

The trouble in Nigeria was mainly caused by the ill-feeling between the Ibo and the Hausa–Fulani. After several political murders and much bloodshed, political power came into the hands of the army and the constitution was suspended. General Gowon, who took over the federal government, thought that one main cause of the trouble was that the Northern Region was too big, and so had too much power in the federal government. He proposed a new constitution which divided Nigeria into twelve regions instead of four. In the East, Colonel Ojukwu refused to accept this, and declared the Eastern Region an independent country under the name of Biafra. The federal government thereupon made war on Biafra.

CHAPTER XV

The Organization of Government

A. *The Civil Service.*
Appointment by patronage replaced by competitive examination. The civil service is (i) permanent. Civil servants serve Governments of different political views; relationship between permanent civil servant and political Minister.
(ii) impartial; civil servants must not allow their own views to affect their professional conduct;
(iii) anonymous; civil servants must not expect to be given the credit when things go well, but they must not be given the blame when things go ill.

B. *Public Finance.*
A state must on the whole live within its income. Revenue: direct and indirect taxes. Taxes voted by the lower House of Parliament; no power of taxation given to executive.
Government estimates of revenue and expenditure: the Finance Bill and the Budget. The Budget's use as an economic tool. Treasury control of expenditure. Government audit.

C. *State Planning.*
Purpose of planning; difficulty of accumulating capital for development. Example of Russia. First object of planning is to increase national income. New manufacturing industries. Limits to sacrifices people will be willing to make. Foreign investment. Dangers in all planning.
Planning in Ghana: the five State planning bodies.
Planning in Nigeria: the eight fundamental principles.
Planning in Sierra Leone: part to be played by private enterprise.
Comparison of Sierra Leone, Ghana, Nigeria development plans: analysis of principles involved.

D. *Local Government and Chieftaincy.*
Need of local government: local government in West Africa before colonial times: position of chiefs.
Indirect rule in British Africa: failure of British to establish effective local government in colonial times.
Decay of local government in 19th-century Britain, and its reconstitution by modern legislation: advantages and weakness of British system. Local government in France and America.
British model followed in West Africa. 1951 Ordinance in Ghana, and the Local Government and Chieftaincy Acts of 1961. Northern Nigeria and Sierra Leone.
How the British model has been modified in West Africa: (i) strict

control by central Government; (ii) shortage of qualified staff. Relationship between councillors and officers.

We have now completed our survey of the constitutional laws of the four Commonwealth countries of West Africa. But laws do not make a government, any more than an architect's design makes a house: the paper design has to be carried out in building materials, and the laws have to be administered by officials. We may press the analogy further, and say that a well-designed house may be uninhabitable because it is so poorly built, and likewise a country with a good constitution and good laws may be an unhappy country because it is so poorly administered. In this chapter we discuss some of the general principles on which the four countries are administered, though we have no space to discuss each country separately in detail.

So far, these general principles are part of the heritage from colonial days. The British introduced into West Africa the principles on which they administered their own country. But since the problems of government are much the same the world over, similar principles are found in most civilized countries; only here and there do we see a distinctively British point of view.

THE CIVIL SERVICE

No Government can do its job without a good civil service; and in a parliamentary democracy, the relationship between the permanent civil service and the people's elected representatives is vitally important.

Centuries ago, when the functions of government were limited, the king himself was the executive; and the clerks and secretaries whom he appointed to help him with his office-work were his private and personal staff, paid (in theory) out of his private pocket. (In practice, what usually happened was that these early civil servants were all clergy, and instead of paying them from his private pocket, the king arranged to have them appointed to well-paid positions in the Church.) As the work expanded, and the staff increased so that the king could no longer know all his servants individually, a young man who wanted to join the service had to find someone who would speak for him to some great man or senior official, and ask as a favour that he should be appointed. This system of appointment by patronage lasted until well into the nineteenth century. It was not till 1855 that a beginning was made with entrance examinations, and it was not till 1870 that all public offices adopted the system of opening their ranks to any candidate, however poor and unknown, who passed their examination for entry. The enormous development of Government activities in the last hundred years would have been impossible without this reform in the service. 'Instead of social qualifications or wealthy friends, trained intellect was to be a young man's best passport.'[1] All this happened before the British came into West Africa, and they brought the civil service examination with them.

The civil service is (i) permanent

The abolition of patronage had another important result as well as increasing efficiency. It established the principle that the civil service was a permanent service. The young man no longer had to fear that the great man who had appointed him to please Lord P might quarrel with Lord P and appoint someone else in his place to please Lord Q: or that a change of Government might cause the great man himself to lose his post and bring in a new chief, who would bring in his own staff to replace those appointed under the previous Government. There had of course been some permanent officials before, men whose work was so good that the king refused to allow them to be displaced. But permanence now became characteristic of the whole service. A civil servant is sure of his post and of his pension unless he misbehaves. There is no such security in the business world.[2] There, a manager may find himself dismissed because his branch is not making big enough profits, or because the directors wish to reorganize the business.

(ii) impartial

One result of this security is that in the course of his career, a civil servant will serve many different Governments. Cabinets come and go, but the permanent civil servant sits in his office through them all. He is not the servant of this Minister or that, he is the servant of the Queen, or of the president. On the other hand, the Minister in office for the time being is the Queen's, or the president's representative. He is responsible for policy, and the policy which he advises the Queen to follow becomes her policy, which it is the duty of her servants to carry out. In fulfilling this duty, the civil servant must suppress any personal feeling or political opinion of his own. He may feel sure in his own mind that the Minister's policy is unwise, and will lead to disaster; but it is his duty to carry

[1] G. M. Trevelyan, *British History in the Nineteenth Century*.
[2] In some very large business firms there is a tendency nowadays to give their staff more security of tenure; but hardly as much as in the civil service.

it out with as much zeal as if he were enthusiastically in favour of it. A civil servant must keep his political views to himself, and not allow them to influence his official conduct.

On the other hand, the Minister, if he is wise, will listen to what his senior officials tell him. He may be a comparatively young man, new to public office; or having been Minister of Education in a previous Government, he may now find himself Minister of Agriculture, a subject new to him. His senior officials in the department may be a good deal older than he is, and they have been dealing with the subject for many years. As a newcomer, the Minister will find that departmental questions are not as simple as they may have seemed to him when he was an outsider making political speeches. He will learn the inside reasons for actions which he has condemned. He will be wise to spend some time in mastering the reasons for the old policy before he begins to introduce a new one; and when he does feel ready to make a move, he will be wise to consult his senior officials carefully before making any public pronouncement. For example, he may summon the head of the department and say, 'Our agriculture is inefficient because so many farms are very tiny, and one farmer has his land scattered in several strips among his neighbours' land. Could we not have a scheme for consolidating these small strips into larger units?' And he may receive this sort of reply: 'Yes, sir, we could do that. Fifteen years ago, when Mr X was Minister, we tried to work out a pilot scheme in one province. It was not very successful, for two main reasons. One was that at that time we did not have a very good community development organization, and we could not overcome the farmers' reluctance to make changes—you know what farmers are, sir! The other reason was that in one district, where we did have some success at first, we were unlucky in having a bad plague of locusts the next year; and everybody said, "See what comes of messing about with land boundaries; the gods don't like it!" But now that the community development organization has developed so much, we might try again; after all, we shall be very unlucky if we get locusts twice. You might like to see the papers about this pilot scheme, sir; I will have them sent to you.'

There we have a scheme which is good in itself, though not as new as the Minister thought it was, and not perhaps quite as easy either. But the Ministry officials will look up the past experience, and will work out a fresh scheme, which will probably have a fair amount of success—quite enough success anyway to enable the Minister and his party to claim great credit for themselves with the voters.

On the other hand, the Minister may propose something which

THE ORGANIZATION OF GOVERNMENT 225

his officials think is unwise, or even impossible. He may suggest breaking up large estates into small-holdings of twenty acres, so as to enable thousands of people who have no land to acquire a farm of their own. The permanent head of the department may say, 'Well, sir, I am all in favour of settling more people on the land. But in all your speeches you have been saying that we must increase the productivity of our agriculture, for our revenue depends on it. Now these large estates are very efficiently farmed; in fact, I think they produce eighty per cent of our export crops. It is certain, I think, that if they are broken up into small-holdings for subsistence farming, our national productivity will fall alarmingly. Of course, we could start a large-scale campaign of agricultural education among the small-holders, but it will be many years before it produces much effect. You want increased productivity, and you also want a programme of land settlement. But as things now are, I think you will have to choose; you cannot have both.' This shows clearly where the functions of the civil servant and of the politician meet. The civil servant has done his duty in pointing out the consequences of the political decision. But the decision itself is a political matter, which must be left to the Minister. The civil servant has said all he has a right to say; he must not go further and add, 'If I were in your place, sir, I would postpone the land settlement scheme.' That would be to enter on politics; and to the civil servant, politics is barred.

The Minister will make his choice (perhaps in consultation with his colleagues in the cabinet) according to his judgment of the political situation; and whatever his choice may be, the officials must do their best to make a success of it, even if they think it certain to fail. If the Minister produces a scheme which his officials think is quite crazy, it is their duty to warn him of the probable consequences. If he laughs at their warning, they may protect themselves by writing him a memorandum and keeping a copy in the file. But they must do their best to work his crazy scheme, all the same.

(iii) *anonymous*

Another feature of the civil service is that it is anonymous. Everyone knows that the detailed work of administration is done by the permanent officials, and no one will expect the Minister, when receiving congratulations on his success, to say modestly, 'I really think most of the credit must go to Mr Smith and Mr Jones of my department.' On the other hand, if the Minister takes the credit for success, he must also take the blame for failure. It is a well-established convention that a Minister who is defending himself against criticism must never say, 'It is not my fault; I received bad advice from Mr Smith in my department. He told me he thought it would work.' There are reasons for this. (a) The policy is the Minister's policy; if it succeeds, he takes the credit, so if it fails, he ought to take the blame. (b) If the Minister blames his officials in parliament, they have no defence; they cannot be there to speak for themselves. (c) If a Minister expects his staff to be loyal to him, he must be loyal to them. Loyalty works both ways. If a subordinate makes a mistake, his superior may reprimand him or punish him in private, but must take the blame himself in dealing with the outside world. No superior who is disloyal to his subordinates can expect that they will give him good service; it is not in human nature. In this special case of the Minister and the permanent officials, a Minister who publicly blames his officials for the failure of his policy will wreck his department in a very short time.

There are dangers of course in this system of permanent officials, safe in their anonymity and in the permanence of their posts. The chief danger is that they may get so absorbed in routine that they come to think office routine important in itself. A civil servant should remember that he is the servant of the public, not its master: and that the bundle of papers on his desk which to him is an unpleasant task, to be disposed of and pushed into his Out-tray, represents someone's hopes and anxieties. Both these are sometimes forgotten.

This system of the anonymous, impartial, permanent civil service is found in Britain and in many other countries. In the United States it has not yet completely replaced the old system, under which thousands of petty civil service posts were regarded as political. Every time a new party came to power, large numbers of sub-postmasters, customs officers, highway surveyors and other minor officials were dismissed, and a fresh set appointed who were members of the party now in power. But the needs of modern administration are causing this old-fashioned and inefficient system to give way to the system we have described.

PUBLIC FINANCE

It is impossible to discuss public finance in great detail without passing from the sphere of politics to that of economics. But there are certain broad principles which every administrator must know.

In its essentials, public finance is no different from private finance. A State, like an individual, must on the whole live within its income. It may over-spend this year and next year by drawing on its reserves, but it cannot do so indefinitely, for when the reserves are exhausted the State will be bankrupt. The Khedive Ismail of Egypt, the ruler who had the Suez Canal cut in 1869, is an example of a ruler who did not understand this. He did much for his country, but he spent money like water, and the time came when he had no more to spend. He borrowed as much as he could, and taxed his people as heavily as he could; he sold his Suez Canal shares, he mortgaged all the profits from the railways and the royal estates, and in the end he could not even pay the interest on the money he had borrowed.

A Government collects revenue by means of taxes. Taxes may be direct, like income tax or death duties, which everyone (or everyone except the very poorest) has to pay, since everyone earns some income, and everyone will die. Or they may be indirect taxes, such as duties on tobacco or gin or petrol or imported goods. Indirect taxes can be avoided; for you can go without these goods if you choose to live so austerely. Since nobody enjoys paying taxes, all countries have made it a rule that taxes have to be voted by parliament, not by the executive; and if parliament has two Houses, they must be voted by the lower House, that which is directly elected by the people. On the other hand, it is also a general rule that no private member of parliament may propose any expenditure of public money; all such proposals must be made by the Government.

The Government draws up its estimates of what money it will need in the coming years. This is a busy and anxious time in all Government departments. Each department has its own plans for development: a new school or hospital or power station or bridge and so forth, and of course all the time the recurrent expenditure on salaries and repairs and maintenance. It is usual to divide departmental estimates into two sections, capital (that is, the new items such as those we have mentioned) and recurrent expenditure. One of the points that the department has to bear in mind is that every item of capital expenditure this year will involve an increase in recurrent expenditure hereafter: thus, if you build a new school, you will always have to pay the salary bill for its staff and the necessary expenses for maintenance and repairs to the building, and for furniture and equipment. The head of the department will consult his officers in the field, and it is probable that when he adds up all the suggestions they have made, he will find the total is bigger than he can possibly hope that the Treasury will accept. If so, he just has to cut his estimates down to what they will accept. The Treasury has the task of co-ordinating all the departmental estimates and working out what revenue will be needed to meet them, and what taxation will be involved. Invariably, departmental officials complain at the parsimony of the Treasury. It is certainly frustrating to a conscientious head of department, who has already cut down his estimates to what he considers the bare essentials, when the Treasury notifies him that it has made a further arbitrary cut of twenty-five per cent. But the Treasury and the cabinet have to think of the general welfare of the country: is the national income rising? are exports balancing imports? can the people stand a five per cent increase in taxation, or a ten per cent? is it better to spend money this year on more schools, or on new factories? These are political and economic questions which the Minister of Education for example does not need to consider within his own department.

When the Government has settled how much money it is prepared to spend, the next question is, how is the money to be raised? It may all be raised by taxation—and if this means increasing the taxes, the Minister of Finance will have to consider how the increase can best be made. Or it may be raised partly by taxation and partly by borrowing. It used to be thought that a good Minister of Finance would always balance his budget; that is, raise all the money he needed by taxation, and borrow little or nothing. But in the last sixty years or so we have found that it depends on circumstances whether it is wise to balance the budget, or to have a surplus, or a deficit, and whether to raise all the money in taxation, or to borrow. The reason for this is that commercial prosperity seems to come in waves. For some years everyone will be busy, the factories producing goods, everyone eager to buy, prices high. Then for some reason (which we have not yet been able to analyse precisely) there comes a bad time: people are shy of buying, so the producers lower their prices; the factories find themselves with stocks of unsold goods, so they dismiss some of their workers. Thus there is unemployment and poverty and general unhappiness. Governments nowadays regard it as part of their job to try and moderate these fluctuations. When everyone is prosperous, that is the time to increase taxation; and the Government may think it wise to go further, and discourage business firms from heavy borrowing. It can do this by raising the rate of interest on bank loans. When the bad times come, the Government will try to restore public confidence and get the wheels moving again by reducing taxation and reducing the bank rate. These questions of high finance are really outside the scope of this book; we mention them briefly to show the sort of considerations which the Treasury has to keep in mind.

So the Government lays its estimates of expenditure and revenue before parliament, and a long and complicated Finance Bill is introduced to authorize the various items of expenditure. Each departmental estimate is scrutinized in turn, and this gives parliament its greatest opportunity of examining and criticizing every aspect of the Government's activity. The process may take several weeks, but there is some urgency about it, because until the Finance Bill has become law the Government is not strictly speaking entitled to collect taxes. In practice however, all parliaments have made standing arrangements so that such taxes as customs and excise duties continue to be collected. It would be intolerable if goods could be imported duty free for six weeks or so at the beginning of the year because parliament had not yet legalized the customs duty. The income tax authorities work out their calculations on the assumption that the finance bill will become law; in any case, they will not send out their demands for some months after the beginning of the year.

Normally speaking, Government financing is carried out a year at a time. Unless there is a long-term programme of development (we shall discuss this kind of state planning later), money voted by parliament for one year cannot be carried over to be spent in the next year. As every head of department knows, money which he has not spent at the end of the year has to be 'returned to the Treasury'. Nor without special permission can money which has been voted for one purpose be spent for another. The Minister of Education may find that he has under-estimated the amount he will need for repairs to school buildings, but that he has over-estimated the travel expenses of his inspectors. He may write to the Treasury and ask for permission to spend an extra £200 on repairing a leaky school roof and the damage which the water has done in the classrooms, and he will point out that he has £375 in hand through saving on travel expenses. The Treasury will almost certainly give him permission; but he will be in serious trouble if he acts without it. This may seem a trivial case. But it is an important principle that parliament votes money to be spent in certain ways. If it were once admitted that the Government could spend the money in any way it liked, there would be an end of parliamentary control of public finance.

Of course, it is impossible to estimate expenditure exactly. Parliament and the Treasury know this, and are reasonable. It may happen that the Ministry of Education places a large order for school equipment, costing say £15,000, which has to be imported from abroad. For reasons quite beyond the control of the Ministry —a shortage of raw materials, or a strike in the docks or in the factory or power station—the order may not be delivered till after the end of the financial year, and the bill come to hand well into next year. Nobody will make any difficulty over sanctioning this expenditure.

Every Government has an audit department, whose business is to go through the departmental accounts and satisfy itself that the money voted has been spent for the purposes authorized. The auditors will inspect all salary vouchers and pay-sheets, and compare the books of the department with the receipts and other papers which confirm that the money has been duly spent. It is another anxious time for the department, especially its accounts branch, as the audit staff sit there day after day ticking items with their green pencils and demanding explanations. The audit department lays its report on Government expenditure before parliament, usually before a Select Committee. It is the duty of the auditor-general to report to parliament any irregularity he has found. More than that: he will draw parliament's attention to any expenditure, even though duly authorized, which seems to him wasteful. Thus, he may report that this year the Ministry of Education has adopted a new set of English readers for the primary schools; this being so, it is a pity that the Ministry ordered fifty thousand copies of the old set only last year, which are now in its stores and will never be used. Or, the Ministry of Health has built a new hospital; when the building was half completed, the Ministry altered the design so that the building cost £100,000 more than the original estimate. It is no business of the auditor-general to say that the Ministry of Education does not need new readers, or that the Ministry of Health's new design for the hospital is wrong. But it is his business to point out that if the officials in the Ministries had looked ahead better, they might have achieved the same result for less expenditure.

When his departmental affairs are being discussed in parliament, in the light of the auditor-general's report, the Minister of course will be present to answer any comments that are made. If his Ministry is criticized, he must take the blame. When he goes back to his office, he will no doubt summon the head of the department and give him an unpleasant ten minutes; and the head of department will make it his business to look into the trouble and give the office a shake-up. The whole affair may result in an adverse comment being made on the confidential files of one or two officers who were mainly responsible; and this of course will affect their prospects of promotion.

This short discussion of public finance leads us straight into the question of state planning.

STATE PLANNING

A Government can do nothing without revenue, and it can have no revenue without taxation. But it can have no taxation unless its people have money in their pockets. There are still some parts of

THE ORGANIZATION OF GOVERNMENT 231

Africa where the people live by subsistence farming; they have very little property, and no money. From such people you cannot collect taxes. This is an extreme case today, for in the last fifty years most African countries have developed some export industries, and there is money flowing. But we all know that compared with highly industrialized countries like Britain, the United States, or Japan, Africa is still poor.

The Government of a poor country finds itself in a difficult position. If it could build roads and airfields, discover oil or minerals, and educate its people, it would raise the national income greatly, and would gain revenue for more projects. But it cannot make a beginning on this work without some money to start with. Since 1945, both directly and through the United Nations, the richer countries of the world have been helping the poorer countries, by lending or giving them material equipment and the services of trained people, and by training their own citizens in modern techniques. But every State wishes to make itself independent of such help as soon as it can. And so Governments draw up plans for using the outside help they are given in the most effective way, so that their national income may be increased and they may be able to raise revenue for further development from their own people.

Japan was probably the first country to plan its development; but the most famous example of State planning is Russia. When the Russian revolution took place in 1917, Russia was economically very backward: it was a very large country with an inadequate system of roads and railways, and very little manufacturing. The great majority of Russians were villagers living by subsistence farming. The revolutionary leaders were determined to make their country into a modern industrialized state. Like the poorer parts of Africa today, they started with the handicap of having very little machinery or equipment, and very few trained men. They decided that they must buy machinery from abroad, and employ foreigners to run it until their own people were trained. But how could they buy it without money? By terrible discipline, the Russian Government made its villagers hand over some of the food they produced on their farms. Large numbers of people in the villages died of starvation; but Russia was able to export wheat and butter and other foodstuffs, and gradually obtained the equipment and training it needed. Since those early days, Russia has had a series of five-year plans, laying the emphasis now on building up heavy industry, now on light industry, now on agriculture, as circumstances changed. Russia's example has been followed by India, and African Governments too now have their development plans.

We can discuss only the broad principles of State planning in this book; a detailed study would take us away from politics into economics.

It is a well-known saying that money breeds money: as a rich man once said, it was very hard for him to make his first ten thousand pounds, but the next ten thousand was easy, and after that, it was impossible to stop the money from coming in. So it is with nations. It is difficult for a Government to accumulate its first small revenue surplus. With skill and patience and discipline, the surplus will grow, until there comes a moment at which the national economy suddenly becomes self-supporting. The process has been compared to the beginning of a flight. The aeroplane begins to move slowly and heavily, moves faster and faster, and suddenly leaves the ground and becomes air-borne.

Skill, patience and discipline—all will be needed. Since the Government will not obtain revenue until its people have money to spare for taxation, the first object of its plan must be to increase the people's income. How that is to be done will depend on circumstances. Russia decided to make a start with heavy industry, with steel works, power stations, and so forth; and Russia's success after nearly sixty years of effort is influencing many other countries to follow the Russian example. But it is not certain that this was the best method even for Russia. If the first object of a plan is to increase the national income, it may be wise to begin by finding out what your country can produce and sell most easily, and to spend your first money on improving the quality and cutting down the cost of its product. If your people grow ground-nuts for example, but grow them only for food, you may perhaps find that the most effective first step you can take is to develop an export trade in ground-nuts: you may introduce improved varieties of the crop, build roads, manufacture sacks from sisal or some other locally-grown fibre, and grade your ground-nuts for overseas marketing. Money spent in this way will produce trade and prosperity—and so, revenue for the next steps in the plan—sooner than money spent on building a steel works.

It is natural that countries which have no manufacturing industries should wish to develop them. But certain things are needed if a factory is to succeed. It must have the raw materials at hand, or at any rate cheaply obtainable; it must have power to run its machinery, a reliable supply of labour, and a sure market for its product. Thus, it is good planning for Nigeria to establish a large ply-wood factory at Sapele. It has plenty of timber and of workers, and the new Nigerian oil-field will supply fuel for its power plant. Ply-wood is easily packed for export, and Europe and America will take all that Nigeria can spare. But it would not be wise for West

Africa yet to begin manufacturing its own railway locomotives, for West Africa's annual requirement of new locomotives would not justify the enormous cost of the factory and the imported steel and other materials. This may come some day, but other things must come first. The right manufactures to begin with are those which can undercut imported goods. Cigarettes, soap, cement are good examples, using locally produced tobacco, palm oil, and limestone, and all of them sure of a large home market. The planner must ask himself, How can I spend my limited money so as to produce the quickest increase in trade and prosperity?

Here we come again to a fundamental political fact: the planner is dealing with people, and in a free country there are limits to what the people will stand. The Russians were able to build their steel works and power stations because they had absolute control over their people. The Government was prepared to allow people to die of hunger, and the people were powerless. But a free parliamentary democracy could not impose such a cruel discipline on its people. The voters will discipline themselves up to a point for the sake of better times to come. But a wise politician will see to it that they do not have to wait too long before seeing the first fruits of their self-sacrifice.

The capital which is needed to build a bridge or a factory can be obtained only by saving up the profits made in some previous undertaking. Every well-run business puts aside some of its profits each year into a reserve fund, and it is this reserve fund which provides much of the new capital which the business needs for its expansion. A poor country can speed up its economic development if it can persuade foreign investors to bring their capital and skill into it. Africa will develop more quickly if it is prepared to welcome foreign investors, with the money which they have made in Europe or America. What happens in this case is that instead of staying at home and spending their money in employing European workers, the foreigners will spend their money in Africa in employing African workers. Foreign investors certainly hope to make a profit out of their business in Africa; if business men cannot make a profit, they close their business and go bankrupt. But African Governments and trade unions can lay down minimum wages and conditions of labour, and the companies' profits can be taxed. Governments can lay down other conditions: for example, that a company must train Africans to take its senior posts, or that a given proportion of the directors should be Africans. It should be easy for an African Government to prevent any exploitation or 'neo-colonialism'.

On the other hand, no foreign company is compelled to come to

Africa; and if foreign companies find conditions in Africa too difficult, they will stay away. If Africa wants their skill and capital, it must offer attractive terms. Ireland too is a poor country with few natural resources. For many years, the Irish Government has been successfully persuading foreign firms to settle in Ireland and establish businesses there. The foreign firms bring their capital, erect factories, bring over a few skilled workers on contract, and train Irish workers to take their places. The Irish Government promises them a number of years in which they will be free of tax. It can afford to do this because from the very beginning, the foreign firms pay wages to their Irish workers and so send money circulating through the country; the Government taxes the workers' incomes, and so makes new revenue. The Irish Government is happy to see employment and prosperity increasing, and thinks the price worth paying.

Countries which are already well developed also carry out some State planning. In Britain for example, a number of public utilities, originally established by commercial companies, have been nationalized: among them, coal, gas, electricity, railways, and car ds. Under national control, these services are being deliberately planned on a national basis so as to provide the best service to the country as a whole. The planning process sometimes causes uncomfortable readjustments, as when branch railway lines are closed, or when a quiet country village finds itself suddenly expanded into a busy commercial and industrial town.

These uncomfortable readjustments remind us of the danger involved in all State planning. State planning must always bring about some restrictions on individual freedom or convenience. I wish to build a factory here, but I am not allowed to, because the town-planning authority has laid down that this area is reserved for private housing. I wish to sell my cocoa to Messrs X and Co., who would pay me a much higher price than the official marketing board; but I am not allowed to, because the State has laid it down that all cocoa is to be sold through the marketing board, and part of the proceeds will be used for national development according to the national plan. I live ten miles from an important railway junction, and once or twice a year I go up to London, taking a slow train from my local railway station, and changing to the London express at the junction. But I shall no longer be able to do this, for in accordance with its plan for the railways, the Government is closing my branch railway line. Or, I have lived in a certain village all my life, and my fathers before me. But now I am told that we must move fifty miles and build a new village, for when the new dam is finished all this area will be under two hundred feet of water. Individuals are bound to suffer in such ways as these; they suffer in order that the community as a whole may benefit. The danger in such planning is that those drawing up the plan may become so enthusiastic over the hoped-for results that they forget the individuals who must suffer: they take no trouble to keep down individual suffering to a minimum, and they are so anxious to have as much money as possible available for the next stage of their plan that they spend as little as they can in compensating the sufferers for the inconvenience, and perhaps financial loss, which they must undergo.

This does not always happen, and no one would suggest that State planning should be avoided because of the fear that it may happen. But it is certainly a danger, which the planners and the public should guard against. The danger lies in human nature. My colleagues and I may have spent months of work in drawing up a plan, and when it is published there are loud protests. If we give way to the protests and admit that we have made a mistake, our work will be torn up and we shall have to start afresh. No one likes making such an admission. There is a great temptation for us to retort to the objectors, 'We have studied the subject and you have not: your objections are selfish and trifling: and anyway, the plan has been approved by the committee and cannot now be altered.' That is the danger which besets all planners. It can be avoided.

We can illustrate State planning from Sierra Leone, Ghana, and the Federal Government of Nigeria. We shall look at the plans in Sierra Leone and Nigeria; in Ghana, we shall look, not only at the plan itself, but also at the State planning organization.

Planning in Ghana

The Ghana Government has an elaborate organization for planning the country's economic development. Five bodies are concerned. They are the National Planning Commission, the State Planning Committee, the Budget Committee, the Foreign Exchange Committee and the State Management Committee.

The National Planning Commission is appointed by the President. It includes Ministers, and representatives of such bodies as the Trades Union Congress, agricultural, co-operative, and women's organizations. Under the Ghana system of the one-party state, many of these organizations are parts of the Party. It would seem that this Commission is primarily a party and a political body, whose function is to draw up the broad outlines of the plan without entering into much detail. This illustrates the fact that economic planning must have its political aspect. When presenting the seven-year plan to parliament in March 1964, President Nkrumah said,

'Ghana has chosen the socialist form of society as the objective of her social and economic development. This choice is based on the belief that only a socialist form of society can assure Ghana a rapid rate of economic progress without destroying that social justice, that freedom and equality, which is a central feature of Ghana's traditional way of life.'

Thus, Ghana's development plan must be designed to encourage the development of this socialist society; this is a political aspect, which it is the function of the National Planning Commission to consider.

The detailed economic planning is carried out by the next body, the State Planning Committee. The committee sits under the chairmanship of President Nkrumah. It includes the Ministers of Finance and of Foreign Affairs and the executive secretary of the ruling Convention People's Party. But then it includes professional economists and bankers: the Government's economic consultant, the deputy governor of the Bank of Ghana and the managing director of the Investment Bank, the Government statistician, the director of the School of Administration, a newspaper editor and others. Although the politics of planning is not neglected in this committee, the committee is much more of a professional body. Its duty is to work out the detailed measures needed to carry out the plan, and to give directions to Ministries, and State enterprises and others who have a share in the duty of carrying out the plan. The committee is responsible not merely for giving directions but for seeing that the directions are properly carried out.

The next planning body is the Budget Committee. The Minister of Finance is chairman of this committee, and its members are the deputy governor of the Bank of Ghana, the Government statistician, the executive secretary of the National Planning Commission, and two senior officials from the Ministries of Trade and of Finance. The chairman and two, if not three, of the members are members also of the State Planning Committee. The committee's duty is to consider Government expenditure from the point of view of the development plan. It has to consider what revenue the Government needs, how the revenue is to be spent, what taxes will be needed to raise it, and what economies the Government can make so as to leave money free for more necessary purposes. The committee has no power to take action on these matters; it can only make recommendations to the State Planning Committee. As we have seen in our discussion of public finance, the Government budget can be a very powerful tool for encouraging or discouraging development in one way or another. The Government is the biggest spender in the

THE ORGANIZATION OF GOVERNMENT 237

country, and the way in which it spends its money is bound to have a great effect on the country's economic pattern. If a country wishes to have a national development plan, the Government budget must clearly be designed so as to serve the purposes of the plan.

The Foreign Exchange Committee has a highly technical task to perform. Every country which needs to import goods from abroad has to face the problem of foreign exchange. If an American firm sells one of its machines to England, it requires to be paid for it; and it requires to be paid in dollars. It must be paid in dollars, because it has to pay its staff; and nothing but United States dollars will be any good to its staff when they come to pay their butcher and baker. Thus, some arrangements must exist whereby the British firm which buys the American machine can arrange payment in dollars. Such arrangements do exist. They are possible, because there is a rough sort of balance between British purchases from America and American purchases from Britain. Britain needs dollars to pay for her imports from America, and America needs pounds sterling to pay for her imports from Britain. (The balance is often not nearly as close as Britain would like it to be.) But if Britain wanted a great deal from America, and America wanted nothing from Britain, a difficult situation would result. Trade would come nearly to a standstill. There would be a great demand for American dollars, and very little demand for British pounds sterling; the value of the dollar would go up, and the value of the pound would go down. In the end, matters might adjust themselves; because the pound would become so cheap that all British goods would be very cheap for Americans to buy, so cheap that the Americans might begin to buy them again, and gradually trade might begin once more. But a great deal of discomfort and suffering would be caused before that happened. We have seen how this problem of the lack of foreign exchange hampered Russia when she began to develop her country, and how Russia obtained foreign exchange at great sacrifices, by exporting food which she really needed for her own people.

This is a short and over-simplified account of an extremely complicated subject; but it gives an idea of the work which the Foreign Exchange Committee of Ghana has to do. Ghana needs to import a great deal from overseas, and therefore needs large amounts of foreign exchange: dollars, pounds sterling, German marks, Russian roubles and so on. She can obtain this exchange by selling her cocoa and timber and diamonds and other products, but she cannot obtain as much as she needs. It is therefore important that Ghana should not waste foreign exchange by importing unnecessary goods—whether they are goods that could be produced in Ghana, or goods which cannot be produced in Ghana but are less necessary than some other goods. To take an extreme case: a Ghanaian lady might visit London and buy an expensive china tea-service, and a Ghanaian bank or business office might spend about the same amount of money in buying an electric typewriter or an adding machine. There is no doubt which of these foreign articles would help the national development more. The Foreign Exchange Committee has to survey the country's position in the matter of foreign exchange, draw up an annual budget of exports and imports, and make recommendations to the State Planning Committee. It may be that as a result of these recommendations, the Government may decide (as other Governments have done, including the British Government) to impose restrictions on the use of foreign exchange, such as forbidding its people to order goods from abroad without a Government licence.

The chairman of the Foreign Exchange Committee is the Governor of the Bank of Ghana, and its membership is much the same as that of the Budget Committee.

Lastly, there is the State Management Committee, which is concerned solely with the management of the various enterprises which the Ghana Government itself runs, such as the State Mining Corporation and the Ghana Housing Corporation. These corporations are not Government departments, but are owned or financed by the Government. The Management Committee is responsible for fixing their annual programmes and seeing that their work is done efficiently and profitably, and in accordance with the State plan.

Planning in Nigeria

State planning in Nigeria is carried out by the National Economic Council, which was established in colonial days. The Prime Minister is chairman, and the regional premiers too sit on the council. Sierra Leone has a Minister of Development.

Nigeria's development plan for 1962-68 is drawn up with eight considerations in mind. (i) The country must have a plentiful supply of cheap electricity; the Niger Dams project will help to supply this, and, like the Volta Dam in Ghana, will help agriculture, fisheries, and internal navigation. (ii) Agriculture must be developed, and there must be research into the country's natural resources. (iii) The Government must encourage industry; two important steps here are to establish a Development Bank, and to develop a steel industry. (iv) Technical, secondary and higher education must be further developed. (v) Transport and communications must be extended. (vi) The Federal Territory of Lagos must be improved, especially as regards housing, sewerage, and traffic. (vii) Defence

THE ORGANIZATION OF GOVERNMENT   239

and internal security services must be strengthened. (viii) Investment outside these fields must be restrained, so that as much money as possible may be available for these important schemes. The total capital cost of the plan is estimated at £412.5 million.

Planning in Sierra Leone

The Sierra Leone plan for 1962-71 is estimated to cost £125 million. The Sierra Leone Government hopes to find a good part of the money from its own resources, especially from its mineral wealth. But much will come from outside the country: from international sources of investment such as the World Bank, the International Development Agency and the International Finance Corporation, and from private overseas capital. The Government says,

'Private enterprise will be encouraged to play a large role in the development of the country, and opportunities (will be) provided in trade and industry for our citizens, in partnership with foreign enterprises in all cases where this is possible. It is also the policy of Government to encourage private foreign enterprise to provide opportunities for participation by indigenous entrepreneurs and investors, as well as for the training of local personnel at all levels and stages of business activity.'

The three plans compared

It is difficult to compare the development plans of the three countries in detail, for they are not set out in the same way, and they do not all use the same headings. Ghana for example groups industry and mining together under one heading, and agriculture, forestry and fisheries together under another. Nigeria groups mining along with agriculture, forestry and fisheries under the heading of *Primary Production,* and separates it from trade and industry. Again, we have to remember that the three countries differ greatly in size and wealth, and are at different stages of their development. Nigeria is so much bigger than the other two, that it is much more expensive to provide her with roads and electricity, and these two items are bound to take a bigger proportion of the development plan. In the Nigerian plan, 3.9% is to be spent on agriculture, whereas Sierra Leone will spend 7.7% and Ghana 14.3%. This does not mean that Nigeria thinks agriculture less important than the other two countries, but that in Nigeria's circumstances, other things (notably electricity) must come first. This short comparative table must therefore be read with caution. The figures given are the percentages of the capital expenditure allotted to the various items.

	Sierra Leone 1962-71	Ghana 1963-69	Nigeria 1962-68
Primary production, plus trade and industry	16.8	37.3	15.7
Transport and communications	21.0	11.3	32.4
Electricity	11.1	9.8 (including the Volta scheme)	23.8
Water	1.9	5.1	0.4
Education	10.5	13.5	11.7
Health	21.4	6.5	2.5
Social Welfare	1.6	2.2	0.7

The table is not complete, but it includes over 84% of the Sierra Leone plan, and still more of the Ghana and Nigeria plans. Sierra Leone is exceptional in spending over one-fifth of its money on health. Apart from this, it is noticeable how large a share of the development plans is taken by the headings of primary production, trade and industry, transport and communications, and electricity: nearly 49% in Sierra Leone, 58% in Ghana, and nearly 72% in Nigeria—and the Nigerian figure would be higher still if we added the expenditure of the regional Governments on roads. Education still takes a moderate share. Trained and educated men and women are essential for a nation's development; and although all three countries are fairly well supplied with primary schools, there is still much to be done in extending secondary, technical and higher education, which is the most expensive part of education in buildings and equipment.

These three national development plans illustrate some of the general principles which we discussed at the opening of this section. The first object of all the plans is to increase the people's income. Ghana says,

'The economy must be developed rapidly and efficiently so that it shall within the shortest time possible assure a high rate of productivity and a high standard of living for each citizen based on gainful employment.'

Nigeria says much the same thing in different words:

'Over four-fifths of the population of Nigeria depend on, and more than half of its gross national product is derived from agriculture, forestry, livestock and fisheries. The expansion and modernization of agriculture and related production is of crucial importance to the development of the Nigerian economy. The proceeds from export products will determine to a large extent the volume of imports which can be made available for economic development in other sectors; the efficient expansion of domestic food production will determine not only whether the Nigerian people will eat better, but also whether they can effectively reduce dependence on imported foodstuffs; the increased productivity of agriculture will determine whether the income of the great majority of the people can be effectively raised, and this will in turn determine the size of the domestic market for the new industries which are expected to spring up.'

Sierra Leone warns its people,

'Because it has been prepared on the basis of the overall needs of the entire country, the plan should not be expected to provide a programme for every area or locality within the country. The aim rather has been to prepare it in such a way that the country as a whole will derive the maximum benefit.'

The plans concentrate on developing easy communications, electrical power, and manufactures which can use local materials. Manufacturing industry is impossible without some source of power, and hydro-electric schemes are a good means of providing the power for industry. The faster and more easily manufactured goods can be distributed, the cheaper they will be. The Nigerian plan includes the beginnings of a steel industry, which will use local iron, limestone, and coal, and will produce a great part of the galvanized iron sheeting and reinforcing rods for structural work which Nigeria at present has to import. It will be noticed that this piece of planning satisfies the requirements we mentioned: there is a demand for the product, the materials are available locally, the power supply will be available—and moreover, the locally produced steel will make it unnecessary to import so much from abroad.

LOCAL GOVERNMENT AND CHIEFTAINCY

Every State has been formed by the grouping together of many local units, and each citizen has local loyalties as well as his national loyalty. Thus, a man may feel loyalty in the first place to his family group; then to his town of Bekwai; then to the state of Ashanti (of which Bekwai is one division); and lastly to his nation of Ghana. He stands, so to speak, at the centre of a number of concentric circles of loyalty. So it is all over the world.

Every State makes use of its citizens' local loyalties. It is impossible for the central Government to control every detail of local administration. It would be absurd, for example, if the Regional Government at Kaduna were to spend time over the details of drainage and street lighting and car parks in Kano. Such local matters are much better left to the Kano people themselves. In Britain and America, and other countries which have based their organization on British or American experience, local government is run by locally elected councils. So it is in many other countries which have their own independent traditions. France has a more centralized system; the central Government appoints the prefect who administers each department, and there are sub-prefects under him. But even in France, prefects and sub-prefects, and the mayors of towns and villages, have locally elected councils to assist them.

Before colonial times, West Africa had its own system of local government. Family heads met together in village councils or clan councils; and where there were larger units, the heads of village councils met together in higher councils. The system is seen at its most complete in such a state as Ashanti, where the 'concentric circles' of loyalty might be, first the family council, then the village council, then the sub-divisional council, then the divisional council (such as Bekwai), and lastly the great council of all Ashanti, with the Asantehene at its head. A great deal of power had to be left to the lower chiefs and their councils. Even in the great civilized states such as old Ghana, Mali, and Songhai, centralized government such as we have today would have been impossible. There were differences of language and of custom, and communications were slow; local authorities had to carry a great deal of responsibility if the state was to hold together at all.

The chiefs were an essential element in the system. A tribe or a village was held together not only by economic and social links—such as living and farming together—but by spiritual or religious links. There was a strong religious element in the chieftaincy; the chief was the link between the living people and the spirits of their ancestors, and he performed many duties (such as making sacrifices and libations) which were essentially those of a priest. Similar conceptions are found in other parts of the world. The kings of England, for instance, were thought to have magical or miraculous powers of healing a certain disease by touch, and as late as the reign of Queen Anne (1702-1714), people were regularly brought to be cured by the touch of the royal hand. Since the chief in Africa and his people were linked in this spiritual way, it was difficult to fit strangers into the system. This may be one reason why strangers tended to live in settlements of their own outside the town, ruled by a chief of their own.

In those days, local government was a personal affair. An Oyo man obeyed his Alafin because of the personal links between them. But when the Europeans came, and trade began to develop, and people began to move up and down the country, this old personal government was no longer adequate. The Europeans introduced a new idea, the idea of territorial government. If the Oyo man came to Accra, there were no such links between him and the Manche as between him and his Alafin at home. But all the same, the Oyo man found that there were local regulations which everyone in Accra had to obey. If he wished to ride a bicycle in Accra, he had to pay a licence fee to the town council and fasten a licence plate to his machine. This conflict between personal and territorial authority, between the personal rule of the chief over his tribesmen and the territorial authority of the town council over everybody who came within its geographical limits, caused a good deal of friction in colonial times. The colonial Governments tried to improve the municipal governments and give them more power, but the chiefs and their elders were afraid that an elected mayor at the head of a strong town council would overshadow their own authority. And since the colonial Governments always tried, as a matter of principle, to work through the chiefs as much as they could, they did not like to force through such a measure against the chiefs' opposition.[3]

This British idea of working through the chiefs and their councils is called indirect rule. It was introduced by Lord Lugard in Nigeria, and soon became the accepted principle of all British colonial government in Africa. There were two parts of the doctrine of indirect rule. The first part was that colonial government would be much more effective and acceptable if the people's natural rulers agreed with what the Government proposed, made its proposals their own, and handed them on to the people with the backing of their own authority. The second part of the doctrine was that the chiefs and their councils must be taught modern ideas, so that they could develop into efficient organs of local administration.

The system of indirect rule was only partly successful. The British administrators were fairly successful in the first part: they refrained from giving orders, and gave advice, which was sometimes taken

[3] The French did not pay nearly as much attention to the chiefs as the British did; we are speaking here of British West Africa.

and sometimes ignored. But, although there grew up a number of 'native administration' hospitals and schools and road-making activities, it cannot be said that the British had much success in the second part of the doctrine. For one thing, few young educated men were admitted to the traditional councils, which kept to their custom of admitting old men and the holders of certain traditional offices. For another thing, few native administrations were able to attract the services of efficient technical staff. Young African clerks, accountants, doctors or engineers usually preferred to make their career in the service of the central Government, not in that of local governments.

Thus, the British never succeeded in setting up an efficient system of local government in West Africa, and when internal self-government was attained, this problem still remained to be solved.

Local government in England itself had fallen into such decay and confusion by the nineteenth century that an entirely new system had to be created by legislation. The old tribal units out of which England was formed had long ceased to have any meaning. Many towns had councils of a very un-representative kind. Local government in the rural areas was carried on by a strange jumble of bodies. Some of them, like the justices of the peace, had added various executive functions to their original judicial duties; others had been created for certain specific purposes, such as maintaining roads, providing water supplies, and administering poor relief. Acts passed in 1888 and 1894 brought some order into this chaos, and set up a system in which the highest unit of local government was the county council. Below the county council there were urban or rural district councils, and below them there were parish councils. By an earlier Act, in 1835, the old-fashioned town councils were reorganized and made much more representative. Local government as we have it in England today is thus a new thing, created by a series of nineteenth-century Acts of Parliament with little or no regard to the relics of what had formerly been. In our own day, the enormous growth of London and some other places is leading us to set up still larger local government units.

This English system is sometimes described as 'three-tier'; it is not a very good name, but it is so commonly used that it is as well to mention it. We speak of the tiers of seats in a theatre or stadium. In England we have the three-tier system of county council, rural district council, and parish council. This is in rural areas. In urban areas there are usually only two tiers; the urban district council works as one unit, and has no parish councils below it. Certain large and important towns in England have the full status of counties in their own right; for them, there is a one-tier system.

THE ORGANIZATION OF GOVERNMENT 245

Local government authorities in England derive their powers from an Act of Parliament. Whatever their size and importance, they are all organized on similar lines. Each has an elected council, which employs professional staff to carry out its functions. The full council sets up a series of committees, each with one separate function, such as the education committee, the health committee, and other committees for highways, housing, libraries and museums, parks, and so on. The committees meet frequently (sometimes as often as once a week) to settle policy and to give decisions on matters referred to them by their specialist officers. Their reports are considered by the whole council, which may accept them or refer them back for reconsideration.

The system has the great advantage that it gives people a very real degree of control over their local affairs. But in modern times it has one great disadvantage. Since the Act of 1894, the functions of local government have increased so much that the councils have far more work to do than was contemplated at that time; and the burden on local councillors is very heavy, and becomes constantly heavier. Councillors are not paid for their services, and indeed it was only in 1948 that they were for the first time allowed to claim out-of-pocket expenses. Many men and women who would make admirable councillors cannot afford to give the necessary time to the work.

This British system is not the only possible way of providing for local government. In France, there is much more control from Paris. The Government appoints its own administrative officers, the prefects and sub-prefects; they make a good many of the decisions, and carry out a good many of the duties, which in England belong to the elected councils. There are in France town councils and other elected local bodies, but they have not nearly the same status as their counterparts in England. There is no official in England corresponding to the French prefect. There is a Ministry of Local Government in London, but its function is to supervise and co-ordinate the work of local government authorities, not to do their work for them.

In the United States, there are different types of local government organization. Some cities govern themselves by a mayor and council much as in England, though the differences between the American and the British traditions of government bring about differences in the ways in which these systems work. The mayor in England is merely the chairman of the council; he holds office only for one year and has no special powers. The American mayor is the city's chief executive, with great powers; his relation to the council is much like that of the president to the Congress, and he holds office for several years.

The work of the city council has increased very greatly in America, as it has in England. Many American cities have decided that it is too much to expect busy men to run the affairs of the city in their spare time, and they have abandoned the system of an elected council. Some of them elect a small board of commissioners, each of whom is responsible for supervising the work of one or more of the city's administrative departments. Some cities go further, and elect a small group of councillors whose main duty is to appoint a permanent full-time city manager, who will hold office as long as his work gives satisfaction.

Local government in Ghana

In the Commonwealth countries of West Africa, the British system of local government has been followed. One of the first actions of the Nkrumah Government in Ghana was to pass the Local Government Ordinance of 1951, six years before independence. There was at that time very little true local government in Ghana. The district commissioners were agents of the central Government, responsible for carrying out the central Government's policy. What local government there was lay in the hands of the 'native authorities', which the British Government had been trying, without very much success, to modernize; the four largest cities had elected councils, whose relationship with the traditional authorities was uneasy and ill defined.

The Coussey commission had reported that Ghana needed a modern system of local government, and had drawn up detailed proposals. It thought that the traditional tribal authorities still had a part to play in local government, and recommended that they should be strongly represented in the new local councils. The Ordinance of 1951 was based on the Coussey proposals, though it did not follow them word for word. It divided the country into thirty-seven districts, each with a district council, and 243 urban or local councils. The Coussey committee had contemplated a three-tier system, with a few still smaller units; but no smaller units were set up by the Ordinance. One-third of all the members of the 243 lesser councils (14 urban and 229 local councils) were to be nominated by the traditional tribal authorities; the other two-thirds were to be elected. All rate-payers of twenty-one years old or more were entitled to vote. The members of the thirty-seven district councils (which correspond roughly to the English county councils) were not to be directly elected; they would be members of the lesser councils, sent up to represent their views. The Coussey committee

THE ORGANIZATION OF GOVERNMENT 247

had proposed that the district councils also should have some of their members directly elected; but this proposal was not adopted.

This system was a compromise between the needs of modern local government and the desire to retain the traditional chieftaincy. It gave the tribal authorities work to do, and prevented them from becoming purely formal and ceremonial bodies. On the other hand, it gave young men and strangers a full share in the government of their locality.

The Ordinance of 1951 however was not completely successful. The relationship between the traditional and the elected councillors was not always happy. Many traditional elders who sat on the councils found it distasteful to be out-voted by the young men, and they found it difficult to take an active interest in much of the up-to-date work which the councils were doing. After ten years, the Government decided that the Ordinance must be drastically amended, and in 1961 it passed two laws, the Local Government Act and the Chieftaincy Act, which revolutionized the whole system.

The Local Government Act of 1961 abolished the two-tier system of district and local councils. It provided that the Minister of Local Government might create a local government authority by an Instrument, which would define the powers of the new council. The whole of Ghana, outside the big towns, was divided into sixty-nine districts, each with its council; thus, the average size and population was much greater than those of the 243 lesser councils established by the Ordinance of 1951. All the members of the council are elected; there are no members nominated by the traditional authorities. It is true that the paramount chief of a district may be nominated as president of a council, but his functions are purely honorary and ceremonial. For business purposes, the council elects a chairman and a vice-chairman from among its members. The members hold office for three years, and the full council must meet at least four times a year. The Act adopts the British system of committees. Every council must appoint three committees: one on finance and staff, one on education, and one on development. The council must appoint these committees, and it may, if it chooses, appoint others. All members of the finance and staff committee must be members of the council, but only two-thirds of the members of the other committees need be councillors; the remaining third may (if the council chooses) be invited from outside the council.

The Act lists 108 duties that may be entrusted to a council, and it will be for the Minister to decide how many of these he will entrust to each council when drawing up the Instrument which creates it and authorizes it to begin work. His discretion is not unlimited. There is a list of duties which every city or municipal council *must* carry out: among them, paving and lighting the streets providing drains and sewers, a fire brigade, and a bus service, controlling traffic and providing car parks, supervising markets and general hygiene, controlling public entertainments and registering births, marriages and deaths. There is another list of duties which *may* be entrusted to a council, such as building schools, hospitals, markets, libraries and museums, providing police, parks, musical concerts, allotments of land for gardening, and making regulations to control hunting and the keeping of livestock, and to control building and town planning. All these are for city or municipal councils; local councils have less extensive powers and duties, but they have in general the duty of maintaining order and good government within their boundaries. The Minister has extensive powers of supervising the work of the councils. If he thinks that a council has failed in its duty, he may direct it to do something that it has neglected to do; and in extreme cases he may take away from a council some function which it is not fulfilling satisfactorily, and entrust it to some other body or individual. He has even the power to suspend or dissolve a council altogether and entrust all its functions to someone else.

This Local Government Act, as we have said, removed from the councils the representatives of the traditional authorities, the chiefs and elders. The Chieftaincy Act, also of 1961, regularized the system of chieftaincy and the relationship between the traditional authorities and the Government. It classified chiefs in four grades and defined their powers. The Act finally abandoned the effort, which had been begun by the British, to modernize the traditional authorities and develop them into efficient local government bodies. Modern functions were transferred to the councils established under the Local Government Act, and the traditional authorities were limited to their traditional functions. Even here they were closely supervised: the Government was empowered to make regulations for the destoolment of chiefs, to withdraw recognition from a chief whose conduct was unsatisfactory, to prohibit him from continuing to act as chief, and to exclude him from a given area and make him reside in exile. The Act also set up a House of Chiefs in each of the eight regions of Ghana. (It must be remembered that Ghana is a unitary state, not a federation; not only is a region in Ghana much smaller than a region in Nigeria, but it has nothing like the same degree of independence; it is an administrative unit of the central Government.)

A local government authority in Ghana draws its revenue from various sources. It collects some in licence fees; in fines imposed for certain offences; in rents obtained by letting public buildings or by building houses for letting to tenants; in receipts from public utilities, such as bus fares; in grants from Government funds; and in rates. A rate is a local tax levied by a local authority; it is based on the value of the house or land which a person occupies. The property is valued by an official valuer as worth so much a year: that is, it would bring in that amount in rent. This official annual value is called the assessment or rateable value. The total value of all the assessments on a council's district is called the district's total rateable value. Let us assume that I live in a house assessed at £100, and that the district's total rateable value is £250,000. The council estimates its expenditure for the coming year at £156,250. This sum works out at five-eighths of the total rateable value, and this fraction is expressed as so many shillings and pence in the pound: in this case, twelve shillings and sixpence. The council then levies a rate of 12s 6d in the pound, and everyone pays accordingly; my share will be a hundred times 12s 6d. Shops, factories, farms and agricultural land, cinemas and all other kinds of occupied land and buildings are rated, as well as dwelling-houses.

One of the duties which are compulsory upon every city and municipal council in Ghana is to contribute from its revenue to the traditional authority. This continues the system of the 1951 Ordinance, which took away from the traditional authorities the management of their lands, but provided that the revenues should be paid over to them by the local government councils.

The system of raising local revenue by rates on property is much criticized. It is said that it may have been all very well long ago to assume that the house a man lived in was a fair indication of his income; but it is not so today. The central Government in England tries to ease the burden of rates on poor districts, by making richer districts contribute something to their poorer neighbours; and sometimes too it makes grants from central revenue. In West Africa, Government grants to local authorities are extremely important, for rateable values in many places are so low. But critics of the rating system say that a system which needs to be patched up like this is a poor system: it would be fairer to base local taxation, like central taxation, on income. It has been suggested that the central Government should collect its revenue from income tax, customs and excise duties, and all the rest; and should then allot to each local authority, as accurately as it can, a share of the revenue in proportion to what the district has contributed. But this would still leave the problem that the poorer the district, the more it would need but the less it would get. Some kind of equalization grant would still be needed.

Local government in Nigeria and Sierra Leone

It is difficult to generalize over such a huge area as West Africa; but the general principles of local government which we have been describing in Ghana apply too in the three southerly regions of Nigeria, though of course with local modifications. In Northern Nigeria and in Sierra Leone, the position is somewhat different. In Northern Nigeria there is a great variety of political organization, from the large and efficiently organized emirates like Kano or Katsina down to small tribes on the plateau whose political organization is of the simplest kind. The Northern Region made no attempt to set up a uniform system of local government all over its area. It has used different types of local authority according to the conditions of each locality. The traditional authorities play a great part, and in many places it is a most valuable part, because many of the emirates had an efficient system of taxation before the British came into the North, and village headmen were accustomed to act as local officers of the emir. This organization has been preserved. Since 1963, every authority must include some members who are elected by the people, and the tendency is for the elected element to grow in strength.

In Sierra Leone also, local government today preserves much more of the traditional organization than in Ghana or southern Nigeria. The unit of local government in Sierra Leone, outside the municipalities, is the chiefdom or native authority. As we have seen on page 172, in 1946 a district council was set up in each of the twelve districts, and in 1954 the district councils were reorganized and given greater powers. The chiefdoms are subordinate to the district councils, and have to provide the district councils with revenue. The chiefdoms levy local taxation. A chief in Sierra Leone is chosen by his people in the traditional way, but he has responsibilities to the Government which make him in fact a sort of civil servant or local government official. In each province there is a resident Minister who has to supervise the work of the chiefs in local government.

There is one striking difference between local government in Sierra Leone and elsewhere. In Ghana and Nigeria, the powers of local government authorities are strictly defined; in Ghana for example there is a list of 108 functions which may, if the Minister sees fit, be entrusted to a council, and it is clear that he may not entrust to it any power not included in the list. In Sierra Leone, on the other hand, the chiefs and the district councils are made generally responsible for development and welfare and good government, so that there is no legal restriction on their powers. No legal restriction, though there may be an administrative restriction: the

THE ORGANIZATION OF GOVERNMENT 251

resident Minister may refuse to sanction a scheme which he thinks unwise or beyond the council's powers.

Local authorities and the central government

In all three countries, the central Government keeps a strict control over the work of the local authorities, much stricter than in Britain. The chief control which the Government in Britain exercises over the local authorities is a financial one: it audits their accounts. The auditor is responsible for seeing, not only that the account-books tally with the receipts and vouchers, but that the authority has spent its money in accordance with its legal powers. He has a special power of control: if he finds that a council has authorized expenditure which is in excess of its powers, he can surcharge the members—that is, he can make them repay the money out of their own pockets. It is not a matter of overspending, but of unlawful spending. Many councils, for example, provide an official car for the use of their mayor or chairman. The auditor will examine the car's log-book to make sure that it has been used only for official purposes, and will surcharge the chairman if he finds that the chairman has been using the car for his private pleasure.

In addition to this financial control, the central Government in Britain supervises certain parts of the work of local authorities by a system of inspection. The local authorities are mainly responsible for the schools, and they have their own school inspectors; but the central Government also inspects the schools. There is a somewhat similar system of inspection in certain matters, such as police and fire brigades, in which it is important that standards of efficiency should be uniform all over the country. But the Government in Britain would not dream of inspecting the paving and lighting of streets and the public libraries; it limits itself to inspecting matters in which uniform standards are desirable and public money from central funds is being spent. It can afford to let other matters alone because the general level not only of councillors but (perhaps more important) of their professional staff is high. A well qualified librarian, for example, is a member of his professional association, and knows well what a good public library should be. He hopes to make a successful career and end as chief librarian in a big city like Manchester, or in a university. We can be sure that if he is librarian in a small town, he will be constantly pressing the library committee of his council to expand and improve its services.

But things are different in West Africa. Professional men are scarce, and so are experienced and competent members of council. The Governments have found by experience that they cannot leave the local authorities as much alone as the Government can in

Britain. At first they did leave them alone; but the result was so much muddle and inefficiency and corruption that they were forced to introduce strict controls. It is usual to find that local estimates of revenue and expenditure must be approved by the Ministry: all contracts (except very small ones) must also be approved: and very often too the Ministry requires to have proposed appointments to the staff submitted for its approval. These controls are not welcomed; but they have been found necessary. They will no doubt be relaxed in future, as the standards of local administration rise; in fact, certain councils in Western Nigeria whose record is good are already being allowed somewhat more freedom by the Regional Government.

In devising a workable system of local government, there are two opposite dangers to avoid. If you make the units too large, you will lose the interest and support of many of the voters; the local government will seem to them almost as remote as the national government. On the other hand, if you make the units too small, you will discourage competent officers from seeking employment with them. Local government, like national government, needs its civil servants; and local government servants want interesting and important work, and prospects of promotion. If a man has been successful as town clerk of a small town, he will begin to look for a vacant post as town clerk of a big town. Thus, in deciding on the size of your local government units, you must consider also what powers you will give them. It would be unwise, for example, to allow the council of a small town to control its education, for no competent educationist would apply for the post of director of six schools with a total of two thousand children. If a man wants to go in for educational administration at all, he will want something bigger than that. Likewise, a doctor will be happy in charge of his own hospital, for he will balance his administrative work with the personal contact with the patients and the chance of doing some medical or surgical work. If you remove him from this personal contact, and turn him into nothing but an administrator, you must give him something to compensate for what he has lost. It is not a question of money, it is a question of interest. You must make him feel that his administrative work is helping many other doctors and matrons and nurses, and through them, large numbers of patients. In other words, if you want to secure the services of a good medical administrator, you must give him enough hospitals to make the job worth his while. And this means that he must serve a large local government authority, not a small one.

As we have seen earlier in this chapter, another feature of the civil service is that it is impartial. A civil servant wants to be left alone to get on with his job, no matter which political party is in power. This is just as true in local government as in national government. A great deal—perhaps most—of the routine work of local authorities is quite unpolitical in character. Streets have to be paved, swept, and lighted; markets have to be inspected; schools have to be built, repaired, equipped and taught; the engineers in the waterworks and the power station, the doctors and nurses in the hospital, have to be at their posts and doing their duty: and their work is the same, whether the local authority they serve supports the People's Party or the National Council, the N.C.N.C. or the Action Group. It is for this reason that in the United States, one of the most highly political countries in the world, so much of the work of local government has been taken out of politics and entrusted to professional administrators, whose job is safe as long as they do their work properly. Even when different parties do have different views on policy, it is the civil service tradition that a man should loyally carry out the council's policy, even if he himself dislikes it. If local government in West Africa is to be a success, local government officials must be allowed to do their work without interference on political grounds. There has in the past been trouble over this: capable men have been dismissed merely because they did not support the majority party in the council. To prevent this, some of the Governments have brought in control over local government service. The Western Region of Nigeria has created a unified local government service, and may transfer an officer from one authority to another as it thinks best. In the Eastern Region, the Government took power in 1955 to control all appointments and dismissals of local government staff; and three years later it took power to transfer staff from one local authority to another. Ghana has not gone quite as far as this; but the Local Government Act of 1961 gives the Government power to lay down staff regulations covering all the conditions of local government service; and the Government has power also to second one of its own civil servants to the service of a local authority.

In making these arrangements, the Governments are trying to ensure that men and women who wish to make their career in local government service shall be free from the fear that they may be hindered in their work, or even dismissed from it, because of political quarrels with which their work is not concerned. One of the reasons why local government did not develop successfully in colonial days was that educated people kept away from it, and preferred to make their career in the service of the central Government. If it is to develop successfully now, a career in local government service must be made attractive.

254 GOVERNMENT IN WEST AFRICA

The countries of West Africa are in a state of rapid development. In this chapter on the civil service, public finance, state planning and local government, we have not attempted to describe the present state of development which each country has attained. That would have been a very long and detailed description, which would have been out of date before the book was published. We have discussed the general principles which affect all these four branches of government organization, and will continue to affect them, however fast and far development may proceed.

ADDENDUM

In line 3 of page 214 it is stated that the regional councils or regional assemblies, to which the National Liberation Movement in Ghana attached such importance (see page 186) never became important. This is the reason. They were established; but for political reasons the Opposition boycotted the elections, so that the councils had an overwhelming majority of C.P.P. members. The general tendency of the C.P.P. was towards a centralized Government, so the regional councils never obtained the importance as spokesmen of local feeling which the Opposition had hoped they would obtain. In this respect, the regional Houses of Chiefs were more successful; but their powers were limited. The regional councils were swept away in 1960; at least, they are not mentioned in the 1960 republican constitution, whereas the Houses of Chiefs are mentioned and given a place.

As we have said on pages 167 and 188, Nigeria was formally divided in 1951 into three regions. This arrangement has been much critized; for the Northern region was much bigger than the others, and was predominant in the federal House of Representatives. This was one reason for the outbreak of civil war; and this is why the federal leader General Gowon proposed to divide Nigeria into twelve regions (or 'states') instead of four.

In 1951, the British authorities in Nigeria foresaw the dangers of making the North too powerful, and would have liked to divide the North into smaller regions. Rightly or wrongly however, they judged that it was politically impossible to do this: that the North would never accept the idea, and there would be very serious trouble. So they reluctantly allowed the North to remain as one region; and they hoped that Nigerian statesmen both in the South and in the North would see the danger, and would work well together to avoid it and to develop one Nigerian nation.

CHAPTER XVI

Liberia

Origins of Liberia: The American Colonization Society, and the constitution of 1820.
The constitution of 1824 and the Plan of Civil Government.
The draft of 1839 and the constitution based upon it. Weakness of the 1839 constitution: (i) no provision for amendment, (ii) limit set to powers of treaty-making, (iii) governor's unrestricted right of veto.
The independence constitution of 1847.
The relations with the peoples of the interior: local government in coastal districts and inland. The regulations of 1923 and 1936. Position of chiefs: President Barclay's unification policy. Comparison between Liberian and British colonial policy in dealing with indigenous peoples.

IN our discussions of the four Commonwealth countries of West Africa, the influence of British constitutional ideas has been plain. It is only in certain features of the constitution of Ghana that we can see any American influence. When we come to Liberia, however, we find ourselves in a country which has taken most of its ideas from America: as, in view of its history, it was natural that it should do.

Liberia began in much the same way as Sierra Leone, as a settlement for freed slaves on land bought for the purpose from the African peoples. It was in 1787 that the British Government sent out the first party to Sierra Leone, and in 1808 that Sierra Leone became a British colony. The settlement of Liberia came a little later. In 1816 a society was formed in the United States, called the American Colonization Society, to settle freed slaves in Africa; and after an unlucky start on Sherbro Island, the society made its first successful settlement at Monrovia in 1821. In 1824, the country was named Liberia ('the land of the free'), and its town Monrovia, after the United States President Monroe.

The American Colonization Society drew up an outline constitution for the new settlement in 1820. It was a purely colonial constitution: the ultimate power or sovereignty was reserved to the Society, though it is plain from the second article that the Society was contemplating the possibility of some day granting the settlement its freedom. The constitution had eight articles: (1) All the settlers were to be free; (2) As long as the Society kept its Agents in Africa, the Society was empowered to make rules for governing the settlements; (3) the Society's Agents in Africa were to form a Board of Government, with all judicial powers except those delegated to justices of the peace; (4) the Agents had power to appoint subordinate officers; (5) there was to be no slavery; (6) the common law of the United States was to apply; (7) all adult settlers must swear to support the constitution; (8) in an emergency, the Agents were empowered to make new rules, subject to the Society's approval.

There could hardly be a simpler constitution than this; and it is to be noted that no provision was made for amending it. It is not surprising that three years later, the Society's Agent in Liberia submitted a revised constitution, with an appendix containing what he called a Plan of Civil Government. For practical purposes, we may regard the revised constitution of 1824 and the Plan as being one document. The Rev. Jehudi Ashmun, the Society's Agent, was tactful in presenting the two documents separately and in treating the Plan as merely an elaboration and explanation of Article Four of the constitution, under which he was empowered to appoint subordinate officers.

The revised constitution followed the 1820 constitution closely. It repeated the eight articles, in the same order, but added two new ones. The new article 9 made it clear that any United States officers were not limited by the Liberian constitution; the settlement was receiving much help at the time from officers of the United States navy. Article Ten provided that amendments to the constitution could be made either by the unanimous vote of the Managers of the Society in Washington at one meeting, or by a two-thirds majority at two successive meetings.

The Plan of Civil Government was worked out in some detail. The Agent (the Society called him the Agent; we should call him nowadays the Governor, and this term was adopted in 1839) was to have sovereign power in Africa, subject to the Society in America. He was to be assisted by a vice-agent, whom he would appoint every year from a list of three names submitted to him by the settlers. The settlers would also elect two members of council, and the Agent had power to approve or reject their nomination. (It is to be presumed that the settlers would hold only one election, and that the three men elected would compose the council, one of them being appointed vice-agent.) Nothing was said as to what would happen if the Agent rejected a nomination. The judiciary would

LIBERIA   257

consists of the Agent and two justices of the peace, whom he would appoint.

There was to be a two-men committee of agriculture, and a three-men committee of public works; these were to be elected annually and approved by the Agent. There was to be a similar committee of health, though its size was not laid down. The militia was to be governed by a committee composed of its commanding officer (a captain) and two lieutenants; these officers were elected by the men but confirmed and commissioned by the Agent. Again, nothing was said about the possibility of the Agent's rejecting a nomination.

There followed a list of officers whom the Agent proposed to appoint at his own discretion, with no election; they range from a colonial secretary down to a court crier.

This constitution was not altogether agreeable to the Society in Washington. 'The Board,' they said, 'think it much too complicated and intricate for the simplicity of a few settlers. The Government in the present state of the colony should be as simple as possible. We wish the settlement to be founded in republican simplicity and Christian plainness. All unnecessary offices and dignities and official titles ought to be avoided.' But they agreed to sanction it as a personal experiment by the Rev. Jehudi Ashmun; and a year later, in May 1825, they finally approved it.

After 1824, the legislative activity of the Council in Liberia increased, and the Society had less and less to do. There were other settlements along the coast besides Monrovia; by 1838 these were all joined into one Commonwealth of Liberia, except for the county of Maryland, which did not join Liberia until 1857. Now that the area of Liberia had been so much extended, and its population was scattered in several settlements some distance apart, it seemed that the 1824 constitution would need amendment; for one thing, a Council of three was clearly inadequate for the needs of the new Commonwealth.

In 1839 a convention was held in Monrovia to consider proposals for amending the constitution. The delegates thought that it would be better to scrap the 1824 constitution altogether and draw up a new one. They drew up a draft, which they submitted to the Society; and the Society granted the new Commonwealth a constitution based largely upon this Monrovia draft, though differing from it in some respects. We shall set out the 1839 constitution as granted, and indicate the main points where it differed from the Monrovia draft.

All colonies and settlements (except Maryland) were united in one Commonwealth of Liberia. The legislative power was placed in the Governor and Council, subject to the supreme authority of the Society. (The constitution was still a colonial one.) The Council

I

was to be elected in proportion to the population: to begin with, four of the counties were to be represented by six members and four others by four; the Governor was to apportion the members. (This council of ten was an improvement on the Monrovia draft, which suggested a council of only six members.) The members were to be privileged. The Governor was to preside over the council, and had the power of vetoing its acts. The Governor and council were empowered to declare war (in self-defence only), to make treaties (with the African tribes only), to control the militia and regulate naturalization. This was a slight restriction on the Monrovia draft, which suggested that any Negro arriving in Liberia should automatically become a citizen if he swore to support the constitution; this would give the Governor no discretion in the matter. But it probably made no difference in practice.

The Governor held the executive power; he was commander-in-chief, controlled all land and property of the Society, and appointed all officers whose method of appointment was not otherwise provided for by the constitution. He was assisted by a lieutenant-governor, who was elected.

The judiciary was to consist of a Supreme Court and other courts; the criminal laws already in force were to continue, and a code of law would be drawn up. The Governor was to be ex-officio Chief Justice. Here we see a startling departure from United States practice, and also from the Monrovia draft, which provided for the separation of powers.

There was to be no slavery or slave-trading. Elections were to be by ballot, and all men of twenty-one were to have the vote. No one was to be denied access to the courts; all citizens were entitled to petition the Government, and were entitled to trial by jury. (This short section on human rights was shorter than that in the Monrovia draft.) The military were to be subject to the civil power. United States standards of weight, measure and money were to be used.

This 1839 constitution had certain weaknesses. It contained no provision for amendment. The Government was given no power to declare war except in self-defence, and this was an embarrassing limitation; for it is not easy to say how much provocation is needed before a Government can claim to be acting only in self-defence. Again, the Government's power of making treaties was limited to the local African tribes, and even with them the power was subject to the approval of the Society in Washington. But Liberia needed to make treaties with her neighbours, the British in Sierra Leone and the other European powers who might later on establish themselves on the West Coast.

At the first meeting of the new Council, a member objected to the Governor's right of veto. In the Monrovia draft there had been no Governor's veto, and in the American constitution, the President's veto could be overruled by a two-thirds majority of the Congress. The Governor transmitted this objection to Washington, and in 1840 the Society agreed to amend the constitution in this respect: a two-thirds majority of the Council could override the Governor's veto.

The independence constitution of 1847

It was in 1846 that the American Colonization Society agreed to hand over to the people of Liberia the control it had hitherto exercised. In July 1847 the people issued their declaration of independence, and in August, their independence was recognized by Britain. The independence constitution of 1847 is clearly adapted from that of the United States; though Liberia is a unitary, not a federal state, and so its constitution is simpler.

After a short preamble, the constitution opens with a Bill of Rights. In so doing, it profits by American experience: the United States constitution was originally drafted without a Bill of Rights, but there was so much demand for one, that a series of amendments was adopted less than four years after the constitution itself had come into force. As we have seen, the Monrovia delegates had included a Bill of Rights in their draft, but it was shortened in the constitution which the Society granted them.

Article One of the Liberian constitution contains twenty sections. Men are born free and in the possession of certain natural rights. Power belongs to the people, and the people can change their forms of government. There is to be freedom of religion, freedom of assembly and petition, freedom of speech and of the press. There is to be no slavery or slave-trading. Justice is to be available to all without delay, and trial by jury is guaranteed. Every one who is accused of a crime is to have a copy of the charge, and the usual facilities for obtaining witnesses in his favour and examining the witnesses against him. No one may be compelled to give evidence against himself, and no one may be tried twice for the same offence. Excessive bail, fines, and punishment are forbidden. There is to be no arbitrary arrest or search, and private property is not to be confiscated without compensation. No taxes may be levied without the consent of the legislature. Elections are to be by ballot and every adult man has the right to vote. The people have a right to bear arms, and the army is not to be maintained without the consent of the legislature. The privilege of habeas corpus is available to all. The Republic may be sued.

Section fourteen of this article expresses in the most uncompromising way the doctrine of the separation of powers. It divides the powers of government into legislative, executive, and judicial, and provides that, 'No person belonging to one of these departments shall exercise any of the powers belonging to either of the others.' An exception is made of justices of the peace; they are left free to use other powers besides their primary judicial powers. Justices of the peace in Liberia, as in Britain, are useful for miscellaneous minor duties.

Article Two deals with the legislature, which is to consist of a Senate and a House of Representatives. The Senate consists of two members from each of the five counties, elected for a six-year term. The House of Representatives is elected on a population basis. The constitution provides that to begin with, there should be eight members, divided between three counties. Any county subsequently admitted (there are now five in all) should have one representative to begin with. Each town of ten thousand people should have one representative, and an additional member should be given to a county for every additional ten thousand people. On this basis, the House now has thirty-nine members, elected to represent the five counties, four territories, and three provinces into which Liberia is divided. Thirteen of the members represent the tribal peoples of the interior. Representatives are elected for four years; it was originally two years, but this was amended in 1908. At the same time, the Senators' term was extended from four years to six.

The President may approve or reject a Bill. If he rejects it, he must state his objections within five days, and if he neglects to do so, the Bill becomes law without his signature. His objections may be overridden by a two-thirds majority in each House. There is an exception to the five-day rule: if the legislature adjourns before the time expires, the Bill dies. All this is similar to the United States procedure, save that the American president has ten days instead of five. Sometimes the legislature avoids a direct clash with the president by adjourning before the time is up, so that the Bill dies. This can happen in Liberia too.

Article Three deals with the executive. The president is commander-in-chief; he makes treaties, though his treaties must be ratified by two-thirds of the Senate; he appoints all public officers; he is responsible for enforcing the law; he must inform the legislature of 'the condition of the Republic'; he has the power of pardoning offenders. As in the United States, he may recommend the legislature to take certain measures, but cannot compel them to heed his recommendation. 'On extraordinary occasions', as in the United States, he may summon the legislature, and may adjourn it if the two Houses cannot agree when to adjourn. As in the United States, the Senate's approval is needed for the appointment of senior public officers such as the secretary of state.

The 1847 constitution provided that the president should be elected for two years, and nothing was said about re-elections. Presidents often were re-elected, and Presidents Roberts, Benson and Johnson held office for eight years each. In 1908 the constitution was amended to give the president a four-year term, and in 1935 it was again amended to extend the term to eight years. The proviso was then made that the president should not serve two consecutive terms, but this proviso has since been removed by yet another amendment. The president is now elected for eight years, and may be re-elected for any number of terms of four years only. The president is directly elected by the people; there is no indirect election as in the United States.

The vice-president is similarly elected at the same time. He presides over the Senate, with a casting vote. The constitution lays down the chief duties of the secretary of state and the secretary of the treasury. In 1847 it was provided that all public officers should hold office either for two years or 'during the pleasure of the president'. This system was clearly unsuited to modern needs, and in 1935 a new provision was added to the constitution. The legislature was authorized to establish a permanent civil service, and the constitutional limitation of 'two years, or during the pleasure of the president' was not to apply to it. There is thus a clear distinction between the permanent civil service and ministerial or other temporary posts.

Article Four deals with the judiciary. In the 1847 constitution it consisted of only two sections. There is to be a Supreme Court, but the legislature may establish other courts. Judges are to hold office during good behaviour, and may be removed at the request of two-thirds of both Houses of the legislature. They are forbidden to take any fees or payment apart from their official salary. In certain types of cases the Supreme Court is to have original jurisdiction, and in certain others it is to act only as a court of appeal. There the original constitution left the matter. In 1908 a new section was added, fixing the number of judges of the Supreme Court, and in 1927 this was again amended by increasing the number. The Court now consists of the Chief Justice and four associate justices. The Supreme Court is established by the constitution, and neither legislature nor executive can abolish or weaken it. The establishment of other courts is left by the constitution to the legislature, which has of course used its power and equipped the country with a complete system of courts of law of different degrees.

Article Five of the constitution is entitled 'Miscellaneous Provisions', and contains seventeen sections, many of which have no interest today. The first three make provision for the continuance of laws and offices which were in force in the Commonwealth of Liberia before it became independent. Section Four provides for the first presidential election, and Section Sixteen regulates Liberia's relations with the Colonization Society in America. Section Sixteen however has permanent importance, for it forbids the legislature to make any law prohibiting migration. Just as the state of Israel today regards itself as the national home to which every Jew from anywhere in the world can claim admittance, so the newly independent state of Liberia in 1847 regarded itself as 'a home for the dispersed and oppressed children of Africa' (the language is taken from the constitution, Article Five, Section Thirteen), and no Negro might be refused entry.

Section Five regulates the conduct of elections; among other things, it prescribes that if no presidential candidate obtains a majority vote, the Senate and House of Representatives shall sit jointly and elect a president from among the three candidates obtaining the highest number of votes. Section Six compels the legislature to meet at least once a year, Section Seven deals with oaths of office, and Section Eight requires elections of public officers to be made by a majority vote. (Public officers mentioned in this section are the president, vice-president, and members of the legislature.) Section Nine is a temporary proviso: if the constitution creates an office but there seems no need for it yet, it may remain unfilled until the legislature thinks it time to fill it. Sections Ten and Eleven deal with women's property rights: a married woman is to keep control of her own property, and is guaranteed a minimum share of her late husband's estate, if left a widow.

Sections Twelve to Fifteen are designed to protect the fundamental purposes which those who founded Liberia had in mind. No one is to hold land in Liberia unless he is a Liberian citizen, though an exception is made of educational or other benevolent institutions, as long as they use the land they hold strictly for its proper purpose. Since Liberia is to be a national home for 'the dispersed and oppressed children of Africa', none but 'persons of colour' are to be admitted to citizenship. (In 1908 this was amended to read 'none but Negroes or persons of Negro descent'.) In order to improve the life of the African peoples of the interior, the President is to appoint officers in each county to tour the county and give the people what help and guidance they can.

Lastly, Section Seventeen deals with the procedure for amending the constitution. A proposed amendment must first be carried by a two-thirds majority both in the Senate and in the House of Representatives. Then it must be submitted to the people, and must be approved by two-thirds of the votes in this referendum, which is to be held at the next election.

The Liberian constitution is shorter than that of the United States, but it follows closely the American model. It is shorter for two main reasons: Liberia is a unitary, not a federal state, and so nothing need be said about the relations of the States with each other and with the federal Government; and secondly, the Liberian people elect their president directly, and so nothing need be said to describe a complicated election procedure.

Section Fifteen of Article Five, which we have summarized above, is important enough to quote in full:

'The improvement of the native tribes and their advancement in the arts and agriculture and husbandry being a cherished object of this government, it shall be the duty of the president to appoint in each county some discreet person whose duty it shall be to make regular and periodical tours through the country for the purpose of calling the attention of the natives to these wholesome branches of industry, and of instructing them in the same, and the legislature shall, as soon as it can conveniently be done, make provisions for these purposes by the appropriation of money.'

The Government and the indigenous peoples

Liberia, like its neighbours, had to face the problem of what to do with the African peoples who inhabited the country before the newcomers arrived. It was the same problem as that between the settlers in the colony of Sierra Leone and the peoples of the protectorate. In its early days, the young state of Liberia had to face a good deal of hostility from some of the neighbouring tribes, and more than once matters came to fighting. When the hostility ceased, there was a long period in which the African peoples decided that they could not throw the settlers out, but at least they could stay in their forests and have nothing to do with them.

It was a long time before the Liberian Government was able to do much to break down this attitude. It was short of competent staff, and short of money; the constitution was realistic in enjoining on the legislature to provide money for improving the lot of the indigenous peoples only 'as soon as it can conveniently be done'. For many a long year it could not conveniently be done. The intention of the constitution was clearly that the Government should develop the interior by something like the British administrative service: the 'discreet persons' who are to tour the country look very like a British district commissioner. It was not until 1912 that very much was done in this way. President Barclay called meetings of paramount chiefs, and his successor President Howard (1912-20) did more. He invited paramount chiefs from the interior down to Monrovia; he took the trouble to learn local languages and was able to gain the confidence of the people. But as in British West Africa, not very much progress with roads, schools, health and agricultural services could be made without money, and Liberia was poor. It was only when the Firestone Rubber Company began making its plantations in Liberia in the nineteen-twenties that Liberia began to accumulate a little money, and development of all kinds began to appear possible.

Rather surprisingly, in view of its American background, local government in Liberia is carried out, not by elected councils, but by officers appointed by the central Government. The officers of the five coastal counties are appointed from Monrovia. The same system was first applied in the interior. The Liberian Government adopted a sort of direct-indirect rule: indirect, because it allowed the chiefs to continue ruling their people, but direct, because it gave the chiefs orders from Monrovia which they had to obey. This system was not a success: it led to warfare, which lasted until 1910. Then, when peace was restored, the Government claimed the right to disallow the appointment of a chief. The interior was divided into five districts, each under a district commissioner. There was a good deal of friction until 1932, when President Barclay enforced a system of true indirect rule: the district commissioner was to work through the chiefs, and the chiefs were to be freely appointed by their people in the traditional way. After the 1939 war, Liberia became more prosperous, and this indirect rule began to work more successfully.

No attempt was made to interfere with the peoples of the interior until 1892. In that year, the Government set up a Department of the Interior and established a framework of local administration. But money and competent staff were short, and not very much was done until 1923, when President King and his senior officers held a conference which was attended by over five hundred chiefs and elders. The conference produced a set of administrative regulations for the government of the interior districts, taking account of tribal custom and tradition.

The 1923 regulations were not completely successful, because the Government did not follow tribal custom far enough: it laid down that all chiefs were to be elected. This was well enough in some areas, but in others, it was contrary to custom that the chief should be popularly elected, and there was a good deal of friction. In 1931,

President Barclay revised the administrative system in the interior. The central administrative unit was now to be the province, governed by a provincial commissioner and subdivided into districts with their district commissioners. Five years later, in 1936, President Barclay went further, and revised the regulations; and these regulations of 1936 form the basis of administrative policy today.

The heart of the matter lies in regulations 50 to 54. There it is laid down that the Government's policy is to administer tribal affairs by indirect rule through tribal chiefs, who shall govern freely according to tribal customs and traditions, so long as they are not contrary to law or regulation or the public interest. Each tribe is regarded as consisting of a number of clans, a clan containing not fewer than twenty villages. The clans elect their own chiefs, and the council of clan chiefs elects a paramount chief to rule the whole tribe. The regulations state that the paramount chief is responsible to the district commissioner. He is to enforce all laws and Government regulations, and 'he shall carry out all such instructions as he may receive from time to time from the district commissioner relating to the collection of taxes, the construction of roads and bridges, and any other matters affecting tribal welfare, such as improvements in agriculture, trade, and sanitation. . . .' The paramount chief must accompany the district commissioner on his regular tours of inspection.

This is not indirect rule according to the Lugard tradition in British Africa, in which the administration was careful not to give the chiefs direct orders but only suggestions and advice. But as Liberia is a Negro country, it is easier for the Government in Monrovia to unite the tribal peoples with the settlers in the counties under one rule than it would ever have been for the British. Lugard and his successors hoped that the British administrative officer would become the trusted adviser of the chief, so that the tribal council would develop into an efficient local government authority. But if once the administrative officer began giving the chief orders, he would destroy, so it was thought, the whole basis of the system. It was better to go forward at the pace the chief and his elders were willing to go, rather than to hurry them unwillingly .

The Liberian Government has no such fears. It quite frankly regards the tribal authorities as organs of the local administration, and responsible to the administrative officers for the good government of their districts. It can afford to take this attitude because it has a definite policy of uniting all the peoples of Liberia. This unification policy was laid down by President Tubman, though his predecessor President Barclay had taken the essential first step by inviting certain tribes to send their paramount chiefs to represent them in the legislature, and by inviting any tribe which paid $100 a year in taxes to send one delegate to represent it when matters affecting tribal interests were being discussed. Since 1944, when President Tubman took office, this policy has been energetically pursued. Thirteen of the thirty-nine members of the House of Representatives represent the tribal people. Thus, if an administrative officer gives an order to a paramount chief, he does so in accordance with a general policy which the paramount chief himself (or, if not he himself, at all events some of his brother chiefs) has had a share in making.

The Government's unification policy is having considerable success. It will not be complete until with wise government and increasing wealth, education and communications have been so much improved that intercourse between Monrovia and the interior peoples has become easy and natural. But it is in the nature of things that each step in such a process makes the next step easier, so that the process of unification is likely to go on faster and faster towards completion.

CHAPTER XVII

The French Constitution

AT the end of the eighteenth century the French people overthrew their absolute monarchy, and established a republic, with the motto, 'Freedom, Equality, Brotherhood'. The ideals which inspired the revolutionaries have never lost their force; but in the effort to achieve them, France has made many constitutional experiments since her first great Revolution. The first Napoleon overthrew the republic and established an autocracy. When he had been defeated at Waterloo in 1815, the victorious allies persuaded France to set up a constitutional monarchy in imitation of the British system. The monarchy was replaced in 1830 by a *Second Republic,* and that gave way to another autocracy under Napoleon III. The 'Second Empire' of Napoleon III did not survive the Emperor's defeat and capture in the Franco-Prussian war of 1870; there was another revolution, and France set up the Third Republic.

The *Third Republic* had a long run; it survived the war of 1914, but collapsed in the disaster of the second world war. France was utterly defeated, and an old soldier, Marshal Pétain, who had won distinction in the first war, had to face the humiliation and responsibility of accepting the terms imposed by the German conquerors. Under Hitler, Germany had no belief in democracy or any form of popular government; Hitler and his colleagues believed that every people needed a leader. It suited them to uphold Pétain as the leader of France, and to control France through him. The Pétain Government thus naturally tended to be authoritarian. But Pétain did not represent the whole of France. There was a large number of Frenchmen who resisted the German forces in every way they could, even when the German forces had occupied the whole of French soil; and outside France, there was a large French army and a Free French government in exile, under the leadership of Charles de Gaulle. When France was liberated from German control, the authoritarian Government of Marshal Pétain was overthrown, and a Fourth Republic was established.

The *Fourth Republic* was established in difficult times. The new Government had not only to restore the unity of the French people and to rebuild the French state after the dissensions and devastations of the war; it had also to deal with the new independence movements in the French colonies, both in Africa and Asia. The difficulties were too great. Government succeeded Government; France had twenty prime ministers in twelve years. Finally, in 1958, General de Gaulle took over the task of ordering the affairs of France afresh. The parliament granted him special powers, and he established a *Fifth Republic*, with a new constitution which provides for a strong executive.

This rapid survey of French constitutional history is necessary if we are to understand the background to the present constitution of France. France, it must be remembered, is the country of Montesquieu and of the separation of powers. As we have seen on page 34, French Governments under the Third Republic were shortlived, partly because the Government had no power of dissolving parliament before the four-year term had expired. Their history has given Frenchmen cause to fear two opposite evils: a parliamentary government which is too weak, and an authoritarian government under which parliament is reduced to a mere talking-shop, with no power of making its wishes felt.

The constitution was established in 1958, but was amended in 1960 and 1962. It begins by reaffirming the Rights of Man as defined by the French declaration of 1789. The first chapter deals with sovereignty, which is declared to belong to the people. The people may exercise its sovereign power either through its elected representatives or by a referendum. Voting is to be by secret ballot, and all adult men and women may vote. All citizens are free to form political parties, provided that they respect the principles of French national sovereignty and of democracy. The constitution does not explain what it means by the principles of democracy; presumably the reference to the Rights of Man is held to cover the point.

The Executive: the President and the Cabinet
The second chapter describes the position of the president. He is elected for seven years by direct universal vote. (This is a change from the original 1958 version, under which the president was elected by an electoral college consisting of some 80,000 people.) In the presidential election, a candidate who wins more than half the votes is of course elected. But if there are several candidates, it may well happen (it did in fact happen in 1965) that no candidate wins as many votes as this. In this case, the weaker candidates are removed from the list, the two strongest candidates stand again, and the electors have to choose between them in a straight fight.

The president appoints the prime minister. He cannot dismiss him; he can only accept the Government's resignation when the prime minister offers it, and formally terminate the prime minister's tenure of office. The prime minister nominates the members of his cabinet, and the president appoints them. In Britain, the conventions of the constitution would prevent the Queen from refusing to appoint a minister if the prime minister insisted on his name. The text of the French constitution does not say what the president is to do if the prime minister proposes a name which is unwelcome to him. Thus, it leaves scope for the development of convention. In 1966, when General de Gaulle was re-elected president, a French commentator imagined him saying to his prime minister, 'I want you to give ministerial posts to the five men on this list. This second list contains the names of some men whom I will not have as ministers at any price. You can fill the rest of your cabinet as you please; I leave it to you.' From this piece of French guesswork, we can imagine how the convention is developing.

France is still the country of Montesquieu, and believes in the separation of powers. Cabinet ministers are not allowed to be members of parliament. If any member of parliament is appointed to a ministerial post, he must at once resign his seat. The president presides at cabinet meetings. He is of course commander-in-chief of the armed forces, and has the usual powers of a head of state. He appoints ambassadors and high officials; foreign ambassadors are accredited to him. One article of the constitution states in general terms that the president negotiates and ratifies treaties, and he must be kept informed of all negotiations which may be the preliminaries of a treaty. But another article qualifies this power by stating that certain kinds of treaty, though negotiated by the president, need ratification by a law. This brings the parliament into the affair. Like the American president, the president of France communicates with parliament by sending it messages; his messages are to be read, but may not be debated. If parliament is not sitting, it may be specially summoned on purpose to receive a presidential message.

The day-to-day work of administration is the responsibility of the cabinet. As we have seen, the cabinet works in intimate association with the president. It has to work in close association with the parliament also. Cabinet ministers are allowed to attend parliament and to speak there; but they are not members, and cannot vote.

The Legislature
Parliament consists of two Houses, the Senate of about 250 members and the National Assembly of about 450. The Assembly is the popular House, directly elected by the people. The country is divided into constituencies of about 90,000 people, each returning one member. The Senate is indirectly elected. As in some other countries, it is elected to ensure that each territorial unit—called in France the department—is fairly represented, whether it returns many or few members to the Assembly on a population basis. The

National Assembly is elected for five years; members of the Senate are elected for nine, but one-third of them retire every three years. The constitution lays down firmly that members of parliament are privileged in respect of their speeches and votes, and they have a very considerable degree of freedom from arrest and prosecution: either House of parliament has a right to stop any legal proceedings against any of its members. On pages 104-5 we have discussed two views on the member's duty to his constituents. The French constitution is firmly on the side of Burke; it lays down explicitly that all binding instructions given to members of parliament are null and void.*

Parliament meets twice a year, on dates which are specified ('the first Tuesday in October', for example) and sits for rather less than six months in all. It may meet in extraordinary session if the prime minister or a majority of the Assembly so desire. If so, the session lasts only as long as the special agenda requires, and in any case, whether the agenda is finished or no, it must be adjourned after twelve days.

One interesting point is that every member of parliament has a deputy or understudy elected to take his place if he is appointed to a ministerial post, or if he resigns his seat or dies. This has the advantage of keeping down the number of by-elections; a by-election will become necessary only if the understudy is unable to take up the vacant seat. But it introduces a danger. In Britain, a member of parliament who leaves a ministerial post remains a member of parliament; he returns to the back benches. But a member of the French parliament cannot do this, for he has had to give up his seat on becoming a minister. It may be that his understudy will resign to make way for him, and his constituency will re-elect him; but he cannot count on this. Thus, a member of parliament who accepts a ministerial post accepts a risk. If he is unsuccessful as a minister, he may lose both his Ministry and his seat in parliament. The risk is likely to make members of parliament cautious of accepting ministerial posts.

Parliament of course is the legislative body, but its legislative power is restricted. It legislates on the details of certain specified subjects, but on other specified subjects it legislates only on the general principles, leaving the details to be filled in by the executive.

* There was a practice before 1958 of requiring a member to write out a letter of resignation, leaving the date blank; the letter could be used by the party organization at its discretion, since all it had to do was to fill in the date and transmit the letter. This is the sort of 'binding instruction' which the drafters of the 1958 instruction had in mind; but the text which they drafted gives the member of parliament complete discretion.

(In Britain, as we have seen on page 52, it often happens that parliament is content to lay down general principles, and leaves the appropriate Minister discretion to fill in the details by statutory regulations. But the British parliament could make the detailed regulations part of the Act if it chose, and it has the power of revising any regulation that it dislikes. The power of the British parliament in this respect has no limits; the French parliament's power is limited by the constitution.) Private members, as well as the Government, may propose Bills, but the Government has the sole right to propose Bills involving questions of finance. The two Houses have a system of committees to help them in discussing the details of legislation. Both Houses must agree to a Bill before it can be submitted to the president for his approval. If they cannot agree, the Bill is referred to a joint committee composed of equal numbers of the two Houses. If the joint committee cannot agree, the Bill goes back to the two Houses separately; and if the disagreement cannot be overcome, the lower House, the Assembly, will settle the matter by one final vote. Thus, the Senate, like the British House of Lords, has power to delay legislation, but cannot in the end prevent the lower House from having its way. There are special requirements governing finance Bills and also 'organic laws', which are laws (like the Presidential Affairs Act of Ghana) working out the details of constitutional procedure. If parliament has not passed the finance Bill within seventy days, the Government is empowered to pass it by decree.

Since there is a time-limit set on the sessions of parliament, there is always a possibility that the parliament may not get through its programme in time. In Britain, one of the Government's means of controlling parliament is that it is able to say in effect, 'You may not want to pass this Bill into law, but we shall keep you sitting here until you do pass it.' The French constitution does not allow this. But it provides for the danger in another way. If the Government sees its programme in danger, it may ask parliament for authority to legislate by decree. Any decrees which the Government makes under this authority must bear a time-limit. They come into force as soon as they are published, but the Government must introduce a Bill into parliament to ratify them, and if the Bill is not passed before the time-limit expires, the decrees become null and void. This power of legislating by decree is much used. In 1960, for example, there was a serious crisis over Algerian affairs. Parliament was completely unable to agree, and granted the Government powers under this article of the constitution for a whole year. In that time, the president and his Government settled the whole matter and gave Algeria its independence. Parliament could of course, if it had chosen, have refused to pass the ratification Bill at the end of the year; but that would have made no difference to the situation in Algeria.

All Bills which have been passed by parliament are submitted to the president for his approval. He may veto a Bill, or any of its clauses; he must signify his approval or his veto within fifteen days. If he vetoes the Bill or any part of it, parliament is bound to reconsider the matter. The constitution says nothing on what may happen if the parliament, having reconsidered the matter, persists in its opinion. No conditions are laid down on which the parliament may override the presidential veto, as Congress can in the United States.

But if matters have reached this point, the deadlock may be resolved in other ways. If one-tenth of the members of the Assembly so decide, they may move a vote of censure on the Government; and if the vote of censure is carried, the Government is bound to resign. When the president receives the Government's resignation, he may either appoint a fresh prime minister and ask him to form a new Government, or he may (if the outgoing prime minister advises it) dissolve parliament and hold general elections. The newly elected parliament may not be dissolved within the first twelve months. This power of dissolving parliament did not exist in the Third Republic (see page 34), nor does it exist in the United States. It does exist in Britain, and is a powerful force making for a strong Government and a disciplined parliament. No doubt, if parliament in France were obstinate in fighting for its Bill against the presidential veto, the president would be much tempted to dissolve it.

The general effect of this part of the constitution is to give France a Government with a strong executive and a legislature which is much weaker than in Britain. The president has much power; in one respect he has even more power than the president of the United States, for he can dissolve parliament, whereas the American president cannot dissolve Congress. This predominance of the executive over the legislature is increased by the character of the persons concerned. It so happens that President de Gaulle is a very strong man, and that the parliament still shows the weaknesses of its predecessors under the Third and Fourth Republics: it is divided into too many parties, and wastes much time over party quarrelling and unimportant matters.

The Constitutional Council
In the United States, the Supreme Court has the important duty (see pp. 36-7) of deciding whether any act of the legislature or of the executive infringes the constitution. In France, this duty is not

entrusted to the Supreme Court, but to a special Constitutional Council. The Council consists of nine members, appointed for nine years; a member is not eligible for re-appointment at the end of his term. Three members are appointed by the president, three by the president of the National Assembly, and three by the president of the Senate. One-third of the members retire every three years. In addition to these nine members, former Presidents of the Republic are ex-officio members for life. The Constitutional Council examines all disputes over the validity of elections: presidential elections or parliamentary elections. It supervises the referendum. All organic laws must be submitted to it, and any other law may be. Its decisions must be published, and there is no appeal from them; any law or executive act which it declares to be unconstitutional is void. Thus, the Council has great powers within its own field. But its field is limited. It can only settle disputes between the legislature and the executive, and make sure that elections and the referendum are properly held. When the legislature and the executive are in dispute and one holds that the other has acted unconstitutionally, there are only four people permitted to call in the advice of the Constitutional Council: the president of the republic, the prime minister, and the presidents of the Senate and of the Assembly. The constitution of France, unlike that of the United States, does not provide that a private citizen may ask the Constitutional Council for a ruling, as a private citizen can ask for a ruling of the American Supreme Court.

The Council of State
But the rights of the individual French citizen are effectively safeguarded. Curiously enough, the body which exists to safeguard them is not described in the constitution. Four articles of the constitution mention it, but mention it in such a way as to make it plain that it is regarded as so important and well-known to all Frenchmen as to need no description or explanation. This body is the Council of State.

The Council of State (*Conseil d'Etat* in French) was established in 1800. The French Revolution had overthrown the absolute monarchy, in which the king was above the law; the revolutionaries were determined that France should be subject to the rule of law. But there was a long tradition in France that the judges were hostile to the Government and its absolute powers. The revolutionaries feared that if the actions of the Government were made subject to the decisions of the ordinary courts of law, this old tradition would be maintained, and the Government would be much weakened. So they established a special body, the Council of State, with the special duty of acting as a check on the actions of the Government and protecting the rights of the individual citizen against arbitrary or inconsiderate action. Ever since that time, the Council of State has been active in carrying out this important duty; and it has won such respect and affection that, as we have seen, the constitution of 1958 takes its existence for granted.

Part of its success is due to the fact that membership of the Council has always been regarded as a distinction, and it has always had first-class men sitting on its benches. To be appointed a member of the Council is often the first step in a distinguished career in the public service.

Today, the Council of State consists of 150 members, who are appointed by the cabinet. There is no fixed term of office, and in theory a councillor could be dismissed by the cabinet. But the prestige of the body is so high that any Government which dismissed a councillor without the very strongest and plainest reason would raise up a storm of protest. In practice, membership is for life, if the member so desires. The Council is divided into five panels dealing with different branches of the administration, and a member of the Council will be moved from one panel to another. Moreover, he may be seconded from the Council to an administrative department of the Government or to take some special temporary post. While he is thus seconded, he cannot of course sit as a member of the Council; but when his period of secondment is over, he returns to his Council seat. A member of the Council cannot be a member of parliament without quitting his seat on the Council; but if he leaves his parliamentary seat he may return.

The Council of State has the double task of advising the Government and of standing ready to rebuke the Government if it has acted unjustly. Any action of the Government may be brought before it by any citizen. This double task may seem difficult. If a man has been seconded from the Council for some years to work in a Government department, how, we may ask, is it possible for him to be impartial when the work of that department is laid before him by an aggrieved citizen after he has resumed his seat on the Council? Will he not inevitably tend to sympathise too much with his former official colleagues? The answer is that experience has shown that the Council is impartial. You have to be a first-class man to be impartial in such circumstances, but then the members of the Council of State *are* first-class men. The advisory and the judicial work of the Council are kept separate; the same man cannot carry out both duties at once, though he will no doubt in the course of his membership pass from one side of the Council's work to the other.

The constitution mentions two important duties which the Council of State has to carry out in its advisory capacity. It has to consider and advise on all Government Bills before they are laid before parliament. Similarly, if the Government has received temporary authority from parliament to legislate by decree, its draft decrees must be submitted to the Council of State before they are enacted. In addition to these important duties, which do not come to any individual councillor very often (since any given Government department is not promoting new legislation all the time), there is of course a mass of day-to-day routine advice which is required of him. Similarly, in its capacity as guardian of the citizen's rights, the Council may have to deal with weighty matters such as racial discrimination, or the unjust decision of an administrative tribunal: or it may deal with matters which by comparison seem trifling, such as the action of a village mayor in banning a film in the village cinema, or some question of discipline among university students. (Mayors and university principals—rectors, the French call them —are Government officials in France, so their alleged misdeeds are official misdeeds, infringing the rights of the citizen.) The power of the Council of State has recently been extended. It is now able to follow up its decisions and inquire what action has been taken upon them. In its annual report, it is entitled to mention such cases and comment on the action taken. This is an important strengthening of the Council's power of protecting individual rights.

Thus in France, the Constitutional Council and the Council of State between them amply fulfil the duty, which the Supreme Court fulfils in the United States, of watching over the working of the constitution and of protecting the constitutional rights, both of the individual citizen against the Government, and of one branch of the Government against another branch.

Other Provisions
The constitution provides that if the president, or any member of the Government, commits high treason or any other serious crime against the security of the State, he shall be tried before a special court composed of members of the Senate and of the National Assembly in equal numbers. The court is to be bound by the laws of the land. A matter of this kind is too serious to be entrusted to the Council of State. The constitution says very little on the ordinary judiciary; this, like the Council of State, it takes for granted. There is a High Council (consisting of the Minister of Justice and nine members appointed by the president) to nominate judges for appointment, and if necessary to act as a disciplinary body.

When the constitution was established in 1958, it was hoped that France and the French oversea territories in Africa and elsewhere would remain united in one French Community. The constitution works out at length the details of the Community's organization. Since all the French territories in Africa (except French Somaliland) become independent two years later, France has now very little in the way of oversea territories, beyond a few tropical islands. Most of this part of the constitution has thus become out of date.

The constitution may be amended in two ways. In either case, the amendment must be passed by parliament. It may then be submitted to a referendum; or if the president so decides, it may be re-submitted to a joint session of the two Houses of parliament, and passed by a three-fifths majority. The president has absolute discretion whether to seek approval by referendum or by a three-fifths majority of a parliamentary joint session. The republican form of government is not to be changed.

CHAPTER XVIII

The Constitution of the Soviet Union

MODERN Russia began with the communist revolution of October 1917. The old Russia, as we have said on page 231, was greatly under-developed, both politically and economically. It was governed by an absolute monarch, the Czar, assisted by the great nobles. In 1905 the Czar gave Russia its first parliament, but the experiment was a failure. Until as lately as 1861, the villagers were serfs: not exactly slaves, but bound to stay in their village and work on the land. They were as much part of a nobleman's estate as his cattle were. In 1917, though free, they were still illiterate, living by subsistence agriculture and governing themselves through their village councils.

The Czar's Government was overthrown by a socialist revolution in March 1917, and the socialist Government which assumed power was in its turn overthrown by the communists in October of the same year. The aims of the socialists and the communists were identical. They wished to overthrow the capitalist system: that is, the system in which the capital—buildings, machinery, lorries and the like—needed to produce or distribute wealth is in private hands, and the man who owns capital pays men to work for him. Both parties wanted to replace this capitalist system by a system in which such capital is owned by the community. 'From each according to his ability: to each according to his need'—this is a quotation from the Communist Manifesto of 1848. Both socialists and communists accepted this principle. The two parties differed in their methods. The socialists were prepared to make gradual progress, to observe the laws in force, and to make changes by constitutional means. The communists, as we have seen on pages 93-4, believed that only a violent revolution would achieve their aims. It was hopeless, they argued, to expect that the people who owned capital would ever give it up voluntarily. They must be compelled to. The socialist party was open to anyone who agreed with the aims of socialism; the communist party was open only to the select few who were prepared to endure the stern discipline that would be needed to carry through the revolution.

The difficulty which faced the victorious communist Government in 1917 was a very great one. Not only had they to reorganize Russia on communist lines so as to begin their work towards the classless society, but at the same time they had to carry out a tremendous task of economic and social development. They had to build railways and factories, educate the illiterate villagers and turn many of them into industrial workers, replace ox-drawn by tractor-drawn ploughs, and generally transform Russia into a modern industrial state. The capitalist world of the West was hostile to them, so they could expect no financial help from abroad, and had to finance their development from their own internal savings. Of the fifty years since the revolution, nearly twenty have been spent in war and in repairing the destruction of war. This great handicap has called forth a great response in the discipline and self-sacrifice of the Russian people. The Russians have made a significant change in the wording of the above quotation from the Communist Manifesto. Instead of saying 'to each according to his need', they now say 'to each according to his work'.

The first constitution of the Soviet Union was drawn up in 1923, and contained several principles which have been preserved in the modified constitution of 1936. The 1936 constitution is still (1966) in force, but the Soviet Union is proposing to revise it again.

The Union of Soviet Socialist Republics, like Nigeria, Switzerland, and the United States, is a federal state. It consists of fifteen equal 'union republics', twenty 'autonomous soviet socialist republics',* and some 'autonomous regions' and 'national areas'. The word *soviet* simply means a council, whether it is a simple council of family heads in a village, or the supreme council of the nation. The fifteen union republics are the Russian, Ukrainian, Byelorussian, Uzbek, Kazakh, Georgian, Azerbaijan, Lithuanian, Latvian, Esthonian, Moldavian, Kirghiz, Tajik, Armenian, and Turkmen. All of them lie in the western and south-western part of the country, which is the most thickly populated and the most developed. The biggest of them is the Russian S.S.R., which contains about half the total population of the U.S.S.R., and is itself a federation. There is as much variation in area and population among these fifteen union republics as there is among the states of the American union. The Russian Federative S.S.R. has $6\frac{1}{2}$ million square miles and 120 million people; it has over 500 times the area and 80 times the population of the smallest of the fifteen, the Armenian S.S.R., which has 12,000 square miles and $1\frac{1}{2}$ million people. (The biggest American state is over 250 times the area of the smallest, and the state with the heaviest population has 90 times as many people.)

Each of the fifteen union republics is a sovereign state, entitled to enter into direct relations with foreign countries. Not all of them do so; but the Byelorussian and the Ukrainian republics have

* We shall abbreviate the words 'soviet socialist republics' into S.S.R.

separate membership of the United Nations. Further, in complete contrast to the United States, which fought a civil war to establish the principle that a state may not secede from the Union, each of the fifteen republics of the Soviet Union has the right to secede. It might in practice be difficult for a republic to exercise its right. In particular, the whole weight of the Communist Party would doubtless be thrown against any secession which might weaken the power or the standing of the Soviet Union as a whole. But the right exists.

The Soviet Union needs this complicated structure because it is a multi-racial society. It was only in the eighteenth and nineteenth centuries that the Russian people conquered Asia; and the Soviet Union today contains many European and Asian peoples of differing languages and cultures, and publishes newspapers in some 120 languages. It is understandable that many of its peoples desire some degree of self-government; and it is a source of strength, not weakness, to the Union that they should have it. The twenty autonomous S.S.R. include such regions as Dagestan in the Caucasus and the Bashkir republic, both of which are parts of the Russian Federative S.S.R., Kara-Kalpak, which is part of the Uzbek S.S.R., and the Buryat-Mongol A.S.S.R. to the east of lake Baikal in Siberia. These autonomous republics have their own constitutions. Each elects its Supreme Soviet and its Council of Ministers, who govern it in accordance with its own constitution and the constitution of the Union Republic of which it forms a part. The autonomous regions have somewhat less independence, and the national areas less still. The national areas are thinly-peopled parts of the Arctic region, not yet sufficiently developed for full republican status.

As in all federations, the constitution of the U.S.S.R. reserves some powers for the federal Government and leaves others to the member-states: that is, to the fifteen Union Republics. Subject to the rights of the fifteen republics, the federal Government naturally deals with external affairs. It also deals with war and peace, the establishment and admission of new republics, defence, security, currency, foreign trade, railways, shipping, the national plans for economic development, and certain fundamental legislation. Except that, the U.S.S.R. being a socialist state, all foreign trade is strictly controlled by the Government, this list is much the same as the list of federal powers in any other federal state.

The fifteen Union Republics administer (among other things) health, culture, education, their internal communications, defence, and their own finance. There is a tendency for the federal Government to relax some of its control over economic affairs and legislation, and to allow the fifteen republics more powers in these matters.

The Legislature

There is a federal legislature, the Supreme Soviet of the U.S.S.R. Like the American Congress, this consists of two Houses: the Soviet of the Union, which is directly elected by the people, and the Soviet of Nationalities, which represents the member republics. The Soviet of the Union contains over 1,400 members. The Soviet of Nationalities is made up of 25 members from each of the fifteen union republics, eleven from each of the autonomous republics, five from each autonomous region, and one from each national area. Like the United States Senate, the Soviet of Nationalities gives equal representation to all member-states of the same political status, regardless of their area or population; there are fifteen Armenians to represent their small country, and only fifteen Russians to represent the Russian republic, which is more than 500 times as big and has 80 times as many people. Both Houses of the Supreme Soviet are equal; either may introduce legislation, and a Bill needs the assent of both Houses to become law. If the two Houses disagree, the Bill is referred to a joint commission of the two; if the commission cannot agree, the Bill goes back to the two Houses for reconsideration; if they still cannot agree, the Supreme Soviet is dissolved and a general election held. The Supreme Soviet is elected for four years, and holds two sessions a year. But much of its work is done through standing committees, which sit throughout the year, even when the Soviet itself is in vacation.

The Soviet of the Union is elected on a basis of universal voting by secret ballot. Elections in the U.S.S.R. differ from those in Britain or the United States in that by the time the voting takes place, the voters in each constituency have only one candidate **to vote for,** instead of having a choice between two or more. It seems that although elections are nominally direct, they are in fact indirect. Candidates may be nominated by all kinds of groups: trade unions, factory or office or farm organizations, local branches of the communist party, and so forth; there may be many candidates nominated in a constituency. When all the nominations have been received, representatives of the various groups that have made nominations get together and go through the list to pick the best candidate. It is a process very like the process by which a party in the United States picks its presidential candidate out of several possibles. Thus, when polling day arrives, the voter finds only one candidate's name printed on his voting paper. He can vote for him, or he can abstain from voting; but he can vote for no one else.

On page 75 of this book, it is argued that a free choice between candidates and their different policies is one of the requisites for obtaining a truly representative parliament. As we have said on

THE CONSTITUTION OF THE SOVIET UNION 281

page 66, neither the British—nor the Russian—nor any other parliament is perfectly representative. In a British constituency, anyone is free to nominate a candidate; but nowadays, no candidate has any hope of being elected unless one of the principal political parties backs him. Many candidates are sent down to the constituency from party headquarters, and it is seldom that a candidate is personally known to the mass of the voters in his constituency. That is why the candidate has to 'nurse' his constituency (pp. 103-4). The local party organizations make very little impression on the mass of the voters; not one voter in a hundred could tell you the name of the chairman of his local party organization. During the few weeks before the election, the voter will have had party leaflets pushed through his letter-box by which each of the candidates in his constituency introduces himself, and promises the sun, moon and stars if only the right party is enabled to form a Government. The voter usually ignores them all, and votes for Smith because Smith is Labour, or for Jones because Jones is Conservative.

In the Soviet Union, nominations are not made by political parties, but by the voter's own colleagues in farm, factory, or office. The voter has more chance of knowing the candidate and the people who nominate him than the British voter. After the nominations, there follows the period of discussion between the nominating groups, in which one candidate after another is knocked out of the list, and finally only one name is left. The individual voter (let us call him Nikita) may be disappointed that Ivan, who was nominated by Nikita's office association, has been knocked out and Yuri is finally nominated; for Yuri was originally put up by the workers in the cotton-mill, and Nikita personally thinks Ivan the better man. But Nikita's colleagues, his elected representatives who have been taking part in the discussions, have accepted Yuri, and they can explain to Nikita why they have accepted him and why Nikita ought to vote for him. It is in effect a system of indirect election; but we should hesitate to say that Nikita has less real freedom of choice between candidates than the voter in Britain.

But what about choice between different policies? There, the position is very different, because of the difference between the Communist Party and the political parties in capitalist countries: see pages 93-4. The Communist Party in Russia made the revolution. In the beginning, the Communist party was divided into a minority (the Mensheviks) who pleaded for a democratic organization and majority voting within the party, and a majority (the Bolsheviks) who maintained that strict party discipline was essential if the revolution was to succeed. It was not long before the Bolsheviks threw their rivals out of the party and reviled them as traitors and counter-revolutionaries, and since 1918 the Soviet Union has been a one-party state. The job of a political organization in a Western country is to bring together people who think alike, and then persuade the majority of the voters to support them, so that they can form a Government which will do as they wish. The job of the Communist Party is quite different. It is to pick out the best brains and the natural leaders: to set them to work out by free discussion among themselves (within the limitations of Marxist-Leninist doctrine) what policy should be: and once policy is decided, to permit no further questioning, but to enforce it on everyone. Thus, when it comes to electing a candidate to a soviet, it is not Nikita's job (as it would be in the West) to wonder which policy he would prefer and to choose a candidate who agrees with him. Policy is not Nikita's business; that is the business of the Party. Ivan and Yuri and all the other candidates can be trusted to follow the policy which the Party has laid down.

There is no point in discussing whether the British or the Soviet way is the more democratic. As we have said on page 83, much depends on how the Party is organized. As far as mere size goes, the Communist Party of the Soviet Union has over ten million members, and its youth branch, the Young Communist League, has twenty million more; together they contain about one-fifth of their age-group, and this is more than the total of active workers for the three main British political parties together. But size is not everything.

The Executive
The two Houses of the Supreme Soviet, sitting together, elect two executive bodies. One is the Presidium, the other the Council of Ministers.

The Presidium is a sort of standing executive committee of the Supreme Soviet. It holds a great deal of power: partly because it sits permanently, whereas the Soviet is often in vacation, and partly because it is a small enough body to be businesslike, whereas the Council of Ministers and the Soviet itself are too big. The Presidium consists of a President, fifteen vice-presidents (one from each of the fifteen union republics), a secretary, and sixteen members. Its members have no departmental responsibilities; they are free to concentrate on general policy. While the Soviet is in session, the Presidium has to issue ordinances, interpret the laws, hold referendums, and supervise the decisions of the Council of Ministers and of the fifteen similar councils in the fifteen union republics, to make sure that they are constitutionally sound. (This last function is one which in the United States is carried out by the Supreme Court.) It is the Presidium that will have to dissolve the Soviet and hold new elections if there is a disagreement between the two Houses.

When the Soviet is in vacation, the Presidium appoints and dismisses Ministers (on the advice of the Chairman of the Council of Ministers), institutes and awards decorations, pardons criminals, appoints and dismisses the commander-in-chief, declares war, sees to national security, ratifies treaties, appoints Soviet ambassadors and receives foreign ambassadors—in short, carries out most of the functions which in the United States belong to the President. Its appointment and dismissal of Ministers has to be ratified by the Supreme Soviet.

The President of the Soviet Union, like the first President of Nigeria or the Queen of England, is the ceremonial head of the state but nothing more. He may have personal influence, but he has no constitutional power in the day-to-day business of government. The Soviet Union is another example to illustrate the warning we have given on page 143 that a federal constitution need not necessarily involve a president with great executive powers like those of the American President.

In contrast to the Presidium, the Council of Ministers of the U.S.S.R. is a large body, including not only what we should regard in the West as Ministers, but also a number of committee chairmen and others: such as the chairmen of the State radio and television committee, of the cinematography committee, of the Press committee, of the building committee, of the farm-produce buying committee, of the State bank, and of the central statistical board. Not only is it a large body, but its members all have special departmental interests and responsibilities. The fifteen chairmen of the Councils of Ministers in the union republics are all ex-officio members of this federal Council of Ministers. The Council is responsible to the Supreme Soviet, and when the Soviet is in vacation, to the Presidium.

In all this, where does real power lie? The responsibility of the Presidium and of the Council of Ministers to the Supreme Soviet means less than it would in Britain, where a swing in public opinion might bring about a revolt of back-bench members of parliament and overthrow a Government. In the U.S.S.R., the whole system is held together by the discipline of the Communist Party: an admirable example of the force of a constitutional convention. It is because a man stands well with the Party that he is likely to be elected a Minister. Very great power lies in the hands of the Secretary to the Central Committee of the Communist Party: Stalin held that post, and so did Khrushchev, who was both Secretary to the Party and Chairman of the Council of Ministers. If a man is ambitious for power, it seems more likely that he should work his way to the senior positions within the Party, and thence aspire to membership of the Presidium than to membership of the Council of Ministers. If he joins the Presidium, he will have the whole vast field of government under his eye; if he becomes a Minister, three-fourths of his time will be spent on the affairs of his own department.

The Judiciary
The Supreme Court of the U.S.S.R. is elected by the Supreme Soviet for five years; similarly, the fifteen union republics and the twenty autonomous republics elect their own Supreme Courts. District judges and local magistrates are elected by the people. In all courts, the judges are assisted by part-time assessors, who are elected by the people for two years and do two weeks duty in each year. Thus, the judges are amateurs, though the lawyers who plead before them are professionals. This is a contrast to the British system, in which the judges in all the higher courts are appointed from among the professional lawyers. But even in Britain, a very large number of local magistrates in the lower courts are amateurs (though appointed by the Government, not elected by the people). In the United States, federal judges are appointed by the Government, but most of the judges in State courts are elected by the people. Thus the Soviet Union goes much further than either Britain or the United States in relying on amateurs for its judicial work. Decisions in Soviet courts are taken by a majority of the judges and assessors together. The independence of the judiciary is guaranteed by the constitution. In recent years, the Soviet Union has been gradually codifying its court procedure and its civil and criminal law; thus, the judge may be an amateur, but he has to work within the limits laid down for him, and will need professional advice to help him to do so.

Local Government
The whole political structure of the Soviet Union is based on the idea of the soviet, which in its simplest form is a council of village elders. The original village soviets have been replaced by a nation-wide system of regional industrial soviets and regional agricultural soviets, both popularly elected. It is significant of the emphasis which the U.S.S.R. lays on economic development and production, that these local government units are not organized (as in most Western countries) simply on a territorial basis, but also on an economic basis. It may happen that on the outskirts of a town, some people work in industry and others in agriculture. They vote for the local soviet appropriate to the nature of their work. This is because, in addition to the ordinary duties which fall on local government bodies all over the world—health, roads, markets, lighting, libraries,

housing and so on—the local soviets in the U.S.S.R. have important duties in stimulating economic production, whether of crops or of manufactures.

As in other countries, the local soviets have a professional staff to carry out their orders, and they work largely through a system of committees. In some other countries, the elected local councils draw on the voluntary help of members of the public—for example, as local magistrates, school managers, or members of the education committee. The U.S.S.R. also follows this principle, and carries it to very great lengths: so much so, that there seems no very clear dividing line between local government, co-operative societies, and the sort of part-professional, part-amateur (voluntary) sort of community development work that we are familiar with in West Africa.

INDEX

Presidents, colonial governors, Ordinances, and Acts of Parliament are indexed under those four headings.

Aborigines Society, 152-5, 210
absolute government, 15, 16, 43, 54, 64
Action Group, 211
administrative tribunals, 57-9
Acts of Parliament:
  Bill of Rights, 29
  British North America Act, 27
  Chieftaincy Act, 247, 248
  Colonial Development and Welfare Act, 160
  Constitution Amendment Act 1961, 218
  Constitution Amendment Act, 1962, 218
  Constitutional Referendum Act, 218
  Electoral Act, 218
  Ghana Independence Act, 27, 186
  Local Government Acts (Britain), 244, 245
  Local Government Act (Ghana), 247-9, 253
  Mid-Western Region Act, 218
  Native Representation Act, 31
  Nigerian Independence Act, 193
  Parliament Act, 30, 31
  Presidential Affairs Act, 113, 217
  Presidential Elections Act, 113, 217
  Road Traffic Acts, 52
  Separate Representation of Voters Act, 32
  Sierra Leone Independence Act, 203
  South Africa Act, 27, 31, 32
America, *see* United States
American Colonization Society, 255-9
Aristotle, 15, 16, 17, 19, 61
Ashmun, Rev. Jehudi, 256, 257
Australia, 70, 136, 138, 143, 191, 219
Azikiwe, Dr Nnamdi, 161

ballot, secret, 66, 67, 259
Bill of Rights, 29
Bright, Dr. Bankole, 172, 206
Britain, *see* England
Burke, Edmund, 105-7

cabinet, 35, 46, 113-20, 143, 165, 181
  Gambia, 208, 209
  Ghana, 183, 187, 188, 215, 216
  Liberia, 260, 261
  Nigeria (federal), 191
  Nigeria (regional), 191
  Sierra Leone, 205
Canada, 27, 138, 139, 143
Chiefs, Houses of (Ghana), 217
chieftaincy, 241-4, 246-8, 250, 251
city-states, Greek, 13, 14, 62, 64
civil service, 222-6
Colonial Development and Welfare Acts, 160
common law, 51, 52
common roll, 71, 72
communal roll, 71, 72
communist party, 92-4
Convention People's Party of Ghana, 28, 33, 35, 95, 113, 166, 182-8, 211, 213, 214
conventions, constitutional, 32-6, 102, 105, 110, 208
corruption, 80, 81
Coussey commission, 164, 165, 180, 246

Danquah, Dr J. B., 163, 210
delegated legislation, 52
democracy, 19-24

elections, 66-76, 88, 110, 111, 261
England, 15, 29-31, 38-49, 54-9, 65, 66, 76-84, 86, 87, 98-107, 113-20, 124, 125, 134, 135, 143, 244-6
executive council:
  Gambia, 149, 161, 174, 175
  Ghana, 149, 161, 164-6, 183
  Nigeria, 149, 150, 161

Sierra Leone, 149, 161, 171
see also cabinet

federalism, 133-43, 184, 185, 188-93, 214
finance, public, 226-30
France, 15-7, 34, 38-40, 43, 54, 87, 88, 109, 134, 143, 245
franchise, 68, 69, 206, 207

Gambia, 147, 149, 151, 161, 173-5, 181; 1962 constitution, 207, 208; 1963 constitution, 208-10
Gandhi, Mahatma, 18
Ghana, 33, 37, 41, 95, 104, 105, 112, 142, 143, 147, 149, 151-6, 159; 1925 constitution, 153-6; 1946 constitution, 162-4; 1951 constitution, 164-6; independence, 181-8; republic, 214-7; planning, 235-41; local government, 246-9, 253
Gold Coast, see Ghana
Gold Coast Convention, 163, 210
good life, 15, 16
Governor:
  Arden-Clarke, 33, 166
  Burns, 162
  Clifford, 152
  Creasy, 164
  Guggisberg, 153
  Lugard, 243, 265
  Richards, 156-8, 162
  Beresford Stooke, 171

habeas corpus, 54-7
Hayford, J. E. Casely, 152
Hobbes, Thomas, 39, 40, 61

indirect rule, 243, 244, 265

judiciary, 29, 43-5, 49; Gambia, 208; Ghana, 186, 187; Liberia, 261; Nigeria, 201; Sierra Leone, 205. see also Supreme Court

legislative council:
  Gambia, 151, 173, 174
  Ghana, 151-6, 159, 162-4, 182, 183
  Nigeria, 156-9, 169, 170
  Sierra Leone, 151, 159, 171, 172
see also parliament

Liberia: 1820 constitution, 255; Plan of Civil Government, 256, 257; 1839 constitution, 257-9; independence constitution, 55, 56, 259-63; indigenous peoples, 263-6
Locke, John, 40-3, 50, 54, 61
local government, 241-53

Mali, 16, 41
Margai, Sir Milton, 161, 172, 206
Montesquieu, 43-8
Morgan, J. P., 21

National Congress of British West Africa, 152, 153
National Council of Nigeria and the Cameroons, 211
National Council of Sierra Leone, 172, 211
nationalism, 17
National Liberation Movement, 95, 184-6, 211
Nigeria, 41, 55, 123, 125, 126, 139, 141, 143, 147, 149, 150, 156-9, 161, 166-8; 1951 constitution, 168-70, 181; 1954 constitution, 188-91; changes in 1957/8, 191-3; independence, 193-202; republic, 199, 201, 218-20; planning, 232, 238-41; local government, 250, 253
Nkrumah, Dr Kwame, 18, 33, 95, 113, 142, 161, 166, 182-8, 211
Northern People's Congress (Nigeria), 211
Northern People's Party (Ghana), 183, 211

Ofori Atta, Nana Sir, 149, 154
one-party state, 86, 90, 92-8
Ordinances:
  Native Authority (Colony), 162
  Native Courts (Colony), 162
  Protectorate Ordinance, 172
  Protectorate Native Law Ordinance, 172

Paine, Tom, 16, 17, 61
parliament, 121-132:
  British, 43-7, 76-84, 86, 87, 98-107, 124-32

INDEX

Gambia, 207-10
German, 47
Ghana, 113, 187, 214, 215
Liberia, 260
Nigeria (federal), 191-3, 197-201, 220
Sierra Leone, 202-5
United States (Congress), 48, 49, 83, 110-3, 130, 132
see also legislative council
party system, 22, 72-6, 85-107
planning, state, 230-41
Plato, 21, 62, 84
powers, governor's reserved, 163, 177-80, 183, 193, 207, 208
powers, separation of, 43-9, 109, 112, 132, 143, 258, 260
president, powers of, 48, 108-13, 214-7, 219, 220, 260, 261
President:
  Azikiwe (Nigeria), 161
  Barclay (Liberia), 264, 265
  Eisenhower (U.S.), 43
  de Gaulle (France), 109, 143
  Howard (Liberia), 264
  King (Liberia), 264
  Lincoln (U.S.), 131
  Nkrumah (Ghana), *see* Nkrumah
  F. D. Roosevelt (U.S.), 37
  Tubman (Liberia), 266
  Woodrow Wilson (U.S.), 120
prime minister, 114-20, 182, 199-201, 205, 208, 209
privilege, parliamentary, 77, 78
protectorate (Sierra Leone), 172, 173
provincial councils (Gold Coast), 104, 105, 153-5
public service commission, 35, 186, 201, 206, 208

questions, parliamentary, 78, 79

referendum, 106, 214, 218, 219
regional councils (Nigeria), 167-70
regional legislatures (Nigeria), 188, 189, 192, 193
representative government, 63-84
reserved powers, governor's, 163, 177-80, 183, 193, 207, 208
revolution, French, 17, 134
rights, fundamental human, 54, 60-2, 194-7, 204, 209, 210, 217, 259
Rousseau, J. J., 15, 16, 61
rule of law, 50-62

Sarbah, John, 152
second chamber, 121-6
separation of powers, 43-9, 109, 112, 132, 143, 258, 260
Sierra Leone, 118, 147, 149, 151, 159, 161, 171-3, 181; 1958 constitution, 202, 203; independence, 203-7; planning, 239-41; local government, 250, 251
Sierra Leone People's Party, 172, 211
social contract, 15, 16, 39-42
South Africa, 31, 32, 137
sovereignty, 39-43
state rights, 136-40
Statute of Westminster, 32
statute law, 52
statutory regulations, 52
Supreme Court, 32, 36, 37, 49, 138, 214, 215, 261

Uganda, 86, 142, 143
United States:
  declaration of independence, 17, 61
  constitution, 25-7, 36, 37, 48, 49, 109-12, 122, 123, 132, 137, 138, 191
  political parties, 88
  local government, 245, 246

Watson commission, 163
whip, party, 99-103

For Product Safety Concerns and Information please contact our EU
representative GPSR@taylorandfrancis.com
Taylor & Francis Verlag GmbH, Kaufingerstraße 24, 80331 München, Germany

www.ingramcontent.com/pod-product-compliance
Lightning Source LLC
Chambersburg PA
CBHW061435300426
44114CB00014B/1695